Wingshooter's Guide to™

MICHIGAN

Upland Birds and Waterfowl

Titles Available in This Series

Wingshooter's Guide to™

MICHIGAN

Upland Birds and Waterfowl

Tom Pink

Bird Descriptions by
Jason Smith

Wilderness
Adventures
Press™

Belgrade, Montana

This book was made with an easy opening, lay flat binding.

Published by Wilderness Adventures Press
45 Buckskin Road
Belgrade, MT 59714
800-925-3339
Website: www.wildadv.com
email: books@wildadv.com

10 9 8 7 6 5 4 3 2 1

Printed in the United States of America

Library of Congress Cataloging-in-Publication Data

Pink, Tom, 1962–
      Wingshooter's guide to Michigan : upland birds and waterfowl / Tom Pink.
      p.   cm.
   Includes index.
   ISBN 1–885106–57–2 (alk. paper)
      1. Upland game bird hunting––Michigan––Guidebooks. 2. Waterfowl
shooting––Michigan––Guidebooks. 3. Michigan––Guidebooks. I. Title.
SK232.P56   2000
799.2'46'09774––dc21   00-042279
                                                                             CIP

Table of Contents

Acknowledgments

Many considerate folks helped put this book together. The state's chamber of commerce offices, as well as convention and visitors bureaus, provided much information on accommodations, restaurants, area businesses, services, and more. These offices are a wealth of information and are good places for hunters to stop when visiting an area.

Many thanks also to the dozens of helpful staff within the Michigan Department of Natural Resources. The MDNR field biologists and support staff in this state are topnotch. They're knowledgeable and very helpful to hunters with questions.

Thanks to the USDA Forest Service, which, along with the MDNR, gave us permission to reproduce the maps you'll find in this book.

Thanks also to Jason Smith for writing the bird description section; Christopher and Steve Smith for advice and encouragement; to Chris Zimmerman who supplied dozens of color prints and slides; and to Darren Brown, Chuck Johnson, and the folks at Wilderness Adventures Press for allowing me to have this opportunity.

Last, but certainly not least, my heartfelt thanks to family and friends for their patience and encouragement—especially my wife, Holly, and my two favorite hunting partners, Andrea and Alex.

Introduction

If you request outdoor information from a local chamber of commerce or visitor's bureau in Michigan, you will probably find no shortage of information on fishing or other outdoor activities. Finding specific hunting information is sometimes more difficult. This book will be helpful because it is a comprehensive guide with all the information you need to get started bird hunting in any part of the state.

Michigan's welcome mat is always out for tourists in any season, and you will find no shortage of excellent places to sleep or eat. To list every motel, hotel, and resort in good bird hunting territory would require a book 10 times the size of this one. We have listed a few places in each area, most of which have been supplied through local chamber of commerce offices. There are dozens more motels and campgrounds, rustic and modern, scattered throughout the state. Some of the motels, restaurants, sporting goods stores, and veterinarians' offices are located outside the hub city in which they are listed. This provides options for the traveling bird hunter who covers a lot of ground in any particular county.

We attempted to list mostly places that allow you to bring your bird dog inside. A word of caution here: we spoke with many hotel, motel, and resort owners who have either quit allowing dogs in their businesses or are considering banning them. They are fed up with owners who won't clean up after their dogs, let their dogs run without supervision, or lack the common sense to cage their dogs so they can't cause damage. It's tough enough to find a place that welcomes animals, and it's going to get more difficult in the future. Please make sure you clean up after your dog and put it in a cage when you are not in the room with it.

Although there huntable land in all of Michigan's 83 counties, there is generally more elbow room as you head north. There are no state game areas in the Upper Peninsula and few in the northern Lower Peninsula. That's because these areas have abundant state and federal lands that are home to many species of birds and animals. There are pros and cons to hunting every part of the state. For example, heading north, there is more ruffed grouse and public land, but the best pheasant country is found in southern Michigan's farmland, most of which is privately held. But no matter where you go, you'll find no shortage of opportunities.

As with any outdoor pursuit, success largely depends on your willingness to scout —in the field and out. Besides checking out likely coverts, it is necessary to keep an eye out for other hunters in the field and pay attention to what is being said in local establishments. While picking up overheard tips here and there, you might stumble into a friendly local resident who will be more than happy to provide some advice. Write or call the local chamber of commerce before your trip or stop there when you arrive, and you will be able to get more information. The chambers of Michigan have been indispensable in helping to put this guide together, as have the Michigan Department of Natural Resources (www.dnr.state.mi.us) and U.S. Forest Service.

Hunt safely and have fun!

Hotel Fee Key: $ = Under $40; $$ = $40 to $60; $$$ = Over $60

Major Roads and Rivers of Michigan

Michigan Facts

Area	96,810 sq mi (56,809 land, 40,001 water)
Rank	11
Highest point	Mount Arvon, 1,979 feet
Lowest point	Lake Erie, 572 feet
Capital	Lansing
Counties	83
Population	9,863,775
Nickname	Wolverine State or Great Lakes State
State Flower	Apple blossom
State Bird	Robin
State Fish	Brook trout
State Tree	White pine
State Stone	Petoskey stone
State Reptile	Painted turtle
State Wildflower	Dwarf Lake iris
State Mammal	White-tailed Deer
Name Origin	From the Indian word meaning great or large lake
State Parks	96 (265,000 acres)
State Forests	6
State Game Lands	61
National Forests	4
National Parks	5
Wilderness Areas	6

Michigan Hunting Regulations

Highlights

Michigan Department of Natural Resources
Wildlife Bureau
Box 30444
Lansing, MI 48909
517-373-1263
www.dnr.state.mi.us

Identification

It is illegal to destroy the identity of game or evidence of the game's sex while in the field or when transporting in a motor vehicle.

Transportation

You may transport another person's game as well as your own. You may not destroy the identity or evidence of the bird or animal's sex. If you are transporting migratory birds, one fully feathered wing must be left on each of them. If you are transporting another person's migratory birds, the birds must be tagged with the person's name, signature, address, number of all birds by species, dates of kill, and the hunter's small game license number.

Hunter Education Requirement

All hunters born on or after January 1, 1960, must have completed a hunter safety course. When purchasing a license, you must present a hunting safety certificate or a previous hunting license. If you cannot present either of these, you must sign an affidavit stating that you have completed a hunter safety course or have previously possessed a hunting license in Michigan or elsewhere.

Closed Season on Sharp-tailed Grouse

Although sharp-tailed grouse are listed in this book as a game species, the season was closed at the writing of this book. When open, it is limited to a small area in the Upper Peninsula's Chippewa County. Wildlife biologists are monitoring the sharptail population and may decide if it can withstand a hunting season at a later date. Check your hunting regulations.

Posting and Trespass

You must have permission from the landowner or leaseholder in order to hunt on any lands fenced or posted as private or on any farmlands or connected woodlots. Landowners may grant verbal permission. Hunters must show their hunting licenses upon request of the landowner.

Michigan has approximately 2 million acres of commercial forestlands, mostly in the Upper Peninsula, that are private lands where hunting and fishing are allowed.

*The future
of Michigan hunting.*

Commercial forestlands may not be marked or have signs that designate them as such, but they may be fenced or gated. Listings of commercial forestlands are available in booklets available from the Michigan Department of Natural Resources for a fee. You can get a booklet order form by writing DNR Forest Management Division, P.O. Box 30452, Lansing, Michigan, 48909-7952, or by calling 517-373-1275. If you call, the department can send an order form to you by fax.

Other private lands available to hunters include more than 55,000 acres of farmland that the DNR leases in southern Michigan through the Hunter Access Program. The program is funded by hunting license fees. You may hunt on these lands with permission of the landowner, who will issue a tag to you. You can get a free publication, Public Hunting on Private Lands, from southern Michigan DNR offices, license dealers, and other outlets.

Turkeys flock up before winter. (Photo by Chris Zimmerman)

Closed or Restricted Areas

The *Michigan Hunting and Trapping Guide* lists a number of townships that are closed to hunting or restricted to types of firearms or the discharge of firearms. The areas may be posted with restrictions. The township clerk or local police department should also be able to provide information.

Sunday Hunting

Some parts of Michigan are closed to all or some types of hunting on Sundays. In Hillsdale, Lenawee, Tuscola, and Washtenaw Counties, there is no hunting with firearms or dogs except on state lands. Likewise, in Macomb and St. Clair Counties, there is no hunting with firearms or dogs except on state lands, and you can hunt waterfowl in offshore border waters of the Great Lakes and Lake St. Clair.

Off-Road Vehicle Use

It is illegal to operate an off-road vehicle (ORV) on public lands in the Lower Peninsula that are not posted as open. This rule does not apply in the Upper Peninsula yet. Statewide, it is illegal to operate an ORV between 7 and 11AM and from 2 to 5PM in any area open to public hunting. This does not apply during the firearm deer season, and it does not apply to persons using ORVs for an emergency or to travel to a residence or hunting camp that is not accessible by car or truck.

Firearms in Motor Vehicles

Firearms in motor vehicles must be unloaded in the barrel and magazine and either cased or carried in the trunk.

Hunting ducks on a beaver pond. (Photo by Chris Zimmerman)

Number of Shells in the Gun

When hunting woodcock and waterfowl, your shotgun cannot be capable of holding more than three shells, and your gun must be plugged. With other upland birds, a plug is not necessary.

Age Restriction

Hunters under age 17 must be accompanied by a parent, guardian, or person 17 or older who has been designated by the parent or guardian.

Tentative Season Dates

Ruffed Grouse

- September 15–November 14 statewide *and*
  December 1–January 1 in Zones 2, 3
- Daily limit: 5 in Zones 1, 2
            3 in Zone 3
- Possession limit: 10 in Zones 1, 2
                6 in Zone 3

Scott Adams and Jake, a tricolored setter. (Photo by Chris Zimmerman)

Woodcock
- Varies from year to year — mid to late September to early November
- Daily Limit: 3
- Possession limit: 6

Pheasant
- October 10–20 in Zone 1
  October 20–November 14 in Zones 2, 3
  Plus late season, December 1–15 in parts of Zone 3
- Daily limit: 2 males per day
- Possession limit: 4
- Season limit: 8

Bobwhite Quail
- Varies from year to year: If open: late October to early or mid-November; open only in parts of Zone 3
- Daily limit 5
- Possession limit: 10

Ducks and Geese

- Varies from season to season: Ducks generally open on first Saturday in October in Zones 1 and 2; second Saturday in October in Zone 3
- Goose opens in late September; a special late season is held in Zones 2 and 3 in January and February
- Bag limits vary from season to season; possession limits are generally twice the daily bag limit

Early Canada Goose Season

- September 1–10 in Zone 1
  September 1–15 in Zones 2, 3
- Daily limit: 5
- Possession limit: 10

Snipe

- September 15–November 14, statewide
- Daily limit: 8
- Possession limit: 16

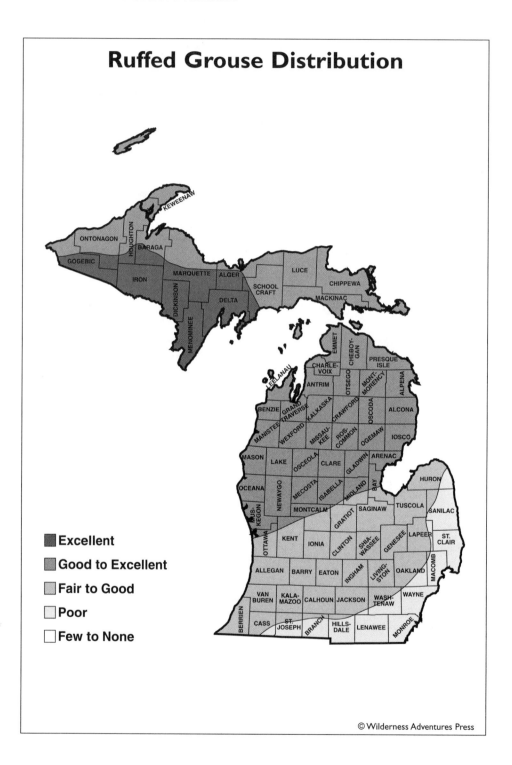

Ruffed Grouse Distribution

■ Excellent
■ Good to Excellent
■ Fair to Good
□ Poor
□ Few to None

© Wilderness Adventures Press

Ruffed Grouse

Bonasa umbellus

FIELD FACTS

Local Names
Partridge, pat, wood grouse

Size
Ruffed grouse are chicken-like birds of the deciduous forest, ranging in weight from 1 to 2 pounds, and around 17 inches long.

Identification in Flight
The thunderous flush from thick cover is the best indicator of a ruffed grouse, as well as the large fanned tail with a black bar near the tip that is very evident in flight. In Michigan, most ruffed grouse have a gray appearance, common for grouse in the northern tier of states, however, some red-phased birds can be found.

Appearance
Ruffed grouse are considered by many upland hunters to be the king of the uplands, and for hunters of the north and northeastern woods, they are perhaps the most prized gamebird. In northern Michigan, this is certainly the case. In the southern parts of the state, ruffed grouse sometimes take a backseat to the more highly sought ring-necked pheasant.

Ruffed grouse have a spectacular patterning of grays, browns, whites, and blacks throughout their body. The ruff, from which the bird got its name, is a black collar of feathers around the neck—large in males and greatly reduced in females—that the male puffs out during displays of courtship or aggression. Besides the ruff, the most characteristic feature of a ruffed grouse is its large fanned tail, a true prize for the bird hunter who bags a grouse. This tail has a black bar near the tip, with white or gray bands on either side of it, and finer dark bands down each tailfeather.

Though ruffed grouse have two color phases—red and gray—hunters in Michigan more often see the gray phase, and this color in the tail is very evident. However, some red-phased birds can be taken throughout the state, and these birds have a reddish-brown hue to the feathers, especially in the tail. Though many people claim to be able to age or sex ruffed grouse by the tail fan, the most reliable clue as to the sex can be found in the rump feathers at the base of the tail. These feathers have one white dot for a female or two white dots for a male.

*Ruffed grouse. (Photo
by Deb Cook)*

Ruffed grouse also sport a crest on their head, and in the winter, their feet develop natural snowshoes, with the feathers extending down toward the base of the legs and tiny projections off the toes.

NOTE: Do not confuse ruffed grouse with spruce grouse, which are found throughout the Upper Peninsula. In Michigan, spruce grouse are not recognized as game birds, and they are illegal to shoot.

On the Wing

The mighty roar of wings while flushing signals a ruffed grouse. The tail fan should be very evident in flight—if you can get a good look at the bird—and an overall gray or reddish-brown appearance with a lighter belly shows in flight. Ruffed grouse are extremely fast flyers—they can reach speeds up to 40 miles per hour—and in the woods, they seem to fly even faster. They are quick to dodge and duck around trees, finding their way through thick forests with ease.

Daily Habits and Food

Depending on the season, male ruffed grouse may spend much of the day "drumming" (an advertising and territorial display in which the male beats his wings ferociously against his breast) on a fallen log or stump. Drumming is interrupted for dusting, feeding, and roosting.

Ruffed grouse are known for eating a wide variety of foods, such as insects; buds of aspen, birch, willow, and other trees and herbaceous plants; berries of all kinds; and green leaves. Young ruffed grouse feed almost entirely on insects and then move on to an herbivorous diet, although adult ruffed grouse still eat insects. Some researchers feel that the population cycle (periods of highs and lows) of ruffed grouse may be tied to a major food source (aspen buds), although there are other theories that are equally plausible.

Seasonal Patterns

The spring season finds the woods filled with the sound of drumming. Males stake out a territory and advertise their position to females—and other males—with the drumming. The male then usually struts along his drumming log with his ruff and tail fanned out, and females approach. The two copulate, she lays the eggs, and he searches out more mates.

Nests are usually located in mature hardwood stands, under low-hanging branches or fallen logs. Between 9 and 12 eggs hatch a little over three weeks after the laying of the last egg. Upon hatching, the young are whisked away into thicker cover that offers more food in the form of insects, and by the age of one week, the young grouse are making their first flights.

Brood dispersal follows approximately four months after hatching, with the males off to find suitable cover for future drumming. With the coming fall and the dispersal almost complete, drumming again takes place, usually to advertise that a territory is occupied. Early in the hunting season, though, it isn't uncommon to flush a brood of grouse underfoot.

Winter can be a devastating force on ruffed grouse. If the snow has a lot of crust to it or there are some severe ice storms, the mortality rate on grouse can be very high. Ruffed grouse are "snow roosters" and burrow into the snow to keep warm and evade predators. The burrows provide excellent insulation for winter protection, staying almost 50 degrees warmer than the outside temperature. Therefore, it is not of critical concern if the winter brings large amounts of snowfall—it depends on the type of snow.

If an ice storm hits while a grouse is in the burrow, the bird may be buried alive, or ice can actually clog the nasal passages and the bird can suffocate. While evading predators—namely goshawks and great horned owls—ruffed grouse dive into snow-banks to escape. If the snow is crusty, grouse can break their necks while trying to dive, or the crusty snow may just push the grouse into thinner cover where avian predators can hunt more easily. Ruffed grouse are adapted to the snow, and as long as there is a powdery snow throughout the winter, even in large amounts, then grouse can move around, feed, and roost relatively easily.

Preferred Habitat and Cover

The best ruffed grouse habitat is a stand of aspen that includes trees of different ages. This mosaic creates edge, and the different age classes of the trees—a second-growth stand about as big around as your forearm; a large, more mature stand; and very young trees growing thick—provide habitat throughout the seasons. The mature stand offers excellent winter and nesting habitat; the second growth stands provide an abundant supply of food during the fall and summer; and the young stand is excellent cover for raising broods. Places where these ages overlap or are in close proximity to each other almost always hold ruffed grouse.

Areas of Michigan where logging activity occurs—especially pulp wood cutting in the central and western Upper Peninsula—are very popular with grouse and grouse hunters.

When the winter—or late in the hunting season—has seen a hard snowfall or some ice storms, ruffed grouse may move into pine tree stands, seeking shelter and insulation from low-hanging pine boughs. This type of habitat provides excellent winter cover, and ruffed grouse can be almost like ghosts in the pines.

Hunting Methods

Hunting ruffed grouse is considered by many to be the most frustrating, yet rewarding, form of wingshooting. Ruffed grouse are fast flyers, and shooting consists almost entirely of snap shots with the birds finding their way behind a tree just as you pull the trigger. Grouse do hold fairly well, and if hunting without a dog, you may get some close flushes, especially early in the season if there are still some broods around. But ruffed grouse cover is thick, and if alone, you'll have to bust through it yourself. This may hinder your chances of bagging a grouse.

Hunting with Dogs

Pointing dogs are preferred when hunting ruffed grouse. The cover is thick, and with a flushing dog, you may not be entirely ready for a flush. Because the shots are so quick—unlike a pheasant that can startle you but still give you ample time to calm down and take a shot—ruffed grouse are gone in an instant. Pointing dogs that can pin the birds allow you to approach and get close flushes, sometimes even pushing the birds in the direction of thinner cover so you can get a better shot.

Those who use flushing dogs, though, find that the dog can bust though the thick cover while the hunter skirts the edges, presenting him with clearer firing lanes.

Keep in mind the time of year when hunting with a dog. Ruffed grouse cover usually holds some water—either a stream or some low-lying holes that have collected rainwater—and make sure to let your dog take a drink.

Bells or beeper collars are essential when hunting ruffed grouse with dogs. Again, because of the thick cover, it may be hard to keep an eye on your dog all the time. When the bell falls silent or the beeper collar goes into the point mode, move up and get ready for a quick shot.

Table Preparations

Ruffed grouse offer some of the most excellent upland gamebird meat there is. The white meat of the breasts and thighs can be very tender—especially with young birds early in the season—and a roasted grouse stuffed with apples is hard to beat.

Chris Zimmerman with Chip, Zack, and a handful of grouse.
(Photo by Chris Zimmerman)

You can also fillet the breasts and fix them as you would boneless chicken breasts. If you've hung them for a few hours or a day, you'll get a hint of wild flavor that will add to the meal.

Gun and Shot Suggestions
- **Gauge**   20, 16, or 12
- **Choke**   Cylinder and Improved for doubles, or either choke for single barrels. Later in the season, when the foliage has dropped, you can go to the tighter choke.
- **Shot**   Spreader loads available from various companies are useful. A load of ⅞ to 1 oz. No. 7½ or 8 is recommended.

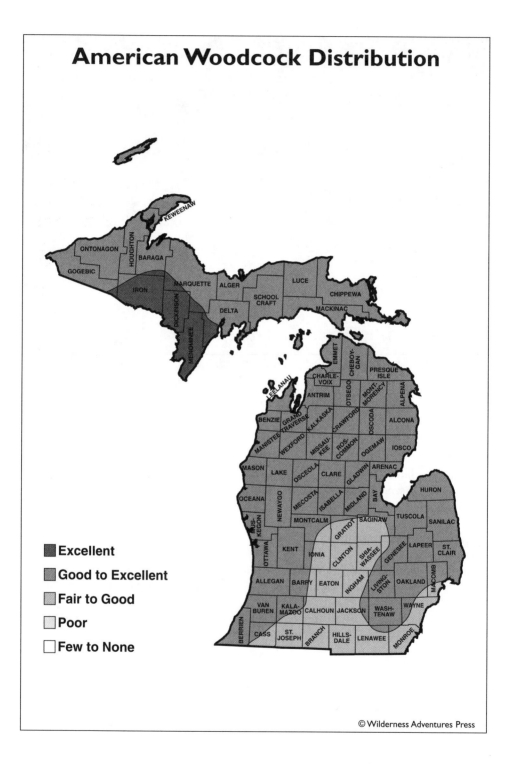

American Woodcock Distribution

Excellent

Good to Excellent

Fair to Good

Poor

Few to None

© Wilderness Adventures Press

American Woodcock

Scolopax minor

FIELD FACTS

Local Names
   Timberdoodle, becasse, night partridge, big-headed snipe

Size
   Woodcock are stocky migratory upland gamebirds. The females are larger than the males, averaging around 8 ounces and 6 ounces, respectively. They are between 10 and 11 inches in length, with bills over 2 inches long.

Identification in Flight
   The twittering sound upon being flushed—the sound of air passing through the primary feathers as the bird takes off—and the long bill and plump shape are key indicators of a woodcock. Flight is typically quick through the cover, as the bird twists and dips in and out of openings.

Appearance

A woodcock is a beautiful mix of browns and blacks, with bold black markings on the head, a long bill, and large black eyes. This stocky bird—which is actually in the sandpiper (shorebird) family but is found in the moist uplands—is closely associated with ruffed grouse, and very often, a hunter will encounter both on the same hunt. Woodcock are well camouflaged with their surroundings of brown leaves, and if they hold tight, they are very often passed by.

On the Wing

While in the woods after ruffed grouse, you might flush this smaller, plumper bird that twitters upon taking flight. Woodcock make sharp twists and turns through the trees or head straight to the top of the cover and head for other places once in the clear. They are not fast flyers in the open, under 15 miles per hour, but through the thick cover, they appear quick. During their courtship display in the spring, male woodcock do a "sky dance," begun by a *peenting* sound on the ground, followed by a high spiral flight ending in a warbling song at the top, and terminating in a nosedive back to the original spot where the *peenting* took place.

Daily Habits and Food

Woodcock sit tight in the cover during the day when hunters are out, and they do their feeding in the evening and after dark. Like the common snipe, they also eat

Ted Morand of Tawas City holds a nice Michigan woodcock. (Photo by Chris Zimmerman)

invertebrates—namely earthworms—and they locate them in the mud with their long probing, prehensile bills. The ears on woodcock are positioned forward of the eyes so that they can hear the movement of the worms, and their large eyes are positioned back in the head, allowing them to watch for predators in all directions while their bills are in the mud. If walking down a dirt trail with puddles in the mud, scout the edges for woodcock tracks, probe holes, and droppings—you may find an indication of a good woodcock covert nearby.

Seasonal Patterns

Woodcock are migrating upland gamebirds, passing through their range in what are called the "flights." Though woodcock do not migrate in flocks, a large number of birds can be found in a very small area at this time, usually in late fall. They migrate at night, following river courses and using a strong north wind for aid in flight. If the winds calm after a strong blow from the north, they might stick around a while, providing fine hunting. Because of the woodcock's migratory habits, southern Michigan lands that may not hold large numbers of birds during the year can still provide good hunting in the fall.

Woodcock draw many hunters to Michigan. (Photo by Chris Zimmerman)

The courtship display marks the return of woodcock in the spring, and after copulation, nests are laid close to a male's *peenting* ground in a cuplike depression in an alder cut. Four eggs are usually laid, with an incubation period of three weeks, and the young making their first strong flights between three and four weeks of age.

Preferred Habitat and Cover

Young aspen and alders found in good ruffed grouse cover are a good spot for woodcock, but a series of medium to tall alders bordering an overgrown pasture or hayfield provides consistent shooting, especially during the flights. In order to be good woodcock cover, though, there must be water close by—this keeps the surrounding soil moist so the bird can forage for worms—and the ground vegetation can't be too grassy, which impedes walking because of the bird's long bill. A hillside of alders with a stream at the bottom is ideal cover.

Hunting Methods

Walking after woodcock is easier than it is for ruffed grouse, simply because woodcock don't run as far or as fast—but holding tight can almost be as bad. Without a dog, expect to walk past most birds.

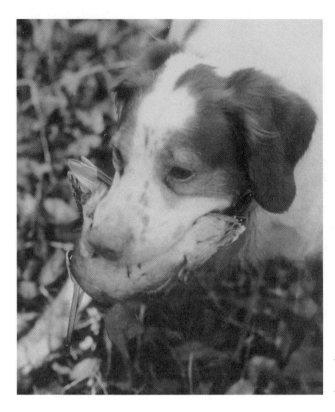

Zack brings a woodcock to hand. (Photo by Chris Zimmerman)

If you can push through a good covert, though, especially during the flights, you can move up to 50 birds in a day, even without a dog.

Hunting with Dogs

Pointing dogs are ideal for woodcock hunting, and many fine English setters, shorthairs, Brittanys, and pointers are trained in their first year on woodcock during the flights. The birds hold well for dogs, allowing the hunter to flush the bird toward a clear shooting area, and a dog that retrieves helps find the heavily camouflaged bird.

Flushing dogs work well, also, but stay close. The thick cover provides almost entirely snap shots, so if hunting with a flushing dog, you need to be on its heels to get a shot off. A bell or beeper collar is strongly recommended.

Don't forget to let your dog take a dip and a big drink in that stream you found flowing through ideal woodcock habitat.

Table Preparations

There is not a lot of meat on woodcock, but they are some of the most delicious gamebirds. Fillet the dark breasts, marinate overnight in Italian dressing, and the next

Woodcock are present in much of Michigan. (Photo by Chris Zimmerman)

day, place each breast on a wedge of onion, wrap in bacon, secure with a toothpick, and throw them on a hot grill. Place the white thighs on a skewer, brush with barbecue sauce, and put them on the grill as well. It is a very rich meal; served with wild rice, it's one of the finest wild game meals.

Gun and Shot Suggestions

- **Gauge**   20, 16, or 12
- **Choke**   Cylinder and Improved for doubles, or either choke for single barrels.
- **Shot**   A light field load of ⅞ oz. No. 8 or spreader loads of the same size is preferred.

Ring-necked Pheasant Distribution

Legend:
- Excellent
- Good to Excellent
- Fair to Good
- Poor
- Few to None

© Wilderness Adventures Press

Ring-necked Pheasant

Phasianus colchicus

FIELD FACTS

Local Names
Ringneck, rooster

Size
Males have long tailfeathers that can account for two-thirds of the overall size of a pheasant. Excluding the tail, pheasants are a little over a foot long and weigh a bit more than 2 pounds.

Identification in Flight
Male pheasants cackle upon flushing, usually running well ahead of hunters and taking flight when cover has run out. The long, barred tailfeathers are very obvious, as is the dark bronze body, green head, and red wattles (cheeks). Females —not legal game in Michigan—very often flush underfoot. They may utter faint cackles, but they have shorter tails and a dull brown appearance.

Appearance

Ring-necked pheasants are perhaps the most sought after—and harvested— upland gamebird in the country, and Michigan is no exception, particularly in the south. Male pheasants—roosters—are brightly colored with long, flowing tails that can't be missed in flight. The body is bronze colored with an array of blues, greens, and yellows on the back. The head is an iridescent green with a red wattle surrounding the eye and cheek; a stark white ring around the neck gives the bird its name. Mature males have small ear tufts and a silver cap on top of the head.

Female, or hen, pheasants are a mottled light tan color. Hens also have long tails, but not as long as the rooster's. It is important to know that only roosters are legal for harvesting, except on shooting preserves, in which case, hens may be legally harvested.

On the Wing

Roosters are unmistakable in flight. The loud cackle and thunderous wingbeats from the cover are what many hunters live for. The long tail adds to the bird's perceived size, and the white ring around the neck contrasts with the darker body. Hen pheasants flush closer, and they may give faint cackles upon flushing but will usually stay quiet.

Mike Poff and Parker, his Chessie, with two nice pheasant. (Photo by Chris Zimmerman)

Their flight pattern is one of rapid wingbeats and glides, and they achieve their fastest speeds after flying for a short while. A passing pheasant that has been in the air for several hundred yards may be moving faster than 45 miles per hour. Roosters are notorious for running through cover, preferring to escape on foot rather than in the air. But once cornered—by human or a good dog—or at the end of cover, the bird will take flight.

Daily Habits and Food

Pheasants usually roost in fields close by feeding areas. This is a popular way to hunt the birds—early in the morning in thick hayfields before they've moved into cornfields to eat for most of the morning, and then to water if it's available. During late morning and early afternoon, they move back into the grass fields to loaf and dust, and then back again for more food.

Dave Zimmerman is happy with this pheasant. (Photo by Chris Zimmerman)

Corn is the food type most commonly associated with pheasants, but they also eat other waste grains, such as barley, wheat, and oats. Both juveniles and adults consume a large variety of insects.

During the harsh winters that can pound the Midwest, pheasants congregate in areas where food is the easiest to reach. In extremely harsh times, when snow and ice have covered up those food stores, pheasant populations can take a nosedive. But these hardy birds usually bounce back within a couple years of a harsh winter.

Seasonal Patterns

As mentioned, winter can take a devastating toll on the pheasant population. Pheasants use the snow for roosting, and if storms are especially strong, there could be considerable die-off. This can be either from the snow and ice locking them in their snow roosts, the snow covering their food, or harsh conditions pushing the birds to thinner cover where they can be preyed upon.

Dan Zeneberg and his German shorthair, Sheena, have reason to be happy with this catch. (Photo by Chris Zimmerman)

In March, a rooster begins to strut before a female, his wattle greatly engorged, ear tufts raised, and tail fan spread and exposed. After copulation, the hen constructs a nest in hayfields, established wildlife habitat plantings, or even road ditches, and lays between 10 to 12 eggs. Incubation is a little over three weeks, and chicks can make short flights after one week.

When fall rolls around, brood dispersal scatters the pheasants, and many birds join into closely associated flocks. During these times, a hunter may be able to flush a significant number of birds in a small area, especially late in the season when the weather has flattened most of the other available cover.

Preferred Habitat and Cover

No other bird is so closely tied to the cultivation of this country's land as the ring-necked pheasant. Though the mechanization of farming that led to "clean" farms threatened to decimate the population, legislation that brought the 1985 and 1996

Jim Jacobs of Mt. Pleasant with pheasant. (Photo by Chris Zimmerman)

Farm Bill and Conservation Reserve Program (CRP) have given the pheasant popula-tion in Michigan a tremendous boost.

The ring-necked pheasant adapted well after its introduction from Asia in the late 1800s. It is a bird of agricultural land, CRP fields of switchgrass and hay; and wooded creek bottoms, draws, and sloughs. Where these grass fields and draws border corn-fields, pheasants will most likely be found.

Pheasants find cover during the winter in draws and sloughs that offer excellent protection from the elements. Wooded draws and sloughs can provide excellent late-season shooting, except when prolonged or intense blizzards fill in these areas with snow. Shelterbelts also provide some winter cover, but those areas are usually thin and fill with snow fairly fast, especially if there is a significant amount of wind. Wherever there is food available during winter, large flocks of pheasants will be seen.

Hunting Methods

Pheasant hunting is probably one of the oldest upland hunting traditions in the country, and many hunters were raised pursuing these birds. Many a young hunter in southern Michigan has been allowed to skip a day of school on the traditional October opening day of the season.

There are several ways to hunt pheasants, all equally enjoyable. One is to push through fields, plowing through the most likely looking cover. Hunting the roosting fields near feeding areas early in the morning can prove extremely efficient, and limits can be had in a matter of minutes.

Once in standing corn, pheasants can be hard to put up for a close shot, so another method, called blocking and driving, can be effective. More hunters are needed to hunt pheasants in this manner, but it can be extremely effective, especially in cornfields. Three or four hunters (drivers) push through the corn while the rest of the party (blockers) stands ready at the other end. Caught in this pincer action, the birds most often run to the end of the corn, and once out of cover—or when they see the blockers—take to the air. Or, if the drivers flush birds while walking through the corn, blockers might get fast pass shots at the incoming birds. Blocking and driving can also be done in hayfields, CRP areas, and just about anywhere else.

Once in the air, a rooster pheasant is not that hard a target, but once they get going, these birds can really move! It takes a stout blow to bring one down, though, so be very conscious of not only hitting the bird but hitting him near the head and neck. A crippled pheasant for the dogless hunter almost always ends with a light game bag.

And again, remember that only male pheasants can be legally harvested, which makes distinguishing between a male and a female pheasant a must.

Hunting with Dogs

To deal with the possibility of losing cripples, pheasant hunters are almost never seen without a dog. Flushing dogs—Labrador retrievers and springer spaniels—are preferred simply because of their drive to pursue and retrieve downed birds. Because the pheasant is one of the cagiest gamebirds when it comes to running from danger, a hard-working flushing dog will stay hot on its trail.

But pointing dogs also shine on pheasants, especially those that can stick with a running bird and are trained to retrieve. Some of the best pheasant hunts, though, come with a combination of flushing and pointing dogs, especially if the team has a history of working together. One points, the other goes in and flushes.

Dogs also make the work of pushing through the thick creek bottoms a lot easier, and this may be another situation for the flushing dog. The hunter can simply skirt the edges while the dog pushes through. The hunter has to be prepared to take off running after a flushing dog when it hits a scent trail. The pheasant almost always tries running away before flying, so you'll have to keep up if you want a shot when the bird finally decides to flush.

Table Preparations

Pheasants are among the most succulent of all wild game. The white meat of the pheasant's breast and the darker meat of the thighs are a treat to be savored. Phea-

Al Straus of Beal City with a beautiful pheasant and his German shorthaired pointer. (Photo by Chris Zimmerman)

sants can be tough, though, so any crockpot recipe for turkey or chicken breasts works well for pheasants. If baking, you can stuff the body cavity with onions and coat the meat with salt and pepper and poultry seasoning or fillet the breast away from the bone, marinate in Italian dressing, and grill topped with pineapple rings. Any recipe you use for chicken or grouse will also work for pheasant. You may wish to hang the birds for an evening, but when the birds are warm, skinning them is much easier.

Gun and Shot Suggestions
- **Gun**   12, 16
- **Choke**   Improved and Modified for doubles, Modified for single barrels. Many hunters choose full choke, especially late in the season.
- **Shot**   A strong field load of 1⅛ to 1¼ oz. of No. 6 or No. 5 will be your best choice for pheasants. Late in the season, No. 4 is a good choice for long shots.

Wild Turkey Distribution

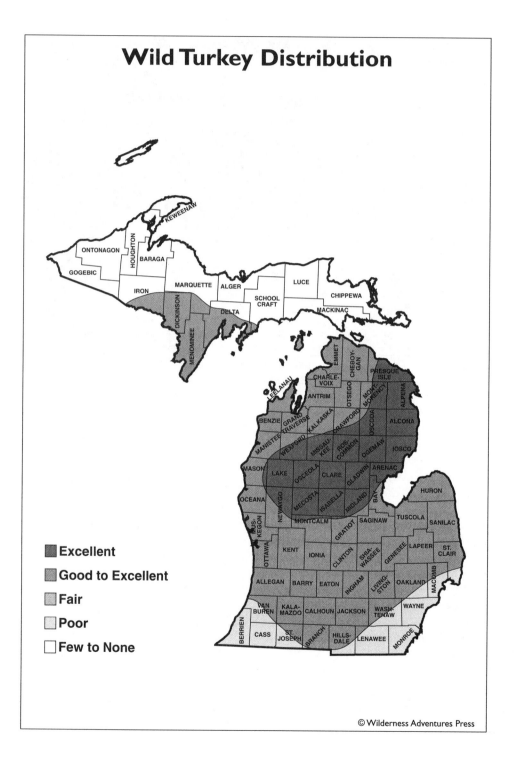

Excellent

Good to Excellent

Fair

Poor

Few to None

© Wilderness Adventures Press

Wild Turkey

Meleagris gallopavo

FIELD FACTS

Local Names
Wood turkey, American turkey, tom, gobbler

Size
These largest of the upland gamebirds (usually considered big game) are 3 to 4 feet in length, and large males can weigh more than 25 pounds.

Identification in Flight
Turkeys are hunted almost exclusively on the ground, so flight identification is rarely needed. On the ground, the bare-skinned, red head of a turkey, combined with the long beard of a mature male, the bronze colored body, and a wide fanned tail are readily identifiable.

Appearance

It is hard to mistake a turkey for anything else: The breast feathers are an iridescent bronze color tipped in black; the wings are black-and-white barred; and the large tail that fans out in courtship and aggressive displays is tipped in brown with black bars down to the body. And of course, there is the signature bare-skinned red head with a fleshy snood—a projection off the top of the bill—and red wattles.

Big males have a beard, and this trophy of turkey hunters can extend anywhere from an inch to over 10 inches from the breast. The hens are a little more pale, and their heads are not as bright red. During the spring, the head of the male (tom) has a blue cast.

On the Wing

A flying turkey is a sight rarely forgotten. Despite their size, turkeys do fly up and down from their roosts, usually in a thunderous clatter of wings, appearing to have trouble getting off the ground. Once they get up a good head of steam, though, turkeys can reach speeds near 35 miles per hour. However, turkeys prefer to run, and for this reason, they are hunted almost exclusively on the ground, using big game, as opposed to traditional bird hunting, methods.

Daily Habits and Food

Turkeys are early risers, flying down from their roosts at dawn. They feed, display, fraternize a bit, dust, and feed some more before returning to their roosts in the evening. Most turkey hunters like to go out the night before to see where the

Author with a spring gobbler. (Photo by Chris Zimmerman)

birds are flying in to roost and then set up with a decoy or two near the roost early the next morning.

Turkeys are voracious eaters of just about everything—primarily seeds, acorns, nuts, berries, and various insects, and even small amphibians and reptiles. Turkeys gather small pebbles to use as grit in their powerful stomachs in order to grind some of the toughest forage.

Seasonal Patterns

Turkeys are nonmigratory birds and make it through the winter in the same type of habitat they occupy the rest of the year. However, they might be found in thicker cover and pine forests, because these areas are less likely to fill up with snow, covering the food supply.

The breeding season is when most turkey hunting takes place, with the large toms being the target during their courtship display of puffed out feathers, fanned tail, strut, and loud gobbles. Females nest near openings in the forest close to some

Chris Zimmerman with a spring turkey season catch.

overhead cover. About one dozen eggs are laid, and they are incubated for four weeks. The young (poults) stick close to the hen for the first few weeks of life—a time of rapid growth—and once the juveniles are making strong flights up to perches and roosts, the broods begin to disperse.

Preferred Habitat and Cover

Turkeys spend a lifetime in hardwood forests bordered by grass, hay, or agricultural fields. Roosting usually takes place in the larger, more mature hardwood or pine trees. Because most of the strutting occurs in open areas, the place to set up a hen decoy is in a field bordering these forests. With the proper calling, a gobbler can be coaxed out of the woods, where he'll head for the decoy, presenting a clear shot.

Hunting Methods

Many hunters argue that there is no finer time to be in the woods than in autumn, but turkey hunters know how wonderful it is to be outdoors during the Michigan

Turkeys flock together on a rise. (Photo by Chris Zimmerman)

spring. The woods are coming to life with budding vegetation and the sounds of migratory birds. Morel mushrooms are popping up, providing the hunter with a tasty side dish to add to his turkey dinner.

The hunting season on turkeys is frequently tied to the breeding season in the spring. This makes it easier to select large, mature toms—adult male turkeys—using decoys and calls of the hen turkey to lure them within range.

The vocabulary of turkeys and turkey hunters is comprised of calls, such as the *putt, cluck,* or *cut, gobble, yelp, kee,* and others. A hunter needs to be fluent with this language to be a successful turkey hunter.

Locating turkeys before actually hunting them is the best way to prepare, though even this may prove unsuccessful. Turkeys are wary creatures, and if they sense something is amiss, they are quick to flee. Therefore, plenty of accurate camouflage is necessary. It is said that a deer sees a man and thinks it's a stump; a turkey sees a stump and thinks it's a man.

Turkeys should be taken by a shot in the head. A crippled bird can get up and fly or easily outrun you, taking multiple hits in the body. Even if you roll a big bird, move up fast and be ready.

For most hunters, shooting a bird on the ground is something out of the ordinary, but hitting and killing a standing bird is actually a lot harder than it sounds. The head should be visible just above the top of the gun barrel, and the trigger needs to be squeezed like a rifle. When you hear a gobbler approaching to your calls, mount the gun and prepare. You might be stuck in that position for quite a while, but turkeys can spot movement with an amazing eye. The bird should be no farther than 30 or 40 yards when you shoot.

If coming to Michigan to hunt turkeys, whether it be for the fall or spring season, you need to be aware that there is a lottery system for obtaining a turkey permit. If

Watch for morel mushrooms while spring turkey hunting— they make a tasty side dish.

your hunt is planned far enough in advance, you can apply before the deadline. But a special permit for a designated part of the state is required to hunt turkeys.

Although there are thousands of acres of state land available to turkey hunters, don't be afraid to knock on a farmer's door if you find some private land that looks promising. Private land turkeys can sometimes be remarkably less wary than birds found on state or federal land.

Table Preparations

A large tom can provide a huge meal, and everyone has his own Thanksgiving recipe for domestic turkeys that will work just as well with a wild bird. The nutty flavor of wild turkey, however, surpasses the supermarket bird.

Gun and Shot Suggestions
- **Gauge**   12
- **Choke**   Full
- **Shot**   Some hunters like a heavy field load of 1⅛ oz. No. 4 , but a load of 1⅛ oz. No. 6 or No. 5 will give you more pellets. Remember, your target is the head —not a very tough part of the bird. Some experienced hunters use No. 6 for the first shot at a standing bird, followed by No. 4 for subsequent shots at a running bird. The largest shot allowed for turkeys is No. 4.

Hunting Turkey Combines Upland Bird and Big Game Skills

For a bird hunter accustomed to shooting at feathered rockets that can weigh anywhere from a half-pound to maybe three or four pounds, bagging a turkey is akin to bringing home a dinosaur. A tom turkey sounds like a dinosaur when it issues its thunderous gobble, and at 20 pounds, it looks more like a prehistoric animal than it does a bird.

Even the method of hunting is more suited to bagging a woolly mammoth than it is to taking birds. Rather than push through cover with a canine companion to see what moves out, the turkey hunter waits in ambush, taking his quarry when it comes along snorting, stomping, and blowing steam.

Turkey hunting is a combination of upland bird and big game hunting, and it packs all of the excitement of those two pursuits into one activity. If you're skeptical, give it a try. I guarantee that the first time a lovesick gobbler answers you, you'll find it difficult to keep from swallowing your diaphragm call, and you'll swear that the approaching tom can hear your heart hammering.

Michigan motorists, accustomed to seeing flocks of wild turkeys feeding along highways, may be misled into thinking that turkeys are creatures of limited intelligence. Let those same birds see an approaching hunter or four-legged predator, though, and they disappear quickly. They're anything but dumb.

I've seen my share of birds on the highway, too, and sometimes I think the turkeys' response to fast-moving automobiles is due to indifference, rather than stupidity. Twice in the past 10 years, my partner, Chris Zimmerman of Mt. Pleasant, and I have called gobblers across highways, and both times the brazen birds nearly became road kill before making it to us.

One "highway gobbler" was particularly memorable. It was during my third year of turkey hunting. After two hours of waiting for a bird on a cold morning, we decided to move to another location. Just down the road from where we were hunting, we spotted several gobblers avoiding the chill by sunning themselves in an open field along the highway. We had permission to hunt the property on the opposite side of the road, so we set up an ambush.

It would be a long pull to get the bird over to us. The birds were 75 yards from the road. Before one of them could be converted to a turkey dinner, it would have to walk that distance, cross the highway, then strut another 100 yards or so to our stand, which was on the edge of a mature maple forest at the top of a good-sized hill. I was not overly confident with our setup, since

Brandon Vaughan in turkey country. (Photo by Chris Zimmerman)

it is very difficult to convince turkeys to cross obstacles such as roads, rivers, and hills, but Zim is a master at calling birds and he had all the confidence in the world.

As soon as Zim began calling, the bigger of the two gobblers expressed his interest. He gobbled and strutted and puffed out his feathers. Finally, slowly, he started to make his way toward us. I lost sight of the bird when he went into the ditch on the far side of the road, then I heard a car approaching.

As the turkey reappeared and stepped onto the pavement, the driver of the car beeped his horn, causing the turkey to gobble three times before running back to the safety of the field where he had been minding his own business and getting a suntan.

For the next few minutes, he gobbled and strutted in the field, hoping to lure the elusive hen over to his side of the road. Zim persisted on the call, begging the tom to try crossing the road again. (I should note that Zim does most of the calling during our turkey outings. He is adept at making the throaty, sexy yelps of a mature hen turkey, while my attempts on the call end up sounding like a pitiful, scrawny bird that might not be old enough to breed.)

I watched as the bird moved our way, again. The mating instinct must really cause turkeys to act crazy, because even after his recent close encounter with a chrome bumper, this turkey stood in the middle of the road again, practically daring another car to approach.

He continued toward us. I had been kneeling behind some brush to watch the highway gobbler, but when he disappeared at the bottom of the hill, I sat back against a large maple tree and, with shaking hands, attempted to steady my shotgun across my knees. A few minutes passed, and I began to think that the bird had come as far as he was going to and that he would get hung up at the bottom of the hill.

After what seemed like an hour, I saw the turkey's bald, red-white-and-blue head appear over the crest of the hill. The bird paused, fanned its tail and ruffled its feathers, then let out a loud gobble. He peered over the top of the hill, looking for the source of the calling, then he gobbled again. When he received no response, he walked closer, and I fired the 12-gauge.

The bird jumped and flapped his wings, then ran down the hill to a thicket near the edge of the road. Thinking I had wounded it, I jumped up and followed, stopping at the crest of the hill to fire another round at the rapidly retreating bird.

We found the gobbler, stone dead, at the base of a pine tree. He had been hit in the head and neck and must have died immediately, but he had run like the proverbial "chicken with its head cut off," and I had thought he was alive. Later, when we reviewed the videotape (Zim is a videographer, besides being a first-rate caller), it was obvious from the way that the bird ran with its wings outstretched and locked, that the shot had killed it, and it was gravity more than anything else that carried the bird down the hill.

Every turkey hunt that I've been on has been filled with excitement, but this particular hunt, since we could see the bird move toward us from such a long way off, was especially exhilarating. A big part of turkey hunting, as it is with any hunting, is getting the chance to see birds. Even during the hunts where I have not been lucky enough to get a turkey dinner, it's been exciting to watch the birds go about their daily routines, with the toms strutting around all puffed up and the hens paying little attention to the macho meatheads.

The chance to enjoy the woods is perhaps the best reason to get into spring turkey hunting. During years when the turkey population is thriving, Michigan

Turkeys in the corn stubble. (Photo by Chris Zimmerman)

opens a fall hunt, too, but classic turkey hunting is best done in spring, when the birds are involved in mating rituals.

Besides the loud turkey conversations, the spring woods are alive with the calling of a variety of songbirds, as well as the drumming of ruffed grouse and the commotion caused by ducks and geese staking out their territories on beaver ponds and small lakes. You'll also hear the buzzing of mosquitoes and blackflies, something the fall bird hunter does not encounter often, so come prepared with bug repellent, gloves, and a headnet. The headgear and gloves are a good idea even if the bugs aren't biting, because they hide your face and hands from the turkey. They may have their heads messed up in the mating game, but turkeys still have incredible eyesight. They can spot movement as well as or better than a deer can. Camouflage yourself from head to toe and keep still.

Another advantage to hunting in the spring is the availability of morel mushrooms. On more than a few hunts, we've come out of the woods with a hat full of morels. Sliced, rolled in flour, and fried in butter, they make a delicious side dish and go well with a heaping portion of roast wild turkey.

Northern Bobwhite Distribution

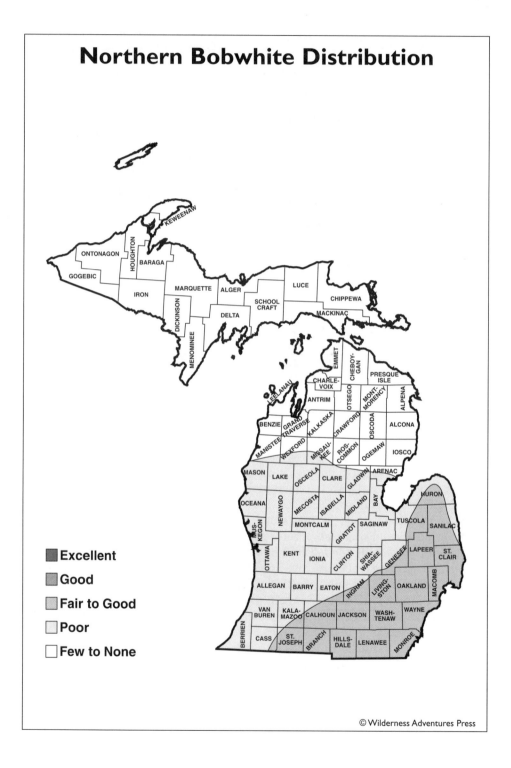

Excellent
Good
Fair to Good
Poor
Few to None

Northern Bobwhite

Colinus virginianus

FIELD FACTS

Local Names
  Quail, Bob

Size
  Bobwhite quail are among the smallest upland gamebirds, approximately 6 ounces and only 9 to 10 inches long.

Identification in Flight
  A burst of numerous birds from underfoot in brushy cover marks a covey of quail, which can contain 10 to 15 or as many as 20 birds. Though not as thunderous as its agricultural/open land cousin, the ring-necked pheasant, the buzzing covey can be just as startling. In flight, both sexes show an overall dark brown appearance.

Appearance

These small gamebirds have an intricate patterning of brown, buff, white, and black. Males have a white stripe through the eye and a white throat, while the same portions on females are buff in color. The breasts of both males and females are predominantly white with a pattern of dark Vs, and the back is covered by dark brown and black spots.

On the Wing

The covey rise of bobwhites is one of the greatest thrills in all of upland bird hunting. A loud whirring of wings upon flight, with birds scattering to all points of the compass easily identifies a covey of quail, even to those who have never seen it before. The birds fly in more or less straight lines, just clearing the top of the brush. Once the covey disperses, singles can be followed up with ease. Where quail are found in or along the borders of woodlots or wooded draws, these small, quick birds darting through the trees can present one of the toughest shots in wingshooting.

Daily Habits and Food

When evening arrives in quail country, the air is filled with the whistle call of the bobwhite—*bob-WHITE!* The call signals a broken covey to reform, and the group of 10 to 15 birds then settles in a tight circle for the night, tails pointing toward the center and heads pointing outward. The tightly bunched birds thus conserve body heat, especially during the winter months. During the autumn hunting season, the covey sticks together, feeding early in the morning, moving to dirt or gravel roads for grit later, and then back to loafing spots around midday. This process is repeated in the afternoon and evening.

Food for bobwhites usually consists of grass seeds, grains, leafy portions of plants, and some wild fruit. Summer months find the quail, especially juveniles, eating a large variety of insects. Coveys (family groups) can be spotted most easily when they move to roadsides for the grit necessary to grind and digest their food. A covey picking grit on the road means that good cover is nearby, because the birds walk rather than fly from cover to food to water to gravel.

Seasonal Patterns

The familiar call of the bobwhite is most often heard in the spring and summer, when males perch on fenceposts or in small trees and call to females or challenge other, nearby males. Pairs form in the spring after courtship, and sometimes intense fighting occurs between males. The nest is formed in a depression in the ground, along weedy fencerows or in brushy cover along fields or woodlots. Both sexes help incubate the 14 to 16 eggs, and after the almost three-and-a-half week incubation period, the young hatch and can fly at just under two weeks of age. The young may begin to covey with adults when they are as young as three weeks old.

Bobwhites are gregarious for almost the entire year, except for pair bonding during the breeding season. Throughout the year they are almost entirely in the covey group, and this becomes even more important in winter when the heat generated by the covey at night helps keep the birds warm. Scientists have found that for a covey to remain viable, there must be at least eight birds. It is a wanton waste to shoot a covey's numbers below eight, because cold and predators will wipe out the remaining birds.

Preferred Habitat and Cover

Though quail is king in the southern United States, Michigan has only small populations in some southern portions of the state, and many years the season is not open. In recent years, Michigan quail hunters have enjoyed a season more often than not, due at least in part to the Conservation Reserve Program (CRP) lands that have been a big help to pheasants, as well.

In most places where ring-necked pheasants are found, bobwhites can also be flushed. During the hunting season, brushy fencerows and thickets bordering fields or woodlots can hold a few coveys, and don't forget to check the thick brush around dilapidated farm homes or farm machinery.

Finding quail in the winter usually involves finding areas with the thickest cover still present in the barren agricultural landscape. The lands in the Conservation Reserve Program have benefitted quail just as much as pheasants.

Hunting Methods

Traditional quail hunts, such as those that take place in the South and Midwest where 20 or even 30 coveys can be moved in a day, most likely never happen in Michigan, but there are still some places where quite a few coveys can be found. Once the covey is broken up, singles can be followed up quite easily, and if hunting without a dog, following up singles is the best bet for putting quail in the bag. Without a dog, coveys can be hard to find, but what can be more difficult is finding a downed bird in the thick grass. The size and cryptic coloration of the bird make it a task to retrieve.

A large covey can fluster many young and experienced hunters, since it can be quite difficult to settle down on one bird and stick with it. It doesn't take a lot of shot to bring a quail down, but a crippled quail can run nearly as fast as a pheasant and, without a dog to trail it, can easily be lost.

Hunting with Dogs

Well-trained pointing dogs (English setters, pointers, and shorthairs) can make a quail hunt most exciting, as the birds, both the covey and singles, usually hold extremely well. But they have been known to scamper out from under a staunch point and flush far ahead of where you think they'll be. Flushing dogs (Labrador retrievers and springer spaniels, especially) can get the birds in the air immediately, and any dog that can retrieve is a valuable asset in the field.

Be sure to keep an eye on the dog, especially early in the season, since quail hunting can be a hot affair. If you check some of the creek bottoms or sloughs, you might find a covey along the edges, as well as a drink for the pooch.

Table Preparations

Baked or roasted quail are truly to be savored. The white, tender meat on the breast and legs, left on the bone, can dry out fairly easily unless you consistently baste throughout the cooking time. Stuffing the body cavity with onions and layering with bacon is a fine recipe, as is barbecuing the whole bird on a skewer, spreading with a favorite mesquite sauce or simply basting with butter.

Gun and Shot Suggestions

- **Gauge** 28, 20, 16, 12
- **Choke** For doubles, Skeet and Skeet, Cylinder and Skeet, or Cylinder and Improved Cylinder are the best choices; either a Skeet or Improved Cylinder choke work for single barrels. Later in the season, switch to slightly tighter chokes, such as Modified.
- **Shot** A light field load of ⅞ or 1 oz. of shot in #8 or #9 is the ideal quail load.

Sharp-tailed Grouse

Tympanuchus phasianellus

FIELD FACTS

Local Names
    Blackfoot, pintailed grouse, prairie grouse, sharptail, sharpie

Size
    Sharp-tailed grouse closely resemble their woodland cousins, the ruffed grouse, in size, being close to 17 inches long and around 2 pounds.

Identification in Flight
    The repeated *kuk-kuk-kuk-kuk* call of a flushing sharp-tailed grouse might get confused with a hen pheasant, but sharptails show large amounts of white from their wings, an obvious eye-catcher. In profile, the pointed tail is evident, and their flight is a series of rapid wingbeats and glides.

Hunting season currently closed—check current regulations handbook for latest information.

Appearance

The two long central tailfeathers gives this bird its name, and during the gaudy courtship dance of male sharptails, the sharp tail is very evident. Like most prairie birds, sharptails display a pattern of browns, tans, whites, and blacks, blending them in well with their grassland habitat; and because they must content with the northern Michigan winter, they have natural snowshoes like the ruffed grouse. The sexes are almost identical—they can be distinguished by the markings on the tail and crown feathers—in both plumage and size. Though sometimes they can be confused with hen pheasants, sharptails have much more white on the wings and belly than the pheasant. Also, sharptails and pheasants are found on opposite ends of the state and their ranges do not, or rarely, overlap.

The wings have white dots along the primary feathers, and on males, even in the fall, a yellow eye comb and purple air sac along the neck will be noticeable is you brush back the feathers. During the courtship dance, the air sac is inflated and very prominent, and the yellow eye comb becomes engorged.

On the Wing

Sharp-tailed grouse will covey up throughout the hunting season, but unlike quail, the covey will flush in staggered ones and twos with a rush of wings and loud

Male sharp-tailed grouse. (Photo by Craig Bihrle)

kuk-kuk-kuk-kuk calls. Flight is composed of a series of rapid wingbeats and glides, and sharptails have been known to fly up to a couple miles, reaching speeds around 30 miles per hour.

Daily Habits and Food

Sharp-tailed grouse will move to feeding grounds early in the morning, and then to loafing spots for most of the late morning and afternoon. They will feed again before roosting.

Young sharptails will consume insects for about the first three weeks of life, and adults will eat grasshoppers, crickets, and other insects found in grasslands. Preferred vegetation consists largely of grassland berries (blueberry, snowberry), as well as the leaves of most grasses and legumes. Winter food is composed almost entirely of the buds of aspen and birch trees, but will include any prairie grasses that are still accessible through the snow.

Seasonal Patterns

The courtship dance of the male sharp-tailed grouse occupies the bird from late March until mid-June. After mating, the females will move within one mile away

Retrievers work as grouse dogs.

from the lek—the arena where up to 20 male sharptails will dance and fight—to nest and raise the brood. The nest will have some overhead cover—either a tree branch, log, or thick brush—and the female will lay nine to 13 eggs, hatching after a three and a half week incubation period. Sharptails will begin to make their first flutter-flights close to two weeks after hatching.

In the summer after dispersal and throughout the fall, sharptails will form covey groups, and these vary greatly in size. There will be a short display period again in the fall, and the birds will stick together throughout the hunting season. During the winter, sharptails will snow roost in burrows or in trees, where they can easily feed on the buds of aspen and birch.

Preferred Habitat and Cover

Sharp-tailed grouse are birds of the grasslands and prairie, however, the grasslands in Michigan have been in steady decline for some time. Consequently, the season on sharptails is under study and, at this writing, is closed. Check the *Michigan Hunting and Trapping Guide* to make certain. Now, sharptails can be found in the remnant patches of prairies and grasslands that are usually ringed or dotted by red- and jack-pine stands or young aspen and alder stands or clusters. The trees are used

Highbush cranberries attract grouse. (Photo by Chris Zimmerman)

extensively for roosting or loafing cover. Where larger patches of grasslands can be found, usually in some of the agricultural areas of the Upper Peninsula, sharptails can thrive. When the grassland and prairie patches become too thick for the birds, periodic prescribed burning of the grassland ecosystem will thin the cover and keep the birds in the area.

Open, exposed ground is preferred for the dancing ground location so the advertising display will be highly visible to females close by. Nesting cover is nothing more than a scratched-out depression in the grassland setting, usually under a short tree or near the edge of a cluster of trees either in a draw or creek bottom.

Hunting Methods

Sharp-tailed grouse are the northern Michigan hunter's answer to the pheasant. The birds have a small but loyal following. The hunting is very similar—open fields with pockets of thicker brush providing shots similar to those offered by pheasants.

The nice thing about hunting sharptails is that when the covey begins to flush—even if they're out of range—you've still got a chance. Some birds hang back—staggered flushes—allowing you to run up and get a closer shot. Keeping that in mind, it may not be the best idea to take a shot at the first birds that get off the ground—they may be too far. If you can hustle up to the spot of the flush, you might find almost half of the covey still present, where they'll present closer shots.

There is a lot of walking in sharptail hunting, and if hunting without a dog, it can be difficult to get sharptails in the air. They'll often just scamper away—like a pheasant—so if you spot some on the ground, you'll have to run to get them to fly.

Hunting with Dogs

Flushing dogs—Labrador retrievers, springer spaniels, or golden retrievers—work extremely well for sharptails. The covey will usually not flush together, so a flushing dog that will root around in the brush will assure that no birds hunker down and lay low until you pass. If the dog starts busting birds, again, get up there and wait for the birds that are late getting off the ground.

Pointing dogs work equally well, but sharptails like to run. A dog that will relocate and pin a running bird will work nicely on sharptails, and in the wide-open country, a dog—flushing or pointing—will cover a lot more ground than a lone hunter ever could and save walking a lot of extra miles.

Sharptail hunting can be a hot affair, so don't forget a bottle of water—for you and the dog. Short, periodic breaks will be better than one long break in the middle of the day. Keep an eye on the dog for signs of fatigue and heat exhaustion.

Table Preparations

The darker meat of sharptails can be very tender and tasty, especially with early-season birds. Field dressing the birds will cool them down in hot country, and hanging until the evening or next morning will age the meat and add flavor. Soaking the birds in a marinade of red wine, or a mixture of herbs, spices, and vegetable oil overnight before preparing will keep the meat juicy. The breasts can either be grilled, pan-fried, or baked.

Gun and Shot Suggestions
- **Gun**   12, 16, or 20
- **Choke**   Improved and Modified or Modified and Full for doubles, Modified or Full for single barrels.
- **Shot**   One to 1¼ oz. No. 6 is preferred, but No. 7½ also works well.

Common Snipe Distribution

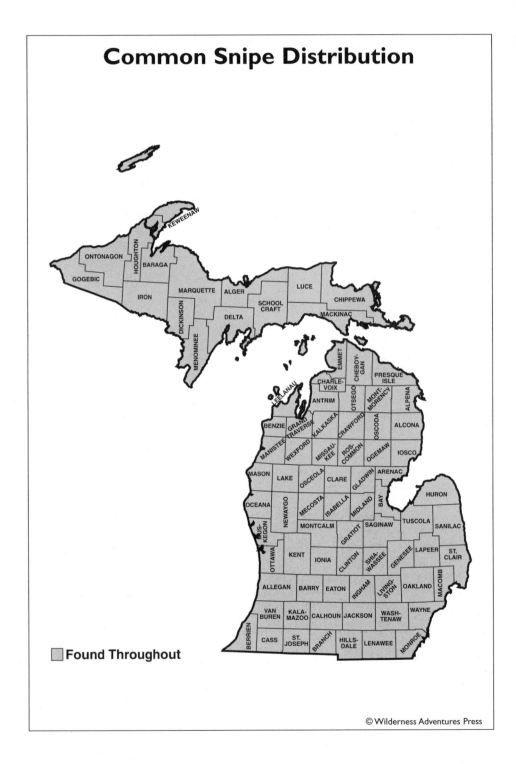

☐ Found Throughout

© Wilderness Adventures Press

Common Snipe

Gallinago gallinago

FIELD FACTS

Local Names
  Jacksnipe, marsh snipe

Size
  Though snipe are sometimes confused with the similarly-sized woodcock, snipe are much more slender, being almost half the weight of a woodcock.

Identification in Flight
  The streamlined body of a snipe differs from the similar-looking woodcock, and the open, marshy habitat where snipe are found should also be an indicator. The bird has a gray-brown appearance, and flight is rapid, composed of numerous twists, dives, and streaks. The birds flush with a cry of *scaip*, sounding almost like two pieces of Styrofoam rubbing together.

Appearance
  Snipe are closely related to woodcock and are often confused with their cousins. But snipe are not as plump and stocky, and the bird has more gray to it than the tan color of woodcock. The head is boldly striped over the crown, and the small rusty tail contrasts with the rest of the gray-brown-white body. They have long legs and bills, and like the woodcock, the females are slightly larger.

On the Wing
  In the hand, snipe are easy to identify, but because of their fast, zig-zaggy flight, they can be tough to get a good look at in the air; the flight pattern is the best indicator—there are many dips, turns, and twists with rapid wingbeats. Snipe take to the air with a flurry of wings, accompanied by a loud shrieking call. Snipe make difficult targets by either divebombing a duck decoy spread or flushing wild in front of a dog, and they can reach tremendous speeds, nearly 40 miles per hour.

Daily Habits and Food
  Snipe are crepuscular, flying near dawn and dusk to feed, and they are associated with wetland habitats, making them an addition to a day spent waterfowl hunting. Snipe eat marsh insects and invertebrates almost exclusively, using their long pointed bills to probe through the soft earth and mud near potholes and marsh

lands. When the weather turns colder, though, snipe migrate, usually a few weeks earlier than most waterfowl.

Seasonal Patterns

During the hunting season, pay close attention to groups of small birds that are strafing your duck decoys. While waterfowl hunting, you may find quite a few snipe. Be careful, though, because many shorebirds are present during the waterfowl season.

Snipe usually come back later than waterfowl, needing the ground to be very soft in order to feed. From April to mid-May is when the snipe begin to return to the North, and they perform an aerial courtship display that is quite dazzling. Males make long, steep dives, and the wind rushing over the last two stiff tailfeathers on the fanned tail produce a winnowing sound. Some often think that the bird is calling, but it is actually the vibrating feathers producing the sound.

Nests are located in dry sections of wet habitat, and it is usually nothing more than a depression in the grass. As is common with members of the sandpiper family, snipe lay four eggs, and incubation and first full flights each take close to three weeks.

Snipe stick around until about mid-October, depending on the weather and availability of food. Usually, they migrate early along with the smaller ducks.

Preferred Habitat and Cover

Anywhere you might find waterfowl, if the water is shallow enough, snipe can usually be found. Shallow swamps, marshes, and flooded fields often hold a fair number, and they have been known to dive in the water to escape danger. If your feet are wet, you will more than likely be in good snipe habitat.

Hunting Methods

If waterfowl hunting, you can wander after snipe if you see them flitting around the marsh, or they may even give your decoy spread a buzz. But a great way to begin a hot early season is to walk after snipe through marshes, around the edges of wetlands, or through a damp field that has collected some water. One of the most important things to remember about hunting snipe, though—and something that most people don't realize—is that you can't shoot lead at snipe. A nontoxic load must be used. Also, the season on snipe opens earlier than the waterfowl season, so be careful to take snipe only.

Hunting with Dogs

Snipe hunting can get a flushing dog in shape for the season. The cover is damp and moist, the dog stays cooler, and you can get some fine shooting. Pointing dogs are not much use; flushing dogs are the ticket when snipe hunting.

Table Preparations

Snipe are often overlooked as table fare, perhaps because there is not a lot of meat on them. But if you like woodcock, you'll like snipe—there is almost exactly the same amount of breast meat, and the taste is almost identical. Follow any recipe for woodcock or dark meat, and snipe will be delicious.

Gun and Shot Suggestions

- **Gauge**   20, 16, or 12
- **Choke**   Improved and Modified, or Modified for single barrels.
- **Shot**   A light field load of 1 to 1⅛ oz. of No. 7 steel or another nontoxic shot is the ideal load.

Finding Upland Birds

My friend and frequent hunting partner, Chris Zimmerman, is a consummate upland bird hunter who gets out a couple times each week from September through December. He lives in mid-Michigan and is able to hunt in both Regions 2 and 3. He knows how to find good grouse, woodcock, and pheasant cover, and when he isn't hunting on state lands, is a master at securing permission from landowners. I asked him what to look for when scouting for upland birds in his neck of the woods.

For ruffed grouse, Zim looks for young aspens with a few balsams or fir trees and plenty of understory, including ferns. Woodcock can be found in the same type of area, as well as along streambeds and in tag alder swamps—damp areas that make it easy for them to probe for earthworms.

"Ferns under aspen is classic woodcock habitat," he said. "Add fruit to that mixture, and you have guaranteed grouse."

When he says fruit, he's talking about hawthorn (thorn apples), beechnuts, acorns, apples, chokecherries, dogwood berries, and highbush cranberries. During the December hunt that is available in Regions 2 and 3, look for wild strawberry leaves that are still green.

"Dogwood is excellent—I think it's number one. From the start of the season through Halloween, it has both food and cover. It's thick, grows in bunches, keeps its leaves fairly long, and has the fruit the birds like. Then, at the end of October when the fruit is gone, it's still excellent cover." Dogwood has berries the size of a pea and is easy to recognize in the fall, when its leaves turn bright purple.

To find grouse and woodcock, look for "edges," such as young aspen stands next to mature hardwoods—these are excellent places to start. Beech stands are good, too, according to Zim. "Beech holds its leaves well into the winter, and grouse like to have something over their heads."

When pheasant hunting, look for croplands next to wetlands and tall grass, like that found in grown-over fields that aren't being cultivated. Wide, brushy fencerows can also be good, especially if they have dogwood in them.

Since pheasants, especially, are found largely on private land, acquiring permission can be an art form. Zim recommends you go in person to inquire about the possibilities of hunting a piece of property as opposed to making phone calls or sending letters.

Explain where you're from and say when you are going to hunt. Be exact about it, because maybe the landowner has friends who will be hunting the property around the same time that you hope to be on it. Make sure you mention that you are interested in birds only, and if the landowner is a deer hunter,

Typical Michigan grouse country.

you may want to suggest that you'll hunt only at midday, since most deer hunters are afield in the morning and evening.

It goes without saying that you must be polite. If you are given permission to hunt, be sure to close gates and don't damage fences when you're crossing them. Offer some of your game to the landowner. Also, make sure you send a thank-you note and maybe a card at Christmas. It will go a long way toward assuring that you have a place to hunt in the future.

The Dabblers

General Characteristics

Dabbling ducks—or "puddle" ducks—are the kind most commonly taken by hunters across the country. These ducks are birds of shallow water, usually no deeper than 5 or 6 feet, and they use their forward-positioned feet for tipping up to feed. Their powerful wings allow for takeoff straight up off the water. The male dabblers are brilliantly colored, and the wings of dabbling ducks have colorful speculums. The color pattern in the wing is a major identification tool, and it is also useful in identifying the bird in flight.

Dabbling ducks are usually hunted in small-water areas (marshes, small wetlands, streams and rivers, beaver ponds, small lakes), however, there are some dabblers that frequent big-water lakes. It is also possible to get excellent dabbler hunting in fields of cultivated grain because this is a major food source for the ducks. Managed wildlife areas throughout Michigan offer some of the best dabbler shooting.

Species and Identification

Mallard (Nickname: Greenhead)
- **Male:** bright green head; chestnut-colored breast; one to three black curls on rump; yellow bill.
- **Female:** overall mottled brown; no curls; orange bill with black spotting.
- **Wing:** large gray wing; purple speculum; white bands bordering both sides of speculum (both sexes).

Black Duck
- **Male and Female:** very similar in appearance; size and bill are distinguishing factors; male is bigger with a yellow bill; female bill dull green with black spotting; large dabbler; darker than female mallard with a very dark brown body and buff-colored head; may hybridize with mallards.
- **Wing:** silver-white underwing contrasts brightly with dark body in flight; purple speculum with no white bands bordering; top of wing is same dark color as body (both sexes).

Wood Duck
- **Male:** considered by many to be the most beautiful bird in the world; unmistakable array of all colors; prominent crest tops a green head with a white chin and neck; chestnut breast and light brown flanks.
- **Female:** also has a crest on head, but head is gray with a white eye ring; may squeal in flight.
- **Wing:** only dabbler wing to have the iridescent purple color of the speculum extend up into the primary feathers; white bar on trailing edge of speculum is straight line in males and a teardrop pattern in females.

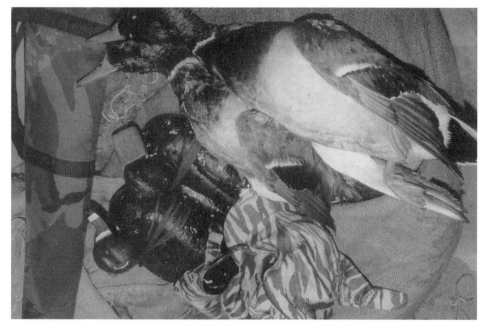

A pair of mallard drakes taken by the author.

Gadwall (Nickname: Grey Duck)
- **Male and Female:** very similar in appearance; male has darker patterning of gray and white on breast and flanks and dark gray or black bill; female has a brighter brown on breast and flanks with an orange, black-spotted bill.
- **Wing:** white patch in speculum in trailing edge of wing; rust color above the white patch is prominent in males and greatly reduced or absent in juvenile males or females.

Wigeon (Nickname: Baldpate)
- **Male:** mature drake is hard to mistake; white streak on forehead; rust-colored breast and flanks; bright white belly; white and black spotted head with a green eye patch that reaches over the eye and extends back behind the head; bill is light blue with black tip; gives a three-whistle call in flight.
- **Female:** lack white forehead and green patch; rust color is lighter and back is mottled brown; juvenile males may be confused with females; bill similar to male but duskier.
- **Wing:** white patch on leading edge of wing distinguishes this duck from gadwall; may hold a velvet green color in speculum with long silver and black tertial feathers close to the body; bright white patch is the best identifier in flight; white patch is greatly reduced in females and juveniles.

John Gierke
with a drake pintail.

Northern Pintail
- **Male:** large duck; long pointed black tail gives the bird its name; white breast extends up into brown head in a thin white line; rest of body is gray, black, and silver; white and black rump; slender light blue bill with black streak down the top; very long neck and long tail evident in flight; also whistles in flight.
- **Female:** mottled brown; similar to female mallard but with gray legs and longer neck; bill similar to male.
- **Wing:** copper colored speculum with white band on trailing edge of wing; overall gray-brown wing (both sexes).

Green-winged Teal
- **Male:** rust colored head with green eye patch; black spotted breast; gray flanks and brown back.

- **Female:** mottled brown over entire body; white underrump and flanks; both sexes are very small (the smallest dabbler).
- **Wing:** bright green speculum with a white band on trailing edge and a buff colored band on leading edge of speculum (both sexes).

Blue-winged Teal
- **Male:** white crescent streak on a blue head is very evident in flight, although in Michigan males are rarely fully colored out during the hunting season; rest of body consists of black spots on a brown background.
- **Female:** mottled brown; comparable to female green-winged teal but with a larger bill and more spotting; juvenile males almost indistinguishable from females; both sexes are small.
- **Wing:** green speculum with a powder blue patch above that shows brightly in flight (both sexes).

Northern Shoveler
- **Male:** mature males have a green head; white breast; rust colored belly and flanks. Rarely colored out during hunting season.
- **Female:** mottled brown; closely resembles female mallard but bill is unmistakable for both sexes; large spoon-shaped bill.
- **Wing:** almost identical to blue-winged teal only larger (both sexes).

Migration

The Mississippi Flyway can host large numbers of dabbling ducks, especially mallards, and Michigan is a major stopping point for many of the Canadian-bred birds. Wood ducks thrive in the many wooded habitats of Michigan, accepting artificial nesting structures readily. Also, flocks of black ducks, especially in the marshes and bigger open water, offer Michigan hunters opportunities at a bird rarely seen farther west.

Teal are the first to migrate south; early-season hunts see large numbers of both green-winged and especially blue-winged teal. Toward the end of the season, expect mostly mallards and black ducks, although there will be some wigeon and gadwall.

Habits and Habitat

Puddle ducks begin flying near sunrise, leaving their watery roosting spots for fields to feed. About midmorning, they return to loaf. Later in the afternoon, they return again to the fields, leaving near sunset for their roosts once again. But when the birds are getting ready to migrate, fat stores need to be built up at a fast rate because the ducks might leave for the South at any moment. At this time, birds feed throughout a clear night, using the early morning to loaf; or if they're stopping over in the state, they may feed all day long to replenish and store energy. By knowing their schedule, you'll know when and where to set up to hunt puddle ducks.

Puddle duck setup in a pothole next to a Great Lakes coastal marsh.

Hunting the Dabblers

Most dabbler hunting in Michigan takes place in the wooded marshes, managed wildlife areas, small inland lakes, and beaver ponds scattered throughout the state. It isn't uncommon in the open-water areas to get dabbler and diver shooting throughout the morning, especially with a mixed decoy spread, but most dabbler shooting takes place over shallow-water habitat or land. Also, the many rivers and coastal marsh areas in Michigan can offer excellent jumpshooting opportunities.

Dabbling ducks are known for dropping from extreme heights in wide spirals, circling the decoy spread numerous times before committing to land. Pintails make huge turns, and just when you think they are leaving, they bank around and circle again—be patient.

Teal, wood ducks, and, to a lesser extent, wigeon and gadwalls, are more apt to buzz the decoy spread, catching you off guard. But once they pass through, they might still bank around and either buzz again, circle, or simply turn around and land.

Dabbling ducks respond readily to the call, and most puddle ducks can be called in with a mallard call. But a pintail whistle is helpful for pintails, and it may also coax in wigeon and green-winged teal.

Puddle ducks make heavy use of the abundant agricultural land in the thumb area of Michigan. Cultivated cornfields and other grain fields are used quite frequently, and hunting ducks over land can present shots at huge flocks of ducks pouring into a field to feed.

A Chesapeake Bay retriever brings a mallard in. (Photo by Chris Zimmerman)

Out-of-the-way places, such as beaver ponds off the beaten path or hidden sloughs and marshes, can provide excellent shooting at puddlers. A small bag of decoys may be all that is needed to get birds in. Also, if you can sit under a flight lane, you can get some excellent pass shooting.

Table Preparations

Dabbler ducks are excellent on the table because most of the birds are vegetarians, unlike some of the fish-eating diver ducks. Hanging the ducks overnight is recommended; however, it may make cleaning them a little more difficult. Either pluck the bird, fillet the breast meat from the bone, or clean the duck whole. There are an almost infinite number of duck recipes, and unless you overcook it, the meat is among the finest the state has to offer.

Gun and Shot Suggestions

- **Gauge**   12, 10
- **Choke**   Improved and Modified for doubles, or Modified for single barrels.
- **Shot**   A nontoxic load (steel, bismuth, or tungsten) is required for all types of waterfowl hunting. For dabblers, loads of 1⅛ to 1¼ oz. No. 4, 2, BB, or late in the season, BBB will work. A light field load of No. 7 steel or bismuth makes a great load for dispatching cripples.

Puddler Hunting Season Is Longer Than Most Think

I'm not sure about my retriever, but I was a bit disappointed. We had just come across two miles of open water that, during the middle of October, was full of scaup, redheads, ringnecks, buffleheads, and goldeneyes. Our boat had moved maybe a dozen birds, most of them mergansers. I had expected to find fewer ducks but still had high hopes that some bluebills or at least some buffle-heads would be around. No such luck.

Then a raft of birds in the back of the bay caught my eye. "The bluebills are all tucked back in this corner of the marsh," I thought to myself. But as we approached the flock, we found it to be at least 200 mallards and black ducks, not the scaup I had expected. Most of them took flight as we drew nearer, but some of them settled back into the thicker cattails and tules, intent on enjoying some sort of feast in the muck.

Thanksgiving is a time of year when most hunters would figure that fair-weather puddlers have moved out of northern Michigan to the south, leaving nothing but hardy diving ducks to weather the bitter, late fall days. That's the way the textbooks tell it, but the truth is that in the northern parts of the state, especially the Upper Peninsula, most divers move out by late season and are replaced by big flocks of northern mallards and black ducks. Farther south, especially in the famed waters of Saginaw Bay, Lake St. Clair, and Lake Erie, Thanksgiving is prime time to find a wide variety of ducks, both divers and puddlers.

My retriever and I are happy to find these birds, regardless of whether they're supposed to be here. Knowing that flight mallards were in the area opened up more possibilities for our hunt. We could set up in the open marsh as we had planned, catching not only the puddlers but also the few divers that might be around. We could explore a little more and put our decoys in a small, shallow pothole that might be more attractive to the puddlers. Or we could forget about the decoys entirely and walk through the shallows, jumping mallards and blacks out of the weeds much like a pheasant hunter would.

With the wind coming through at a pretty good clip and since there were few other hunters in the area, we chose to try the jumpshooting. On a still day, jumpshooting is very difficult because wary mallards can hear your approach from a long way off. Today, we would have the wind to help cover our movements. The more wind the better, especially when hunting with my unruly and less-than-quiet retriever.

After a few minutes of stalking and observing the marsh, I modified our plan again. Farther into the marsh, we spied more blacks and mallards that

*Scott Smith
with blacks
and mallards.*

were feeding, loafing, and preening in an expansive pothole. The water appeared to be only inches deep, but the tall weeds were well back from the edge, making it impossible for me to get close enough for a shot. While I was mulling over the options, I noticed my retriever's head snap to the side as he spotted a couple of birds flying in to join the large group on the water. Behind those ducks, over the open water of the bay, a few more mallards were milling about and making their way into this shallow spot.

We quickly moved well downwind of the roosted birds and took cover on a large muskrat house that was flanked by tall bunches of fragmite. The wind was

Jim Jacobs on a beaver pond.

perfect. Ducks that approached the larger group were flying right over our heads. I coaxed high flyers down with the call, and in short order we had ambushed some singles and small groups that were intent on joining the large bunch of dabblers. We took a couple home to dinner.

Duck hunting is always a game of trying to figure out where the ducks want to be and then setting up in that place. But with puddlers, it seems, waterfowlers have more options. Whereas diving ducks are almost always a big-water endeavor (and sometimes mallards hang out in deeper water, too), puddlers can be closer to shore, in potholes, on inland lakes, or in secluded beaver ponds. And if it turns out that you're not exactly in the place that the birds want to be, you can rely on the gregarious nature of mallards and use your call to pull them over to you. Even if they won't land, you can get them to come in close enough for a shot.

Diver hunters don't always have this option. I'm sure many diver hunters might take exception to the claim, but calling has little effect in bringing diving ducks into your setup. Certainly, diving ducks do make noises, and it is especially evident in large rafts of birds, particularly on quiet days when the purring or skirrling of bluebills or harsh meows of redheads can be heard across the water. But a bluebill's call is a whisper compared to the loud quacking of a hen mallard intent on calling some friends down to feast with her.

A puddle duck hunter is at a significant disadvantage if he forgets to bring along his call. (If he brings his call but hasn't practiced it, he's handicapped, too—but that's another story.) I've been along on many puddler hunts where we relied much more on our calls than we did on our decoys, if we brought along decoys at all.

Likewise, a hunter puts himself at a disadvantage if he doesn't come prepared to modify his plan. On the hunt described above, if we had chosen to stick it out on the open water, hoping for a few divers to show themselves, we would have seen many fewer ducks and most likely wouldn't have gained a duck dinner. In this case, we found a good spot on the edge of the marsh, but sometimes you need to abandon the marsh altogether. We've had wonderful puddler hunts in flooded agricultural fields, tiny beaver ponds, and inland lakes that are near big-water puddler hangouts.

It always pays to be flexible when duck hunting, and it's helpful to hunt in an area where you can take advantage of more than one kind of opportunity. Great Lakes coastal marshes are often crowded during the beginning of the season, and it's not always possible to move around without disturbing other hunters. Later in the season, though, and in secluded parts of the state, all but the diehard waterfowlers will have put their gear away, leaving more elbowroom for the rest.

Michigan waterfowlers are enamored with puddle ducks. They're usually the most plentiful birds around when the season opens. A hunter doesn't need to venture into deep water to find them. And in most years, once the local puddlers have moved out, flight mallards and black ducks move through to keep hunters occupied until the ice makes it impossible to get out.

In spite of the flight ducks, though, most mallards taken by Michigan hunters are locally grown in the state or in neighboring Ontario. Fortunately, the state is very attractive to local puddlers, not only mallards, but wood ducks, which are also hatched in very good numbers here. Besides mallards, blacks, and woodies, Michigan waterfowlers find a good number of green-winged teal and a variety of other puddlers, including wigeon, blue-winged teal, pintail, and some gadwall.

The Divers

General Characteristics

Diving ducks—ducks that dive to great depths under the water to feed—are common on lakes and deep marshes, but they are also known to frequent some of the managed wildlife areas. Diver wings are smaller than dabbler wings, making it easier for them to move through the water when diving but requiring the duck to run along the water to get up enough speed for flight. Their feet are set far back on the body, specially designed for propulsion through the water, but making it a difficult task to walk. For this reason, there is little, if any, diver duck hunting in dry fields. Male divers can be colorful on parts of their bodies, but the wings of both sexes, as opposed to the dabblers, hold no color. The combination of black, white, and gray makes identification by wing difficult except in a few instances.

Divers are fast flyers, approaching a decoy spread low over the water. Rarely do they circle before landing—usually they just buzz in and splash down. Late in the season, divers can store an amazing amount of fat, toughening the skin.

Species and Identification

Ring-necked Duck (Nickname: Ringbill)
- **Male:** mature male has distinct white ring around gray, black-tipped bill; deep crimson ring around neck may be unnoticeable; black breast and gray flanks are separated by a white stripe that reaches down to the water on a sitting duck; back is not vermiculated, which distinguishes it from a male lesser scaup.
- **Female:** white ring around bill is duller; brown duck with faint white eye ring; juvenile male ringnecks closely resemble females.

Lesser Scaup (Nickname: Bluebill)
- **Male:** mature males show an iridescent dark purple/green head and sky blue bill; black breast and bright white belly and flanks; back is heavily vermiculated (spotted) in white; juvenile males can be distinguished from females by the presence of vermiculations on the wing.
- **Female:** has same blue bill as male, but female is an overall brown; white crescent stripe on head near base of bill; juvenile males may also have faint white crescent, but will show flecks of purple in head or vermiculations on back; vermiculations absent in female.

Greater Scaup (Nickname: Broadbill)
- **Male:** very similar to their lesser scaup brothers with dark purple/green iridescent head and sky blue bill; black breast and bright white belly and flanks; back is heavily vermiculated in white; juvenile males can be distinguished from females by the presence of vermiculations on the wing; tell-tale difference between a lesser and

Author and Duke with a goldeneye and ringneck taken in the northwest Lower Peninsula. (Photo by Chris Smith)

greater scaup is in the wing—in greater scaup, the white extends into the primary feathers (both sexes) whereas in the lesser scaup, the white is confined to the speculum (both sexes).
- **Female:** also very similar to lesser scaup females; has same blue bill as male, but female is an overall brown; white crescent stripe on head near base of bill; juvenile males may also have faint white crescent, but will show flecks of purple in head or vermiculations on back; vermiculations absent in female.

Common Goldeneye
- **Male:** mostly white duck; circular white spot on a green head near base of small bill; bright yellow eyes; stark white wing patch is obvious in flight; will produce a whistling sound in flight; back is black streaked with white stripes.

- **Female:** duller white breast and flanks; brown head and yellow eyes; stubby bill may have a bit of orange near tip; bright white neck is obvious when duck sits with head erect.

Bufflehead
- **Male:** white cap; head is a spectacular array of iridescent green and purple; rest of body is mostly white with some black portions on the back; bright white wing patch is evident in flight.
- **Female:** brown duck; white cheek patch; much duller white on breast and flanks than male; both sexes are extremely small.

Canvasback
- **Male:** very large duck; deep crimson head and black bill; forehead is sloped, making the head appear triangular in flight; black breast and white belly.
- **Female:** light brown, also has sloping forehead; white eye ring; flanks and breast a light tan.

Redhead
- **Male:** often confused with male canvasback, but redhead is more gray; red head not as sloped as canvasback; blue bill with white ring near the black tip; black breast and gray flanks.
- **Female:** similar to female canvasback, lesser scaup and especially female ring-necked duck; rounded head; light gray bill with black tip; overall dark brown.

Ruddy Duck (Stiff-tailed duck but included with the divers)
- **Male:** breeding male has clown-like appearance of very big blue bill, white cheek and chin, rust-colored body, and stiff tail; during the hunting season, bill is more gray, and deep rust color has faded to dull brown; still sports white cheek and chin.
- **Female:** very similar to a male during the fall, but cheek and chin not as white; very small duck; not typically hunted.

Hooded Merganser
- **Male:** spectacular plumage of black, white and brown; large white hood with a black rim stands erect when bird is sitting on water; remainder of head is black; bill is long, serrated, narrow, and used for eating fish; white breast and tan flanks separated by black and white stripes.
- **Female:** brown duck; bill same as male; female is easy to pick out from male.

Common Merganser
- **Male:** very large duck; mostly white; green head; narrow bill is long, serrated, and bright red in both sexes; a fish-eating duck; not recommended table fare.
- **Female:** rust-colored head with a white chin; rest of body is ducky white.

Setting up for divers on a small water. (Photo by Chris Smith)

Red-breasted Merganser
- **Male:** large duck; similar to common merganser male but with a dusky gray/red breast as opposed to the stark white breast of the common; green head may have a crest; white ring separates green in head from color in breast; also a fish-eating duck and not recommended as table fare.
- **Female:** can be difficult to separate from common merganser female of which they look almost identical; may also have a small crest on head; rust-colored head with a white chin, grayish body more so than female common.

White-winged Scoter
- **Male:** an almost entirely black duck; white speculum evident in flight; feathering extends over top of colorful bill almost to nostrils; white eye patch.
- **Female:** overall brown; white speculum as in male; lacks white eye patch or is a dusky white; feathering extends over top of bill.

Oldsquaw
- **Male:** stunning pattern of white, black, and brown; long tail is very evident; short bill with a pink band; adult male mostly white with black to dark brown breast and tan and black facial patches; eclipse male has almost entirely black head and breast and light eye patch.
- **Female:** lack long tail; white to dusky white or tan overall; may have dark facial patches.

Migration

Most divers nest in northwestern portions of Canada, and instead of following a southerly migration route, they head diagonally across the continent toward the eastern shore and Great Lakes. The many lakes in Michigan, as well as the Great Lakes, offer ample room for the large flocks of migrating birds to feed, stage, and get a breather on their journey. Larger bodies of water, especially large lakes bordering the Great Lakes, can also receive some of the sea duck species that sometimes trickle through the Mississippi Flyway.

Large rafts of lesser scaup, canvasbacks, and goldeneyes move through the state late in the season, sometimes among the ice floes of the larger lakes and Great Lakes. Though still in decline or at steady population levels, the large flocks of lesser scaup and canvasbacks are eagerly awaited for by many Michigan hunters, especially those around the traditional diver haunts of Lake St. Clair, Lake Erie, and Lake Huron's Saginaw Bay.

Ring-necked ducks are very common early in the season in Michigan marshes, frequenting the same areas as many of the dabbler species. Large flocks can buzz decoys early in the morning and offer excellent shooting.

Habits and Habitat

Michigan is well suited for divers, with its many inland lakes and the Great Lakes and ample supplies of submerged food, both fish and aquatic vegetation. Also, these large bodies of water are ideal loafing spots for the big flocks of migrating birds.

Divers move around a little later in the day than dabblers—some of the best diver hunting is between 9 am and 1 pm. During the migration, though, small flocks of divers can be in the air constantly. The smaller inland lakes, just a stone's throw away from the Great Lakes, offer excellent shelter for birds on windy days when there is severe chop on the big water.

Hunting the Divers

In some of the more open-water areas of Michigan, divers can be hunted in traditional ways, such as layout shooting or hunting decoying birds over large spreads of blocks. Many hunters use blinds constructed on 14- to 17-foot boats, setting up wherever the ducks seem to be hanging out on any particular day. But many times, divers buzz by while you're hunting a small marsh or inland lake for dabblers. In these instances, if you wish to lure some more divers in, a spread of a half-dozen to a dozen scaup, ringneck, or goldeneye decoys, in addition to your dabbler decoys will work just fine. Place the diver decoys off to the side and in a small cluster to simulate feeding birds.

Calling to divers is usually of no use, even though you may hear some birds making sounds. Simply giving some quacks on your mallard call—if you have mallard decoys out—could add some realism to the entire setup. However, if hunting over a large spread of diver decoys, a short trill on the mallard call, like a rapid feed chuckle, can animate your spread.

Chris Zimmerman with a greater scaup.

Table Preparations

Of all the divers, canvasbacks are the preferred duck when it comes to the table. Their flavor is even better than that of many dabblers, and this was one of the reasons for their sharp decline during this century—market hunting. Because most divers incorporate some fish and other aquatic animals in their diets, the meat can have a strong wild flavor. But if dressed right away and marinated at least 24 hours, diver meat can be very tender and juicy, tasting much like any other dark-meated gamebird.

Gun and Shot Suggestions

- **Gauge** 12, 10
- **Choke** Improved and Modified for doubles, Modified for single barrels.
- **Shot**   A heavy load of 1⅛ to 1¼ oz. No. 2, 1, BB, or BBB in nontoxic shot. Later in the season, when the birds have built up a tough fat layer, switch to a heavier load.

Hunting Divers Needs Persistence

It was a day designed for diver hunting—the wind was blasting out of the northwest to the point where we were a bit hesitant about motoring to our blind on a distant island in the middle of an Upper Peninsula lake. The low, gray clouds were on a fast track across the lake. Small bright spots of sunlit blue sky were visible here and there.

Snow squalls were moving over the lake, too, and it seemed that with each one a few squadrons of low-flying bluebills came in. We hurried to put out our spread and move our boat blind into a thick patch of rushes that jutted into the tiny bay. Some of the gusts pushed the reeds flat against the water, and the water was freezing on the weeds in some spots. We found that as the season was progressing, more weeds were being pushed down by frost, and it was becoming more difficult to find a spot to hide the boat.

This was diver hunting at its finest: snow, a hard, cold wind at our backs, the boat blind rocking in the waves, and our retriever on the floor shaking, partly from the icy water but mostly from anticipation and excitement.

Five dozen decoys lay before us, and there was no keeping the divers out of them. It didn't matter if we were standing in the boat or if the dog was out there on a retrieve, every bird that came over the blocks wanted in. Most of the ducks were lesser scaup, but some were greaters and there were even a few ringnecks mixed in with the bluebills.

A nice ring-necked drake. (Photo by Chris Smith)

A popular way to hunt Michigan's diving ducks is using a two-man layout boat. (Photo by Chris Zimmerman)

A half-mile downwind from us a huge raft of divers was getting bigger by the minute. Every now and then some restless birds would break out of the group and head our way, their wingtips nearly touching the choppy surface of the water as they pushed against the wind to see if our little group of plastic fakes was enjoying a better breakfast than they were getting farther out. It was as if they were on a string because they came in with no hesitation. They followed the string of decoys up to the landing zone we'd created, and then one or both of us would stand and greet them.

On most of our days afield, we are lucky to get one man's bag limit, but it soon became obvious that on this morning we would have no trouble filling both our daily bag limits. In fact, they would come too soon.

We were reluctant for the morning's hunt to end. The clouds cleared off and the sun was shining brightly, but the wind didn't slow down. Even as we picked up our decoys, standing there in the bright light in full view, the bluebills circled and dipped and looked for a spot to sit. Some of them landed in the remaining decoys, causing our retriever no small amount of concern. They'd drop in, give a few quick looks at their plastic friends, and then move out.

My partner and I knew that we might never see another hunt like this one. These birds can be here one day and gone the next. That's the nature of northern Michigan waterfowl hunting as opposed to some of the more southern waterfowl staging areas in the state, such as Saginaw Bay, Lake St. Clair, or Lake Erie. In those places, ducks tend to stick around for a while.

A group of lesser scaup drakes sizing up a hen.

Farther north, it's best to hunt every day that you can when the birds are in. You never know how long they'll stick around or how many newcomers will pile in over the next several days. In general, hunters pursuing diving ducks in the Upper Peninsula will see their best days in mid to late October. Farther south, in the middle and southern waterfowl zones of the state, serious duck hunters don't get excited about hunting until November. A handful of diehards enjoy going out in December during years when the season is open into that month.

These days, duck hunters are seeing a decline in scaup, the bread and butter of diver duck hunting. Biologists are still attempting to determine the cause of the decline. Meanwhile, redheads and canvasbacks, two species that were closed to hunting for many years because of low numbers, are more numerous than they have been in years. These three are the diving ducks most commonly found in hunters' bags. Michigan plays host to thousands of buffleheads, another common popular diving duck, but not nearly as popular because of its diminutive size.

Because of the greater number of birds and more generous bag limits in recent years, diver hunting is seeing renewed popularity. Layout boats that hadn't seen use in years have been dragged out of barns and garages and are being pressed into service. Because of the hunting conditions and the huge number of decoys that must be deployed, some hunters dropped out of the diving duck game when the bag limit was reduced. But diehard diver hunters, including me, can't imagine a season going by without sitting next to 50, 75, or more decoys on a choppy lake under clouds that are spitting snow, even if the chances of bringing home a duck dinner are slim.

The Geese

General Characteristics

Geese are voracious eaters in agricultural fields and are seldom solitary—they gather in tremendous flocks, especially during migration. Snow geese are presently at dangerous population highs, and Michigan, although not in the traditional snow goose flyway (Central), might begin to see increasing numbers if the snows start to spill over into the adjacent Mississippi Flyway. Because geese eat a wide variety of grains, the cultivated portions of the state provide an abundant supply of food for the large birds.

Geese are constantly chattering to each other, both in the air and on the ground. While feeding on the ground or loafing on the water, there will always be a few birds —sentinels—with their heads erect, on the lookout for danger. They will often feed into the wind so they can take off quickly if danger approaches. Early in the season, a flock of birds may be smaller, consisting of only one or two family groups.

Species and Identification

Canada Goose (Nickname: Honker)

Dark goose; species of goose most often hunted; distinctive honk in flight and on ground; black head and long black neck; white cheek patch; pale brown breast and flanks; white rump; many subspecies of which size is the best determining factor.

Snow Goose

White goose; flies in tremendously large flocks; hard to hunt because of gregarious nature; high-pitched bark is characteristic; subspecies of lesser and greater snow geese are distinguished by size. Greaters are not usually found outside the Atlantic Flyway.

White Phase: goose is completely white; pink bill and legs; black "grin" on bill; black wingtips are obvious in flight.

Blue Phase: often incorrectly thought to be a separate species; white head, pink bill, and same black grin; rest of body is an intricate patterning of black, gun barrel blue, gray, and white; black wingtips not as obvious because the rest of body is also dark.

Ross' Goose

Very similar to snow goose, but smaller; about the size of a large mallard; also has two color phases that are similar to color phases of snow geese; lacks the black grin on bill; may be rare visitors to Michigan.

Migration

Michigan is home to large populations of resident giant Canada geese for which there is an early season in September and a late season in January and February,

Author's father, Tom Pink, with geese taken during the early season, decoy setup in background.

before and after migrant flocks appear in the state. These seasons were experimental for some time, but now have been declared regular seasons. They are meant to control the population of the giant resident geese as a means of reducing the nuisance problems of the birds.

Michigan, under the Mississippi Flyway, can receive large numbers of migrating birds, but these migratory populations have been in decline, especially the Mississippi Valley population of Canada geese. Currently, seasons and bag limits are very conservative, as Michigan and other states in the flyway are attempting to reduce the harvest of these migrants. Consequently, most goose hunting takes place in September, when most of the shooting is at the resident populations.

The customary formation for migrating flocks is the V, and on clear days, flocks can be very high. If the weather keeps them in the area for a while, flocks may begin to join in staging areas, leading to fields full of thousands of geese.

Habits and Habitat

The complex of marsh systems, managed wildlife areas, and inland lakes in Michigan offer geese plenty of loafing areas, and on some of the larger bodies of water or in some of the agricultural portions of the state, large flocks rest and stage during migration. There can be considerable nesting and brood rearing of geese in Michigan. The burgeoning resident population shows no signs of slowing. In recent years, the resident population has been nearly a half-million birds, and hunters have taken upward of 90,000 geese in the early and late seasons. Michigan is currently one of the top states in the nation to hunt Canada geese.

Geese fly to feeding areas early in the morning, and later that morning, head back to marshes, rivers, or lakes to loaf. Early afternoon finds them again in the fields, and toward sunset, the birds head to roosting spots. Large migrating flocks sometimes stay through the night in fields to eat and store energy for an upcoming flight.

Hunting Geese

Most goose hunting is done in cultivated grain fields. The birds' habits make them somewhat predictable concerning fields they use from day to day, with the exception being snow geese. Scouting a few flocks for a day will give you an idea of where to hunt—not only which field but where in the field.

Hunting Canadas is a little easier than hunting snow geese, simply because they do not congregate in such large flocks. However, because Michigan is not under the main snow goose flyway, the tremendous flocks that are seen in the Central Flyway are rarely seen here. With smaller flocks, the snows might decoy, but they are still wary birds.

Geese can also be hunted on marshes or large lakes. The birds use these areas for loafing, and later in the morning and evenings, they return to loaf and roost after feeding in the fields most of the day. Also, if you can sit below a flight lane between a field and a water area being used, you can get excellent pass shooting opportunities.

Because the birds are so large, they can take a lot of shot, especially in the belly. Therefore, your target should be the head and neck. The big body can be an easy target to shoot at, but it may not result in a killing shot. A shot to the head and neck will bring a goose down on the spot; however, there will be times when a dead goose—or a crippled bird—sails hundreds of yards. If you are consistently hitting geese in the head and neck, this will rarely happen.

Managed waterfowl areas have flooded crops. (Photo by Chris Zimmerman)

Table Preparations

The dark meat on geese can be very strong, especially the snow geese. Prepare geese any way you would other waterfowl. Grilled goose breast is similar to grilled venison or beef steak.

Gun and Shot Suggestions

- **Gauge** 12, 10
- **Choke** Improved and Modified for doubles, or Modified for single barrels. Since shot patterns vary widely with the use of large-sized shot, especially steel, make sure you pattern your shotgun at the shooting range.
- **Shot** A stout load is needed to bring geese down. Nontoxic shot is required, and a load of 1¼ oz. No. 1, BB, BBB, or larger shot is recommended.

Michigan Offers Excellent Goose Hunting

Michigan is one of the best places in the Midwest to hunt Canada geese, and it's not necessarily because of the tremendous flocks of migratory honkers that pass through the state in the fall, although those flights are substantial. It's because of the burgeoning population of resident Canada geese that only migrate as far as necessary to be able to satisfy their needs for food, water, and shelter. During most years, some Canada geese remain in the state all winter.

In recent years, Michigan has been at the top or near the top of the list for numbers of Canada geese harvested among the northern states. This includes

Mike Poff of Mt. Pleasant and Parker with early season geese. (Photo by Chris Zimmerman)

giant Canadas and other subspecies harvested during the statewide seasons in early September and October, as well as the special late season in January and February that targets local giant geese and is restricted to portions of the southern Lower Peninsula.

On the other hand, Michigan hunters shoot very few geese of other species. Several subspecies of Canada goose migrate through the state, however, few snow geese (compared to the thousands that migrate through other states) and few, if any, white-fronted geese pass through the state and are taken by hunters.

Several areas of the state are well known among goose hunters, including the following goose management units (GMU): Tuscola/Huron, Saginaw County, Muskegon Wastewater, and Allegan County. These units have quotas, and the season is closed once the quotas have been reached, even if goose season is still open.

The southern zone of Michigan's waterfowl hunting units (essentially, the lower half of the Lower Peninsula except for the above-mentioned goose management units) is open for a special late Canada goose season through the month of January and usually into the first week of February.

Michigan goose enthusiasts do most of their hunting in harvested agricultural fields, but some also hunt marshes, lakes, and river systems. Like anywhere else that geese are hunted, the need for larger decoy spreads becomes greater as the season progresses. Early in the season, if a hunter is positioned in the right field, as few as a dozen decoys might work just fine.

Hunting Waterfowl

There are several ways to hunt waterfowl in Michigan: over decoys, jump-shooting, or pass-shooting. Dabblers, divers, and geese can all be taken at certain times by each method. If you have a favorite method, then stick with what you enjoy and what works.

Hunting over decoys is the traditional way to hunt waterfowl, but pass-shooting can provide a nice change of pace and can actually be more relaxing. Little in the way of gear is needed, and you can just sit down and wait for something to pass by. Jumpshooting is nice if time is limited or if you want to get some exercise. Many people compare jumpshooting waterfowl to "wet upland hunting," and Michigan's miles of coastal marsh are well suited to this type of hunting.

Portable boat blinds are the way to go. (Photo by Chris Zimmerman)

Duke carefully brings in a wigeon at Keweenaw Peninsula.

Just remember that each method presents different types of shots at the ducks and geese. Decoying shots, whether on water or land, will mostly be incoming shots at the head and neck portion of the bird—the best killing shots. Pass-shooting presents fast crossing or incoming shots, and you'll need to adjust your lead. Jumpshooting offers the least likely killing shot because the bird can get its back and rear toward you very quickly. If jumpshooting, try to take the bird within the first few wingbeats off the water when the head and neck are exposed.

Boats and Blinds

Most waterfowl hunting in Michigan requires some sort of blind, and very often, a boat. Along the large rivers, lakes, and marshes, a boat allows you to get out where the birds are. A boat can be made into a floating blind by a variety of methods, but simply draping a camouflage tarp over the hull and staying low often does the trick.

A belly boat (an innertube with a tough nylon covering and a seat in the middle) allows you to paddle around a deep marsh. If you don't have a dog, this may be the

Diver duck decoy setup.

only way to retrieve a downed bird. These tubes are lightweight and can even provide a little concealment. Some belly boats that are made especially for hunting allow the hunter to sit among the decoys and lower his profile. Or, if setting out decoys or exploring a marsh, a belly boat can give you a little confidence, knowing that something is there to catch you if you happen to step on a false bottom.

When hunting smaller marshes, you can simply stand in the tall weeds and cattails that line the shore. If the shore is sparsely vegetated, a pop-up blind or fencing, woven with brush, provide the necessary concealment. When field hunting, fencing can be bent into a "coffin," woven with the surrounding vegetation, and pulled over your body as you lie down in the field. Simply throw the fencing off and shoot when the birds are in range.

While pass-shooting, you might be able to lay low, hold still, and wait. If there are trees surrounding a marsh, lean up against one and try to blend in. More often than not, the ducks and geese know where they're going, and if you are not too much of an eyesore, you won't flare them. Scouting a marsh or small lake to find the flight lanes that birds take in traveling back and forth can aid in increasing your pass shooting opportunities.

There are also managed wildlife areas in Michigan open to waterfowl hunting. These are usually in a marsh type setting, and if they are in proximity to a waterfowl refuge, the shooting can be tremendous. The areas are divided into numbered sections, and hunters gather to register at a check-in station well before

Could I keep it, please? Chris Smith's lab, Maggie, brings a black duck to hand. (Photo by Jason Smith)

shooting time. Through a lottery system, hunters choose their section for the morning hunt, with another lottery for the afternoon hunt. Boats in managed wildlife areas greatly aid in moving hunters to their sections, and small flat-bottomed boats or canoes are the most maneuverable. Not much may be required in the way of a blind, as these areas usually leave some standing vegetation for hunters to hide in.

Decoys and Decoy Spreads

For ducks, floating decoys are the most useful in most situations. They come in a variety of shapes and sizes, but all work pretty much the same on the potholes, rivers, and lakes, and in fields if silhouette decoys aren't available. Be sure to have the species of ducks you intend to lure represented in your decoy spread.

Goose hunting in the fields requires large decoy spreads, and this is best accomplished through lightweight decoys that can be hauled easily. Silhouettes, shells, foam-bodied decoys, or rags allow you to set up a lot of decoys quickly. There are many ways to set decoy spreads. The horseshoe spread is ideal for dabblers in marshes, but you

Ready, willing, and able, but where are the ducks? (Photo by Jason Smith)

might also find that simply scattering the decoys around near the blind, leaving an area for the birds to land, works well enough. The open-water setup, or "J," is a popular spread for hunting divers from a boat blind. This is useful in big lakes or rivers where you are not near the shore. The field spread, sort of a "horseshoe" on land, is well suited for geese.

An important factor to remember about setting decoy spreads is to always leave a landing area for the birds within killing range, usually 30 yards or less.

Dogs

The retrieving breeds (Labrador retrievers, Chesapeake Bay retrievers, golden retrievers, and springer spaniels) are excellent additions to any duck blind. Some of the versatile breeds, such as wirehairs, also perform well, and even some pointing dogs that have been trained to retrieve work nicely on waterfowl. Their thin coats (compared with retrievers) may restrict them to the early season.

The best way to deal with the possibility of losing crippled birds is to use a well-trained retriever—marshes are often deep in the center and can have thick vegetation throughout. Unless you have a small boat or belly tube, retrieving dead birds in the middle of the marsh is difficult and wet. Dogs simply make waterfowling easier by taking care of one end of the whole job—and it's what they live for.

Paraphernalia

There is probably more gear involved in waterfowling than in most other outdoor pursuits. But some things are essential.

Proper camouflage (plain drab colors work well also), a good flashlight, dependable waders (unless you're hunting in a dry field), durable waterproof and warm jacket and clothing, gloves, and a hat all make the hunt smoother. In addition, a field bag, camera, and binoculars are handy to have along. A first aid kit for both you and your dog should be nearby, and if you're hunting with a dog, don't forget a couple of dog bones, a dog vest for older dogs, and a leash if you'll be heading back to the car near a busy road.

A mallard call will be the most useful in a Michigan duck blind. Nearly all dabbler species, and even some divers, respond to a mallard call. A pintail whistle is a nice addition for the occasional pintail, wigeon, or teal, and if geese are a possibility, then of course, pack a goose call.

Dress in layers—you can always take something off if you get too warm. Keep weather predictions in mind for the day and play it smart. There will always be more ducks and geese.

Region I

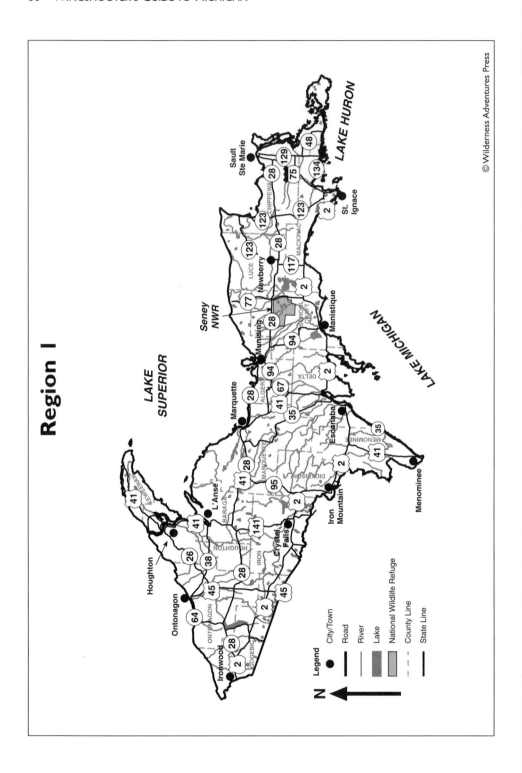

© Wilderness Adventures Press

Region I

Many things come to mind when one thinks of Michigan's Upper Peninsula: rugged country, tough winters, short summers, and few people. But for the thousands of hunters who reside here or travel to this region each fall, the thought that first crosses their minds are the abundance of wildlife and thousands upon thousands of acres of forest and marshland, providing almost unlimited opportunities to pursue grouse, woodcock, waterfowl, and turkey.

The Upper Peninsula holds no state game areas and only a few state wildlife management areas open to public hunting. The Upper Peninsula is, in some ways, one big piece of public hunting land. Where one state or federal forest ends, another begins. There are nearly two million acres of federal forest and just as many acres of state forest. The Upper Peninsula also contains more than two million acres of commercial forestlands—private lands open to hunting and fishing.

National forests include the Hiawatha, 860,000 acres in the east and central Upper Peninsula; and the Ottawa, 927,000 acres in the west. State forests include Lake Superior, the largest at more than one million acres in the east and central Upper Peninsula; Escanaba River, 416,000 acres in the central Upper Peninsula; and Copper Country, 430,000 acres in the west. Seney National Wildlife Refuge is located in the Lake Superior State Forest of Schoolcraft County.

This region is home to thousands of miles of Great Lakes shoreline, as is the rest of the state. Add that to the many public lakes, rivers, and streams, and you have one of the best places in the Midwest to hunt upland birds and waterfowl.

Many hunters would argue that the west end of the Upper Peninsula offers the most opportunity for grouse and woodcock. Likewise, the hundreds of hunters who travel to the eastern end of the peninsula would tell you that that area is best for waterfowl. The truth may lie somewhere in between; in fact, each section of the Upper Peninsula is unique and known for certain types of bird hunting.

It is true that the western Upper Peninsula is best known for its grouse and woodcock hunting. Iron County is perhaps the hub of the western Upper Peninsula's grouse and woodcock territory. In general, grouse habitat is best all along the southern half of the Upper Peninsula because that's where the logging operations are more prevalent. But there are pockets of grouse and woodcock throughout the Upper Peninsula, and you can't find a county that doesn't hold these birds.

The central part of the peninsula is home to the region's only turkey flocks large enough to be hunted. Menominee, Dickinson, Delta, part of Marquette, and now part of Iron County, are all open to turkey hunters who get licenses through

Andrea Pink and her pal, Duke, on an overnight duck hunting trip on Munuscong Bay with decoys in the background. Take the kids along to learn the joys and responsibilities of hunting.

annual lotteries. This is also the only part of the Upper Peninsula that holds pheasants, although the population is small. You'll find plenty of grouse and woodcock here, too.

The eastern Upper Peninsula, bordered by the St. Mary's River system and dotted with hundreds of islands and marshes, is the best place for waterfowl hunters. The west and central Upper Peninsula have traditionally been hotspots for Canada goose hunters who eagerly await the migrant geese that fly through the region each fall on their way to Wisconsin's Horicon Marsh and points south. But the eastern end's burgeoning resident honker population might provide as much or more opportunity for those who love the geese. Chippewa County is by far the best, along with Mackinac and other counties bordering the Lake Michigan shoreline. But resident geese are expanding their range west and north. Statewide, the flocks have grown to the point where the state has for years supported a special 10- to 15-day season in September for local birds. Canada geese have presented such a problem in local parks, golf courses, and beaches that in 1999 the U.S. Fish and Wildlife Service allowed Michigan and other states to take greater steps to control them.

While Michigan has very few sharp-tailed grouse, the eastern Upper Peninsula is home to most of them and is the only place in the state that offered a hunting season

Ruffed grouse. (Photo by Chris Zimmerman)

before it was closed a few years ago. A recent increase in the sharptail population has many hoping there will again be a season. Consult your hunting guide to be sure.

As far as hospitality goes, even the largest Upper Peninsula cities are small towns at heart. A hunter can find many great places to stay and eat among friendly people who are often willing to offer advice and tips.

Depending on the species you hunt, you may find other places in Michigan that hold more birds than the Upper Peninsula, but you won't find a better place to hunt that has prettier country, fewer hunters, and such an abundance of public land.

Ruffed Grouse

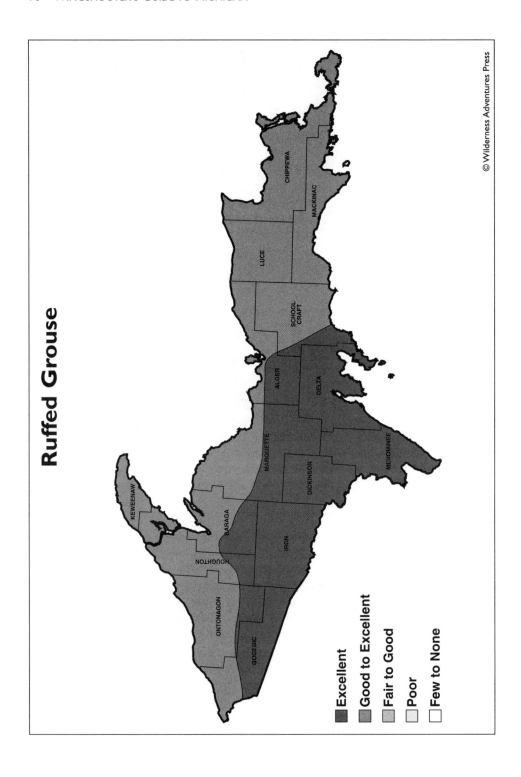

- ■ Excellent
- ■ Good to Excellent
- ■ Fair to Good
- ▫ Poor
- ☐ Few to None

© Wilderness Adventures Press

American Woodcock

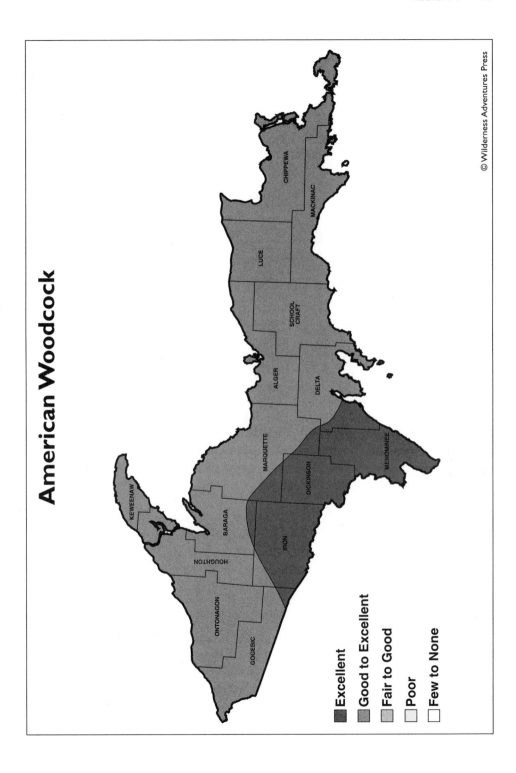

Excellent
Good to Excellent
Fair to Good
Poor
Few to None

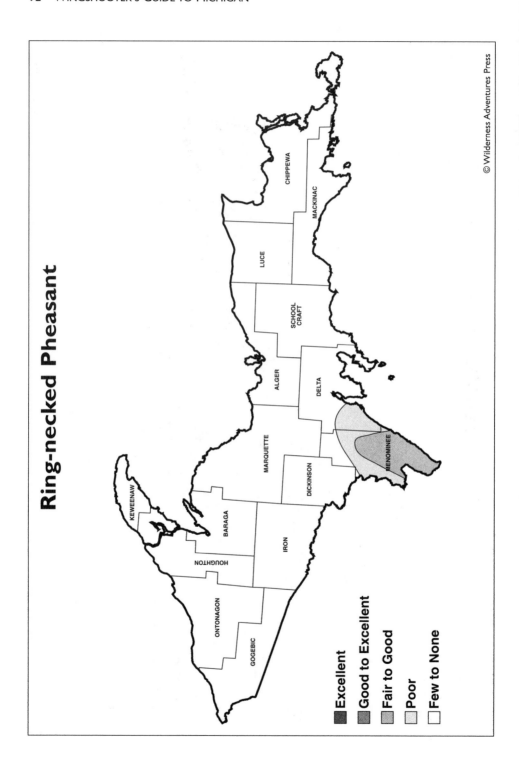

Ring-necked Pheasant

■ Excellent
■ Good to Excellent
■ Fair to Good
■ Poor
☐ Few to None

KEWEENAW
ONTONAGON
GOGEBIC
HOUGHTON
BARAGA
IRON
MARQUETTE
DICKINSON
ALGER
MENOMINEE
DELTA
SCHOOL CRAFT
LUCE
MACKINAC
CHIPPEWA

Wild Turkey

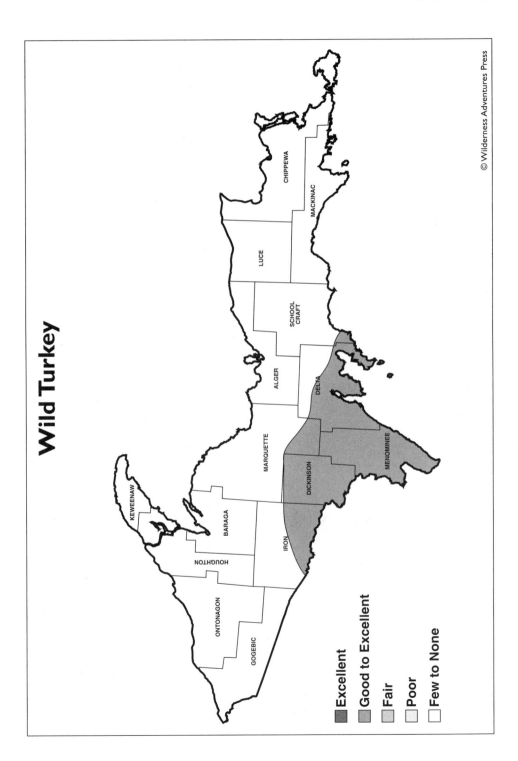

- Excellent
- Good to Excellent
- Fair
- Poor
- Few to None

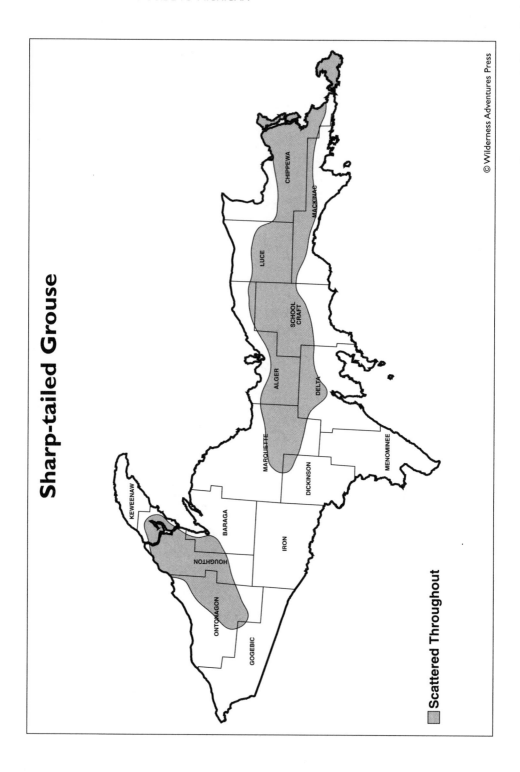

Sharp-tailed Grouse

Scattered Throughout

© Wilderness Adventures Press

Common Snipe

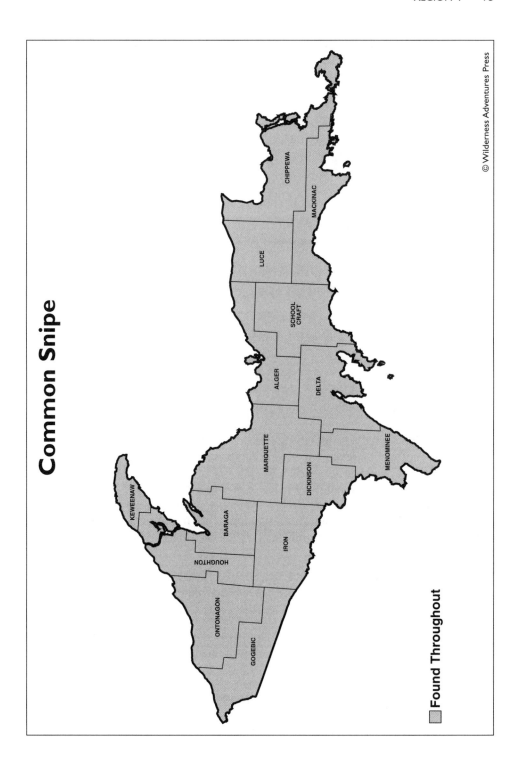

Found Throughout

Ironwood and Gogebic County

Population–6,849	October Average Temperature–56°F
County Population–17,894	Elevation–1,430 ft
County Area–1,102 sq mi	State Land Acres–10,900
	Federal Land Acres–311,500

Gogebic County is at the western tip of the Upper Peninsula, where Michigan, Wisconsin, and Lake Superior come together. This is "big snow country," receiving more than 200 inches of snow annually. The county is home to the 18,000-acre Sylvania Wilderness, part of the Ottawa National Forest. The national forest is home to very good grouse and woodcock hunting. Best bets are in the central part of the county, around Lake Gogebic, and farther east.

UPLAND BIRDS
Ruffed Grouse, Woodcock

WATERFOWL
Ducks, Geese, Snipe

ACCOMMODATIONS
Bear Track Cabins, N-15325 Black River Road / 906-932-2144 / Kitchenettes, restaurant nearby, cable TV / Dogs allowed / $$

Ironwood Motel, 112 West Cloverland Drive / 906-932-5520 / Cable TV / Dogs allowed / $$

Nine Pines Resort, HC1, Box 99SN, Marenisco / 906-842-3361 / On Lake Gogebic; cottages, convenience store, licenses, boat rental, information / Dogs allowed / Guide service / $$$

Root Cellar, East Shore Road, Marenisco / 906-842-3534 / On Lake Gogebic; 5 fully equipped houses which sleep 2-14 people, weekly & daily rates, restaurant & lounge / Dogs permitted with restrictions (not in rooms) / $$

Super 8 Motel, 160 East Cloverland Drive / 906-932-3395 / Sauna, whirlpool / Dogs allowed / $$

CAMPGROUNDS AND RV PARKS
Curry Park, US 2, Ironwood / 56 sites, electricity, water, showers

Eddy Park, M-28, Wakefield / 906-229-5131 / 79 camper and 15 tent sites, water, electric, showers

Lake Gogebic State Park, M-64 / 906-842-3341 / On west shore of Lake Gogebic; 127 sites, water, electricity, showers, boat launch

RESTAURANTS
Branding Iron, Silver Street, Hurley, WI / Steaks, ribs, seafood / 715-561-4562

Hunter's Inn, 111 East Sellar, Bessemer / Homemade pizza, Friday fish fry, cocktails / 906-667-0919

Joe's Pasty Shop, 116 West Aurora / Known for pasties since 1946 / 906-932-4412

Mike's Family Restaurant, 106 East Cloverland Drive / Breakfast, lunch, dinner / 906-932-0555

VETERINARIANS

Ironwood Veterinary Clinic, 601 East Cloverland Drive / 906-932-2060

Lake Road Veterinary Clinic, N-10499 Lake Road / 906-932-4070

Range Animal Hospital, E-6116 US 2 / 906-932-3531

SPORTING GOODS STORES

Black Bear Sporting Goods, 100 West Cloverland Drive / Guns, ammunition, guide service / 906-932-5253

AUTO REPAIR

C & M Oil Co., 605 East US 2, Bessemer / 906-667-0222 / 1301 East US 2, Ironwood / 906-932-0700

Greg's Towing & Repair, 301 West McLeod Avenue / 906-932-9953

Northwestern Auto Co., 200 East Lead, Bessemer / 906-667-0205 / Towing available

AIR SERVICE

Gogebic County Airport, E-5560 Airport Road / 906-932-3121

United Express Airlines, E-5560 Airport Road / 906-932-5808

MEDICAL

Grand View Hospital, US 2 / 906-932-2525 / Between Ironwood and Bessemer

FOR MORE INFORMATION

Western Upper Peninsula Convention & Visitor Bureau
P.O. Box 706
Ironwood, MI 49938
800-272-7000
www.westernup.com

Lake Gogebic Area Chamber of Commerce
P.O. Box 114
Bergland, MI 49910
906-575-3265

Ontonagon and Ontonagon County

Population–2,040	October Average Temperature–55°F
County Population–8,639	Elevation–1,300 ft
County Area–1,311 sq mi	State Land Acres–67,200
	Federal Land Acres–279,600

Ontonagon County is home to some of the most rugged country in the Upper Peninsula, including the Porcupine Mountains Wilderness State Park. The 60,000-acre park stretches along Lake Superior for more than 20 miles and is full of opportunity for hunters, fishermen, campers, backpackers, and in the winter, skiers and snowshoe enthusiasts. The region has a rich mining heritage. Grouse and woodcock numbers are good to excellent, with some of the best hunting in the Ottawa National Forest on the county's southern reaches.

UPLAND BIRDS
Ruffed Grouse, Woodcock

WATERFOWL
Ducks, Geese, Snipe

ACCOMMODATIONS
Scott's Superior Inn and Cabins, 277 Lakeshore Road / 800-884-4866 / 12 room motel & 4 cabins; whirlpool, sauna, cable TV / Dogs allowed / $
Inn Towne Motel, 314 Chippewa / 906-884-2100 / Cable TV, restaurant nearby / Dogs allowed / $
Sunshine Motel & Cabins, 1442 M-64 / 906-884-2187 / 20 units, kitchenettes, satellite TV / No dogs / $-$$

CAMPGROUNDS AND RV PARKS
Porcupine Mountains State Park, M-107 / 906-885-5275 / 199 sites, electricity, water, showers
River Pines RV Park & Campground, 600 River Road / 906-884-4600 / 46 sites, color TV, game room, electricity
Ontonagon Township Park, Lakeshore Drive / 906-884-2930 / 40 sites, water, electricity

RESTAURANTS
Candlelight Inn, 2077 M-38 / 906-884-6101
McMiles Restaurant, M-64 / 906-884-2991
Syl's Cafe, 713 River / 906-884-2522
Wagar's Restaurant, 227 River / 906-884-4475

VETERINARIANS
Copper Country Veterinary Clinic, 904 Sharon Avenue, Houghton / 906-482-1771
Keweenaw Veterinary Clinic, US 41, Arnheim / 906-353-7575

SPORTING GOODS STORES
Autumn Sports, 1755 M-64 / 906-884-2464
Holiday Station Store, 103 Greenland Road / 906-884-4718
Wilderness Supply Ltd., 638 River Street / 906-884-2922

AUTO REPAIR
Bob's Auto Repair, 114 Johnson Road / 906-884-4216
M-64 Truck & Auto Repair, 1001 M-64 / 906-884-4150

AIR SERVICE
American Eagle / 800-433-7300
Northwest Airlines / 800-225-2525
Ontonagon County Airport, Airport Road / 906-884-9958

MEDICAL
Baraga County Memorial Hospital, 770 North Main, L'Anse / 906-524-6166
Portage Hospital, 200 Michigan, Hancock / 906-487-8000

FOR MORE INFORMATION
Ontonagon County Chamber of Commerce and Tourism Council
P.O. Box 266
Ontonagon, MI 49953
906-884-4735

Lake Gogebic Area Chamber of Commerce
P.O. Box 114
Bergland, MI 49910
906-575-3265

Porcupine Mountains Promotional Chamber
P.O. Box 493
White Pine, MI 49971
906-885-5885

Western Upper Peninsula Convention & Visitor Bureau
P.O. Box 706
Ironwood, MI 49938
800-272-7000
www.westernup.com

Houghton and Houghton / Keweenaw Counties

Population – 7,498	October Average Temperature – 52°F
County Population:	Elevation – 1,074 ft
Houghton – 36,140	
Keweenaw – 1,967	Public Land by County (Acres):
County Area:	Houghton State Land – 45,500
Houghton – 1,011 sq mi	Houghton Federal Land – 156,600
Keweenaw – 541 sq mi	Keweenaw State Land – 4,400

The Keweenaw Peninsula competes with the rest of the western Upper Peninsula for the prettiest and most rugged country in Michigan. If you don't pull a trigger in the Keweenaw (and there's no reason you won't), you'll still enjoy the scenery. Copper Harbor and Brockway Mountain Drive at the northern end of the peninsula are worth seeing. This region is visited by a considerable population of Canada geese that stop after making their way across Lake Superior. Many of the birds linger in Houghton County agricultural fields before moving farther south to Wisconsin's Horicon Marsh and beyond. Ruffed grouse and woodcock numbers are good in both counties, especially if you look into recent timber cuttings.

UPLAND BIRDS
Ruffed Grouse, Woodcock

WATERFOWL
Ducks, Geese, Snipe

ACCOMMODATIONS
Best Western Kings Inn, 215 Shelden Avenue / 906-482-5000 / Continental breakfast, sauna, whirlpool / Dogs allowed, $6 fee / $$
Chippewa Motel, US 41, Chassell / 906-523-4611 / Kitchen unit, cable TV, restaurant; near grocery store, boat ramp, Portage Lake / One room where dogs are allowed; all rooms have covered porch for dogs outside / $$
Downtowner Motel, 110 Shelden Avenue / 906-482-4421 / No dogs / $$
Pines Resort, US 41, Copper Harbor / 906-289-4229 / Motel units, cabins for overnight & housekeeping; restaurant, lounge / Dogs allowed / $-$$$
Vic's Cabins, Kearsarge / 906-337-3703 / One & two bedroom units, kitchens, cable TV / Dogs allowed / $-$$

CAMPGROUNDS AND RV PARKS
Lake Fanny Hooe Resort & Campground, 2nd Street, Copper Harbor / 906-289-4451 / Northernmost campground in Michigan, motel and cottages; 64 wooded campsites with trout stream, electricity, bottled gas, laundry facilities, sauna, boat rental / Dogs allowed
F.J. McLain State Park, M-203, 10 miles north of Houghton / 906-482-0278 / 90 sites, electricity, water, showers

RESTAURANTS

Armando's and Douglas' Saloon, 517 Shelden Avenue / Breakfast, lunch, dinner; Friday fish buffet, Saturday Italian buffet, cocktails / 906-482-2003

The Landing, 216 Gay-Lac Labelle Road, Lac Labelle / Famous for omelets, roast beef sandwiches; open 365 days, 9AM–9PM, cocktails / 906-289-4359

The Library, 62 Isle Royale Street / Restaurant, bar, brew pub; daily specials, pizza, sandwiches / 906-487-5882

Suomi Home Bakery & Restaurant, 54 Huron / Finnish specialties, pasties; breakfast served all day / 906-482-3220

VETERINARIANS

Copper Country Veterinary Clinic, 904 Sharon Avenue, Houghton / 906-482-1771

Keweenaw Veterinary Clinic, US 41, Arnheim / 906-353-7575

SPORTING GOODS STORES

Dick's Favorite Sports, 1700 West Memorial Drive / 906-482-0412 / Guns and ammo, supplies

Harter's Party Store, 511 Pine Street, Calumet / 906-337-0913 / Guns and ammo, licenses, supplies

AUTO REPAIR

All Auto, 479 US 41, Chassell Twp. / 906-523-4255 / Domestic and import, all repairs

Keweenaw Automotive, M-26 / 906-482-7988 / Domestic and import, all repairs

Precision Automotive, 911 Evergreen Drive / 906-482-6911 / Major and minor repairs on most domestic cars and trucks

Osceola Service Center, US 41, Calumet / 906-337-5960

AIR SERVICE

Houghton County Memorial Airport / 906-482-3970

MEDICAL

Keweenaw Memorial Medical Center, 205 Osceola, Laurium / 906-337-6500

Portage Hospital, 200 Michigan Avenue, Hancock / 906-487-8000

FOR MORE INFORMATION

Keweenaw Peninsula Chamber of Commerce
326 Shelden Avenue
Houghton, MI 49931
906-482-5240

Keweenaw Tourism Council
1197 Calumet Avenue
Calumet, MI 49913
906-337-4579

L'Anse and Baraga County

Population–2,151	October Average Temperature–55°F
County Population–8,493	Elevation–1,565 ft
County Area–904 sq mi	State Land Acres–78,800
	Federal Land Acres–44,913

Baraga County has it all for the bird hunter. There is plenty of elbowroom in thousands of acres of Copper Country State and Ottawa National Forest lands, and the grouse and woodcock hunting are good to excellent. Canada goose enthusiasts will want to investigate the Baraga Plains, where the state plants grain crops with the hope that migrating geese will linger in the area to provide opportunities for hunters.

UPLAND BIRDS
Ruffed Grouse, Woodcock

WATERFOWL
Ducks, Geese, Snipe

ACCOMMODATIONS
Carla's Lake Shore Motel, US 41, Baraga / 906-353-6256 / 10 rooms, restaurant and lounge, sauna, casino package / Dogs allowed / $$
Cozy Country Hideaway, Pequaming Road / 800-524-5682 / 1 cabin with cable TV, casino package, boat rental / Dogs allowed / $
Hilltop Motel, US 41 / 800-424-2548 / 20 rooms, cable TV, casino package, restaurant / Dogs allowed / $$
Ojibwa Casino Resort Motel, M-38, Baraga / 800-323-8045 / 40 rooms, restaurant and lounge, cable TV, hot tub, sauna, casino packages / No dogs / $$

CAMPGROUNDS AND RV PARKS
Baraga State Park, US 41, Baraga / 906-353-6558 / 137 sites, water and electricity, showers
Craig Lake State Park, US 41, 6.5 miles east of Nestoria / 906-339-4461 / 25 sites, vault toilets, no electricity, water or showers; wilderness area, hike in only

RESTAURANTS
Baraga Lakeside Inn, 900 US 41 South, Baraga / Breakfast, lunch, dinner / 906-353-7123
Canteen Bar & Grill, 9 South Front Street / Burgers, Mexican, Friday fish fry / 906-524-6211
Tony's Steak House, US 41 / Steaks, fish and seafood, cocktails, open 7 days / 906-524-9900

VETERINARIANS
Keweenaw Veterinary Clinic, US 41, Arnheim / 906-353-7575

Another grouse favorite food is wild grape. (Photo by Chris Zimmerman)

SPORTING GOODS STORES
Brewster's Oasis, Nisula / 906-338-2828 / Hunting and fishing supplies, licenses, open 7 days
Indian Country Sports Inc. / 906-524-6518 / Supplies, licenses, information

AUTO REPAIR
Ken's Service, 821 Superior Avenue, Baraga / 906-353-6507 / After hours call 906-353-6021 (Menge Automotive Service), US 41 / 906-524-4400

AIR SERVICE
American Eagle / 800-433-7300
Northwest Airlink / 800-225-2525
Houghton County Memorial Airport / 906-482-3970
Ontonagon County Airport / 906-884-9958

MEDICAL
Baraga County Memorial Hospital, 770 North Main Street / 906-524-6166

FOR MORE INFORMATION
Baraga County Tourism & Recreation Association
755 Broad Street
L'Anse, MI 49946
906-524-7444

Crystal Falls and Iron County

Population–1,922	October Average Temperature–57°F
County Population–13,177	Elevation–1,560 ft
County Area–1,166 sq mi	State Land Acres–84,600
	Federal Land Acres–178,800

Maybe every Upper Peninsula county could argue the point, but Iron County is the heart of Upper Peninsula grouse and woodcock hunting. Bird hunters can wander through tens of thousands of acres of Copper Country State Forest and Ottawa National Forest, as well as a great deal of commercial forestlands. Upper Peninsula turkey flocks have been expanding into Iron County, and a season has recently been opened here.

UPLAND BIRDS
Ruffed Grouse, Woodcock, Turkey

WATERFOWL
Ducks, Geese, Snipe

ACCOMMODATIONS
Hardwood Hotel, 1986 US 41, Amasa / 906-822-7713 / Cable TV / Dogs allowed / $$

Hilberg's Cabins, 231 Hilberg Road / 906-265-2982 / Four cabins with cooking facilities, TV. Boats included

Iron Inn Motel, 211 West Cayuga Street, Iron River / 906-265-5111 / Dogs allowed / $

Iron River Motel, 3037 East US 2, Iron River / 906-265-4212 / Dogs allowed / $

Valley View Motel, 509 South US 2 / 906-875-3762 / Catering to hunters / Dogs allowed / $

CAMPGROUNDS AND RV PARKS
Bewabic State Park, West US 2 / 906-875-3324 / 144 wooded sites four miles west of Crystal Falls

Iron County Pentoga Park, 1630 County Road 424 / 906-265-3979 / Seasonal or daily, full facilities, on Chicaugon Lake between Crystal Falls and Iron River

Iron River RV Park, 50 East Genesee, Iron River / 906-265-3443

RESTAURANTS
Fob's Fine Food, West US 2 / Breakfast, lunch, dinner / 906-875-4200

Club Felix, 2465 South US 2 / Famous for steaks; open 5–10PM Mon–Sat / 906-875-3779

Partners Diner, 320 Superior Avenue / Breakfast, lunch, dinner / 906-875-6788

VETERINARIANS
Highway 2 Animal Clinic, 106 Bernhardt Road, Iron River / 906-265-5891

Iron County Animal Clinic, Iron River / 906-265-3111

Another turkey for the table. Iron County now has a turkey season. (Photo by Chris Zimmerman)

SPORTING GOODS STORES

DJ's Sport Shop & Marine, 31 Superior Avenue / 906-875-3113
Luckey's Sports Shop, 209 19th Street, Stambaugh / 906-265-5339 / Licenses, ammunition

AUTO REPAIR

Champion Auto Stores, 135 Zavada Street / 906-875-4327
Ted's Service Center, 17 Superior Avenue / 800-491-2929

AIR SERVICE

Iron County Airport, 408 County Airport Road / 906-875-9914
Midwest Aire / 800-227-5666

MEDICAL

Crystal Falls Community Hospital, 212 South 3rd / 906-875-6661
Iron County General Hospital, 1400 West Ice Lake Road, Iron River / 906-265-6121

FOR MORE INFORMATION

Iron County Chamber of Commerce
50 East Genesee
Iron River, MI 49935
906-265-3822

Marquette and Marquette County

Population–21,977	October Average Temperature–56°F
County Population–65,442	Elevation–1,415 ft
County Area–1,821 sq mi	State Land Acres–261,000
	Federal Land Acres–18,000

Marquette is the largest city in the Upper Peninsula, and together with the neighboring cities of Negaunee and Ishpeming, provides everything the bird hunter needs in lodging, food, and supplies. There is no shortage of public land available to the hunter in this region. Bird hunters will find good places to hunt grouse and woodcock, waterfowl, and even turkey in the southern part of the county.

UPLAND BIRDS
Ruffed Grouse, Woodcock, Turkey

WATERFOWL
Ducks, Geese, Snipe

ACCOMMODATIONS
Big Bay Depot, 301 Depot Road, Big Bay / 906-345-9350 / Six units, full kitchens / Dogs allowed / $$

Edgewater Motel, 2050 US 41 South / 800-435-2502 / 49 units, restaurant and lounge / Dogs allowed / $$

Holiday Inn, 1951 US 41 West / 906-225-1351 / 203 units, restaurant and lounge, pool, jacuzzi/sauna; group rate available / Dogs allowed /$$$

Village Inn, 1301 North Third Street / 800-800-8909 / 40 units, efficiencies, continental breakfast / No dogs / $$

CAMPGROUNDS AND RV PARKS
City of Marquette Campground, County Road 550 / 906-228-0465

Gitche Gummi Campground & RV Park, 2048 East M-28, Chocolay Twp / 906-249-9102 / electricity, LP gas, laundry facilities

RESTAURANTS
The Garden Room, 2050 US 41 South / Prime rib, seafood, cocktails; breakfast, lunch, dinner / 906-225-1305

Grama T's Pasties, 801 North Teal Lake Avenue, Negaunee / Traditional and not-so-traditional Upper Peninsula pasties / 906-475-6828

Steer & Stein Steakhouse, US 41 West / Grill your own steaks; beer and wine / 906-228-7011

Villa Capri, US 41 West / Opens at 4:30PM; Italian cuisine, steak, pizza; lounge / 906-225-1153

VETERINARIANS

Animal Medical Center, 3145 Wright Street / 24 hr emergency service /
906-226-7400

Bayshore Veterinary Hospital, 1202 South Front Street / Emergency service /
906-228-8775

Marquette Veterinary Clinic, 2270 US 41 South, Harvey / Walk-in hours /
906-249-1456

SPORTING GOODS STORES

ABC Bows & Guns, 2250 US 41 South / 906-228-3030
Johnson Sport Shop, 1212 North 3rd Street / 906-226-2062
Tom's Hunt & Fish, 2162 US 41 West / 906-228-8667

AUTO REPAIR

Affordable Automotive of Marquette Inc., 630 South Lake Street / 906-225-0669
Anthony Automotive, 1919 Enterprise Street / 906-2250102
Autowerks, 3150 Wright Street / 906-226-2700 / Import specialist
Forty One 4x4 & Auto Repair, 6573 US 41 South / 906-249-9252 / 4x4 specialist
Marquette Automotive Inc., 730 West Washington Street / 906-228-6116

AIR SERVICE

Great Lakes Airlines, 198 Airport Road, Negaunee Twp / 906-475-7853
Marquette County Airport / 906-475-9651
Midwest Aire / 906-228-5666

MEDICAL

Bell Memorial Hospital, 101 South 4th Street, Ishpeming / 906-486-4431
Marquette General Hospital, 580 West College Avenue / 906-228-9440
Superior Walk-In Center, 1414 West Fair Avenue / 906-226-2233

FOR MORE INFORMATION

Marquette Area Chamber of Commerce
501 South Front Street
Marquette, MI 49855
906-226-6591
www.marquette.org

Marquette Country Convention and Visitors Bureau
2552 US 41 West
Marquette, MI 49855
906-228-7749

Iron Mountain
and Dickinson County

Population–8,525	October Average Temperature–57°F
County Population–27,176	Elevation–1,060 ft
County Area–766 sq mi	State Land Acres–223,300

One of the smallest of the Upper Peninsula counties, Dickinson has much to offer the bird hunter. The northern portion is covered by Copper Country State Forest and few roads. Turkeys range throughout the county, from the thickest swamps in the central parts to the agricultural lands of the south. Grouse and woodcock hunting are good to very good, especially along the Dickinson/Iron County border.

UPLAND BIRDS
Ruffed Grouse, Woodcock, Turkey

WATERFOWL
Ducks, Geese, Snipe

ACCOMMODATIONS
Best Western, 1518 South Stephenson Avenue / 906-774-2040 / 57 units, cable TV, deluxe continental breakfast, pool / Dogs allowed / $$ / Ask for hunter's rate for up to four in a room / $6 one-time charge for dogs
Hillcrest Motel, US 2, Quinnesec / 906-774-6866 / 15 units, one kitchenette, cable TV, continental breakfast, multiple night discount / Dogs allowed / $
'R' Cabins, N12178 M-95, Channing / 906-542-6995 / Cabins with kitchenettes; 4–6 hunters per cabin; daily or weekly rentals / Dogs allowed / $

CAMPGROUNDS AND RV PARKS
Rivers Bend Campground, N3905 Pine Mountain Road / 906-779-1171
Iron Mountain Campground, W8576 Twin Falls Road / 906-774-7701 / 70 sites, water, electricity, laundry and shower facilities, daily, weekly, monthly rates
Lake Antoine County Park, 1 mile east of US 2 & 141 / 80 sites, electricity, water, showers

RESTAURANTS
B's Country Cafe, 629 South Stephenson Avenue / 906-774-4401
The Blind Duck Inn, Cowboy Lake, Kingsford (across from the airport) / 906-774-0037
Gleason's 1891 Restaurant, 206 East Ludington / Seafood, steaks, southwestern; cocktails / 906-779-5300

VETERINARIANS
Iron Mountain Animal Hospital, 315 Kent / 906-774-5961

SPORTING GOODS STORES

Jim's Sport Shop, North US 2 / 906-774-4247 / New and used guns, licenses

Whispering Pines Outpost, N-4200 M-95 / 906-774-1277 / Open seven days

AUTO REPAIR

Auto Tech Service Center, 701 Carpenter Avenue / 906-779-1699

Brian's Auto Sales & Service, 401 South Carpenter Avenue / 906-774-8844

D & L Auto Repair, 1208 North Stephenson Avenue / 906-776-0846

Dave's Auto Service, 1137 South Stephenson Avenue / 906-774-7717 / Foreign and domestic

AIR SERVICE

Ford Airport, 700 South Stephenson Avenue / 906-774-4830

Superior Aviation Inc., 250 River Hills Road, Kingsford / 906-774-0400

MEDICAL

Dickinson County Healthcare System, 1721 South Stephenson Avenue / 906-774-1313

FOR MORE INFORMATION

Dickinson County Area Chamber of Commerce

600 South Stephenson Avenue

Iron Mountain, MI 49801

906-774-2002

Menominee and Menominee County

Population–9,398	October Average Temperature–58°F
County Population–24,569	Elevation–710 ft
County Area–1,043 sq mi	State Land Acres–94,800

Unlike most of the forested Upper Peninsula, private agricultural lands characterize much of Menominee County. There are large tracts of public land, including Escanaba River State Forest along the east, west, and north portions of the county. For the hunter who is looking for Upper Peninsula pheasants, Menominee County is the best bet, although the population is very small. Good grouse and woodcock numbers are found in state forestlands. Don't hesitate to ask a farmer's permission to hunt a private covert that appears as if it might have possibilities. Across the river from Menominee is sister city Marinette, Wisconsin.

UPLAND BIRDS
Ruffed Grouse, Woodcock, Turkey, Pheasant

WATERFOWL
Ducks, Geese, Snipe

ACCOMMODATIONS

Bay Breeze Motel, N-1055 M-35 / 906-863-6964 / Kitchenettes, cable TV / Dogs allowed / $

Howard Johnson Express Inn, 2516 10th Street / 906-863-4431 / 50 units, cable TV, sauna, continental breakfast / Dogs allowed / $$

Stephenson Motel, US 41, Stephenson / 906-753-2552 / 13 rooms, cable TV / No dogs / $

CAMPGROUNDS AND RV PARKS

Acorns and Pinecones Campground, W-6182 Co. Road G-12, Stephenson / 906-753-2695

Shakey Lakes Park, N-8390 County Park Road, Stephenson / 906-753-4582 / 103 sites, electricity, water, showers, laundry facilities.

Menominee River Park Campground / 52 sites, electricity, showers, laundry facilities

Wells State Park, M-35 / 906-863-9747 / 155 sites, electricity, water, showers, laundry facilities

RESTAURANTS

Regent Chinese Restaurant, 824 10th Avenue / Chinese and Szechuan; lunch and dinner buffet / 906-863-5300

Pat & Rayleen's, 2812 10th Street / Breakfast anytime; open at 6AM / 906-863-6241

Roadhouse Grill, US 41 / Sandwiches, pizza, fish fry; lunch and dinner / 906-863-1159

VETERINARIANS

Bayshore Veterinary Clinic, 2514 10th Avenue / 906-863-2237

Mid-County Veterinary Clinic, E111 South Drive, Stephenson / 906-753-6312

Town and Country Veterinary Clinic, W1292 US 41, Marinette, WI / 715-735-9511

SPORTING GOODS STORES

Dad's Sporting Goods, 2005 10th Street / 906-863-4650

Acorns and Antlers Archery, 2400 13th Street / 906-863-8026 / Some guns and ammunition

AUTO REPAIR

Auto Pro's Service Center, 4120 10th Street / 906-863-4444 / Foreign and domestic work

Jim's Auto Repair, 4317 10th Street / 906-863-9491

Last Stop Auto Repair, 4701 10th Street / 906-863-3464

AIR SERVICE

Twin County Airport, 2801 22nd Street / 906-863-8408

JP's Flying Inc., 2100 22nd Avenue / 906-863-2206

Midwest Aire / 800-227-5666

MEDICAL

Bay Area Medical Center, 3100 Shore Drive, Marinette, WI / 715-735-4200

OSF St. Francis Hospital, 3401 Ludington, Escanaba / 906-786-3311

Northern Menominee Health Center, East US 2, Spalding / 906-497-5263

Stephenson Medical Clinic, E807 Gerue, Stephenson / 906-753-2321

FOR MORE INFORMATION

Menominee County Chamber of Commerce

1005 10th Avenue

Menominee, MI 49858

906-863-2679

Munising and Alger County

Population–2,783	October Average Temperature–56°F
County Population–9,846	Elevation–680 ft
County Area–918 sq mi	State Land Acres–97,100
	Federal Land Acres–128,600

Alger County offers tremendous upland and waterfowl hunting with thousands of acres of forestland in the Hiawatha National Forest and Escanaba River State Forest. Waterfowl hunters will be especially interested in the Cleveland Cliffs Basin. Alger County is home to the Pictured Rocks National Lakeshore on Lake Superior and some of the prettiest country the Upper Peninsula has to offer.

UPLAND BIRDS
Ruffed Grouse, Woodcock

WATERFOWL
Ducks, Geese, Snipe

ACCOMMODATIONS
Best Western, M-28 East / 906-387-4864 / Restaurant and lounge, pool, spa, sauna / Dogs allowed / $$
Comfort Inn, M-28 East / 906-387-2592 / cable TV, pool, hot tub, sauna / Dogs allowed / $$$
Days Inn, M-28 / 906-387-2493 / Cable TV, pool, hot tub, sauna / Dogs allowed / $$$
Hillcrest Motel and Cabins, M-28 East / 906-387-2858 / Free coffee; we love bird hunters / Dogs allowed / $

CAMPGROUNDS AND RV PARKS
Deer Lake Lodge, Shelter Bay / AuTrain / 906-892-8362
Otter Lake Campground, H-09 / 906-387-4648
Pictured Rocks National Lakeshore / 906 -387-3700 / 67 sites
Wandering Wheels Campground, M-28 East / 906-387-3315 / 89 sites, electricity, laundry facilities

RESTAURANTS
Brownstone Inn, M-28 West, AuTrain / Lunch and dinner, cocktails; closed Mondays / 906-892-8332
Dogpatch Restaurant, East Superior / Breakfast, lunch and dinner / 906-387-9948
Main Street Pizza, 114 Maple / Pizza, subs / 906-387-3993
Sydney's, M-28 East / Food and drink / 906-387-4067

VETERINARIANS
G.L. Hoholik, 321 East Superior Street / 906-387-2369

Guns, ducks, and dogs just go together.

SPORTING GOODS STORES
Holiday Station Store, 301 East Munising Avenue / 906-387-4872
Curly's Hilltop Grocery, H-58 / 906-387-3056 / Hunting & fishing licenses

AUTO REPAIR
Lare Auto Repair, Box 187, Ridge Road, Christmas / 906-387-3091
Munising Auto Repair Inc., E-9051 M-28 / 906-387-5490

AIR SERVICE
Marquette County Airport, 198 B Airport Road, Negaunee / 906-475-4463
Midwest Aire, Marquette / 906-228-5666
Northern Michigan Aviation, 199 B Airport Road, Negaunee / 906-475-4400

MEDICAL
Munising Memorial Hospital, 1500 Sand Point Road / 906-387-4110

FOR MORE INFORMATION
Alger County Chamber of Commerce
P.O. Box 405
Munising, MI 49862
906-387-2138

Escanaba and Delta County

Population – 13,659	October Average Temperature – 54°F
County Population – 38,655	Elevation – 600 ft
County Area – 1,170 sq mi	State Land Acres – 67,400
	Federal Land Acres – 241,600

Upper Peninsula bird hunters will find a bit more variety in Delta County. There is a very good population of turkeys and some opportunity to hunt pheasants. Grouse and woodcock hunting are excellent, helped along by a thriving paper and pulp industry. Waterfowlers will find a variety of places to hunt: agricultural fields, the bigger waters of the Bays de Noc, and smaller rivers and floodings. Between the Hiawatha National Forest and Escanaba River State Forest, the county is covered in public land.

UPLAND BIRDS
Ruffed Grouse, Woodcock, Turkey, Pheasant

WATERFOWL
Ducks, Geese, Snipe

ACCOMMODATIONS

Days Inn, 2603 North Lincoln Road / 800-548-2822 / 120 units, restaurant, lounge, pool, hot tub, casino package / Dogs allowed / $$$

Hiawatha Motel, 2400 Ludington Street / 800-249-2216 / 20 units, cable TV, efficiencies, casino package / Dogs allowed / $

Memory Lane Motel & Delta Inn Annex, 2415 Ludington Street / 906-786-7171 / 54 units, cable TV, kitchenettes, daily and weekly rates / Dogs allowed / $

North Land Motor Inn, 4131 M 35 South / 906-786-5771 / 20 units, cable TV, continental breakfast / Dogs allowed

Sall-mar Resort, 7989 US 2, Rapid River / 906-474-6928 / Motel, cabins, kitchenettes, store, licenses, ammunition / Dogs allowed / $–$$

CAMPGROUNDS AND RV PARKS

Gladstone Bay Campground, 37 Michigan Avenue, Gladstone / 906-428-1211

Park Place of the North, M-35 / 906-786-8453 / At Ford River mouth / 20 sites, electricity, laundry facilities

Pioneer Trail Park, 6822 US 2, Gladstone / 906-786-1020

RESTAURANTS

The Carriage Restaurant, 2635 Ludington Street / Breakfast, lunch, dinner; cocktails; award-winning chef / 906-786-0602

Drifter's, 701 North Lincoln Road / Ethnic foods; breakfast, lunch, dinner / 906-789-0508

The Stonehouse, 2223 Ludington Street / Baby-back ribs; cocktails; lunch and dinner / 906-786-5003

VETERINARIANS

Delta Animal Clinic, 2715 South Lincoln Road / 906-786-6260 or 786-4512 / 24-hour emergency service

Escanaba Veterinary Clinic, 618 Stephenson Avenue / 906-786-8020 / Appointment only

Your Front Door Mobile Veterinary Clinic, 2702 Weston Avenue, Gladstone / 906-428-3990 / They come to you

SPORTING GOODS STORES

Holiday Station Store, 700 North Lincoln Road / 906- 786-8199 / Ammunition; licenses

Land 'n Lakes Sports, 845 North Lincoln at Lincoln Fair Plaza / 906-786-LAND / Buy, sell, trade guns; footwear; ammunition

Supply Sergeant, 1115 Ludington / 906-786-7861 / Hunter clothing and more

AUTO REPAIR

Bero Motors, 5273 US 2 / 906-786-0861 / Full service; towing

D&B Equipment Truck & Auto Repair, 2305 9th Avenue North / 906-789-0047 / Complete repairs; trucks, vans, 4 x 4s

Lake Forest Auto Center, 5224 11th Road / 906-786-3072 / General auto repairs, motor and transmission

AIR SERVICE

Mesaba Airlines, 3300 Airport Access Road / 906-789-4330

Midwest Aire / 906-789-5666

Skyway Airlines, 3300 Airport Access Road / 906-789-3066

MEDICAL

OSF St. Francis Hospital, 3401 Ludington / 906-786-3311

OSF Walk-In Clinic, 3409 Ludington / 906-789-4427 / No appointment needed

FOR MORE INFORMATION

Delta County Area Chamber of Commerce
230 Ludington Street
Escanaba, MI 49829
906-786-2192

Manistique and Schoolcraft County

Population–3,456	October Average Temperature–55°F
County Population–8,700	Elevation–620 ft
County Area–1,178 sq mi	State Land Acres–288,200
	Federal Land Acres–122,500

Schoolcraft County is home of the Seney National Wildlife Refuge, a haven for migrating waterfowl. Parts of the refuge are open to hunting grouse and woodcock, but waterfowl hunting is not allowed. Waterfowl hunters might want to explore Indian Lake, near Manistique. Grouse and woodcock hunters will find good to very good numbers of birds in the surrounding Lake Superior State Forest, especially on the western edge of the county.

UPLAND BIRDS
Ruffed Grouse, Woodcock

WATERFOWL
Ducks, Geese, Snipe

ACCOMMODATIONS
Manistique Motor Inn, East US-2 / 906-341-2552 / No dogs / $$
Star Motel, Lakeshore Drive / 906-341-5363 / Dogs allowed / $
Sunset View Cabins, County Road 441 / 906-341-6756 / On Indian Lake, cable TV, 4-6 hunters per cabin / Dogs allowed / $$

CAMPGROUNDS AND RV PARKS
Indian Lake State Park, County Road 442 / 906-341-2355 / 301 sites in two units, electricity, showers
Indian Lake Travel Resort, County Road 455 / 906-341-2807

RESTAURANTS
The Big Spring Inn, M-149 / 906-644-2506
Harbor Bar & Inn, 242 South Cedar / Serving until 9PM / 906-341-2456
Jax Bar and Restaurant, 223 South Cedar / lunch and dinner / 906-341-6179
Sunny Shores Restaurant, East Lakeshore Drive / breakfast, lunch and dinner / 906-341-5582

VETERINARIANS
G.L. Hoholik, DVM, M-149 / 906-341-2813

SPORTING GOODS STORES
Top O'Lake Sport & Gift Shop, 206 South Cedar / 906-341-5241

AUTO REPAIR
Bill's Automotive, 1001 West Lakeshore Drive / 906-341-6736
Scotty's Muffler & Brake Shop, 103 River Street / 906-341-5248

AIR SERVICE

Midwest Aire, Escanaba / 906-789-5666
Skyway Airlines, 3300 Airport Access Road, Escanaba / 906-789-3066

MEDICAL

Schoolcraft Memorial Hospital, 500 Main Street / 906-341-3200
St. Francis Hospital, 3401 Ludington Street, Escanaba / 906-786-3311

FOR MORE INFORMATION

Schoolcraft County Chamber of Commerce
U.S. 2
Manistique, MI 49854
906-341-5010

*Chris Zimmerman
and Duke in a
no-nonsense boat blind.*

Newberry and Luce County

Population–1,873	October Average Temperature–54°F
County Population–5,599	Elevation–875 ft
County Area–903 sq mi	State Land Acres–297,265

Luce County waterfowlers will find beaver ponds that hold good numbers of flight ducks when a northwest wind howls across Lake Superior, as well as small lakes and some small impoundments that offer good waterfowl hunting. Grouse hunters should check out Lake Superior State Forest along the Lake Superior shoreline. It is good grouse and woodcock territory, and there are fewer hunters. Luce County is home to the famous Tahquamenon Falls.

UPLAND BIRDS
Ruffed Grouse, Woodcock

WATERFOWL
Ducks, Geese, Snipe

ACCOMMODATIONS
Comfort Inn, Junction of M-28/M-123 / 906-293-3218 / 54 units, cable TV, hot tub, sauna, deluxe continental breakfast / No dogs / $$$

Evening Star Motel, 965 Newberry Avenue / 906-293-8342 / Microwave, refrigerator / Dogs allowed / $$

Deer Park Lodge, County Road 407, Deer Park / 906-658-3341 / Cabins for 2–6 people / No dogs / $$

Seasons Lodgings, Main Street, Curtis / 906-586-3078 / housekeeping units / Dogs allowed / $-$$

CAMPGROUNDS AND RV PARKS
KOA Kampground, M-28 / 906-293-5762 / Indoor pool, sauna, cabins, showers

Muskallonge Lake State Park, County Road 407, Deer Park / 906-658-3338 / 179 sites, RV parking, electricity, showers

North Country Campground & Cabins, M-123 / 906-293-8562 / 50 sites, RV parking, water, electricity, cabins, lodge

RESTAURANTS
Falls Hotel, 301 Newberry Avenue / Food and drink / 906-293-5111

Pickleman's Pantry & Pub, M-28 & M-123 / breakfast, lunch, dinner, lounge / 906-293-3777

The Poor Boy, M-28, McMillan / Breakfast, lunch, dinner / 906-293-3151

Timber Charlie's, 110 Newberry Avenue / breakfast, lunch, dinner, lounge / 906-293-3363

VETERINARIANS
Newberry Animal Clinic, Foley Hill Road / 906-293-3306
Curtis Veterinary Clinic, County Road H-33, Curtis / 906-586-6821

SPORTING GOODS STORES
Duke's Sport Shop, 202 Newberry Avenue / 906-293-8421
Hilltop Sport & Bait, South Newberry Avenue / 906-293-8856
Mark's Rod & Reel Repair, M-123 / 906-293-5608
S & J Archery, 222 Newberry Avenue / 906-293-9330

AUTO REPAIR
A & A Auto Supply, 680 M-28 / 906-293-3261
Burbach Service, 202 East Helen / 906-293-8391
Curtis Service, Curtis / 906-586-9832

AIR SERVICE
Luce County Airport / 906-293-2926

MEDICAL
Helen Newberry Joy Hospital / 906-293-9200

FOR MORE INFORMATION
Newberry Area Chamber of Commerce
Newberry Area Tourism Association
P.O. Box 308
Corner of M-28 & M-123
Newberry, MI 49868
906-293-5562

Sault Ste. Marie and Chippewa County

Population–15,689	October Average Temperature–53°F
County Population–36,859	Elevation–718 ft
County Area–1,561 sq mi	State Land Acres–216,400
	Federal Land Acres–243,900

Located at the east end of the Upper Peninsula on the St. Mary's River, Sault Ste. Marie is home to the famous Soo Locks that are so important to upper Great Lakes shipping. The town is a good base for bird hunters. Chippewa County has miles of coastal marshlands and thousands of acres of state and federal lands. It contains the only population of sharp-tailed grouse in the state that may be hunted, although the population is very small and the area open to hunting is limited. (Season may not be open at this writing. Consult the *Michigan Hunting and Trapping Guide*.) Grouse and woodcock hunting are very good, especially in the western part of the county and near the Mackinac/Chippewa county line.

UPLAND BIRDS
Ruffed Grouse, Woodcock, Sharp-tailed Grouse

WATERFOWL
Ducks, Geese, Snipe

ACCOMMODATIONS
Budget Host Crestview Inn, 1200 Ashmun Street / 800-955-5213 / Cable TV, casino package / Dogs allowed / $$
Little Munuscong River Resort, 3831 East Mills Road, Pickford/ 647-2024/ Housekeeping cabins, guide service/ Dogs allowed/ $$
Quality Inn, 3290 I-75 Bus. Spur / cable TV, indoor pool and spa, restaurant and lounge / Dogs allowed / 906-635-1523 / $$$
Riverview Resort & Marina, South Scenic Drive, Barbeau / Cabins on St. Mary's River / Dogs allowed / 906-647-3033 / $
Twin Cedars Resort, off M-123, Trout Lake / 906-569-3209 / 5 cottages and 2 motel units on Frenchman's Lake / Dogs allowed during bird season only / $-$$$

CAMPGROUNDS AND RV PARKS
Aune Osborn Campground, East Portage Avenue / Water, electricity, showers / 906-632-3268
Chippewa Campground, 412 West 3 Mile Road / RV parking, water, electricity / 906-632-8581

RESTAURANTS
Abner's, 2865 I-75 Business Spur / Breakfast, lunch, dinner, lounge, "Backwoods Buffet" / 906-632-4221

The Antlers, 804 East Portage Avenue / Lunch and dinner, cocktails / 906-632-3571

Clyde's Drive In, Riverside Drive / Lunch and dinner, burgers / 906-632-2581

Freighters, 240 West Portage Avenue at Ojibway Hotel / Breakfast, lunch, dinner, lounge / 906-632-4100

Lockview, 329 West Portage Avenue / Breakfast, lunch, dinner, cocktails, whitefish / 906-632-2772

Palace Saloon, 200 West Portage Avenue / Lunch, dinner, cocktails, Mexican / 906-632-7721

VETERINARIANS

Animal Kingdom Veterinary Clinic, 305 West 3 Mile Road / Emergency service / 906-635-1200

Chippewa Animal Clinic, 1554 East 3 Mile Road / 24-hr. emergency service / 906-635-5814

Hiawatha Veterinary Hospital, 8247 South Mackinac Trail / 906-632-3141

Sault Animal Hospital, 2867 Ashmun Street / 24-hour emergency service / 906-635-5910

SPORTING GOODS STORES

Hank's Sporting Goods, 3522 I-75 Business Spur / 906-632-8741

J & E Sports & Hobbies, 3127 West M-80, Kinross / 906-495-5815

The Great Outdoors Sport Shop, M-134, Cedarville / 906-484-2011

Leitz Sports Center, 2512 I-75 Business Spur / 906-632-8291

AUTO REPAIR

Delta Tire Center, 700 West 3 Mile Road / 906-635-1122

Quality Automotive Repair, 956 East Portage Avenue / 906-635-6887

Soo Automotive, 301 Maple Street / 906-635-1555

AIR SERVICE

Twin Cities Air, 228 West 14th Avenue / 906-635-0252

Chippewa County International Airport, Kinross / 906-495-5631

Drummond Island Air, Townline Road, Drummond Island / 906-493-5767

MEDICAL

Bay Mills Medical Clinic, Lakeshore Drive, Brimley / 906-248-5527

War Memorial Hospital, 500 Osborn Street / 906-635-4460

FOR MORE INFORMATION

Sault Area Chamber of Commerce
Sault Area Convention and Visitors Bureau
2581 I-75 Business Spur
Sault Ste. Marie, MI 49783
906-632-3301
800-MI-SAULT

St. Ignace and Mackinac County

Population–2,568	October Average Temperature–56°F
County Population–10,978	Elevation–588 ft
County Area–1,021 sq mi	State Land Acres–214,250
	Federal Land Acres–152,000

St. Ignace is one of several towns in Mackinac County that make a good base for a hunt. Like most Upper Peninsula counties, Mackinac is home to thousands of acres of public land, most of which have good to excellent numbers of grouse and woodcock. Best hunting is in the western half of the county. St. Ignace, where the mighty Mackinac Bridge takes visitors from the Lower Peninsula across the Straits of Mackinac, is the gateway to the Upper Peninsula.

UPLAND BIRDS
Ruffed Grouse, Woodcock

WATERFOWL
Ducks, Geese, Snipe

ACCOMMODATIONS
Driftwood Motel, 590 North State Street / Restaurant, lounge / 906-643-7744 / Dogs allowed / $

Howard Johnson Express Inn, 913 West US 2 / 906-643-9700 / Continental breakfast, pool, sauna, jacuzzi / Casino shuttle and packages / Dogs allowed / $$

CAMPGROUNDS AND RV PARKS
KOA Kampground, 1242 West US-2 / 906-643-9303
Lakeshore Park Campground, 416 Pte. LaBarbe Road / 906-643-9522
Straits Area State Park, East US-2 / 318 sites / 906-643-8620

RESTAURANTS
Clyde's Drive-In, US-2 / Lunch and dinner, burgers / 906-643-8303
Driftwood Sports Bar & Grill, 590 North State Street / Breakfast, lunch, dinner / 906-643-9133
Galley Restaurant & Lounge, 241 North State Street / Breakfast, lunch, dinner, whitefish, steaks / 906-643-7960

VETERINARIANS
St. Ignace Animal Clinic, 843 Portage Street / 906-643-9332

SPORTING GOODS STORES
Ace Hardware & Sporting Goods, 7 South State Street / 906-643-7721
The Great Outdoors Sports Shop, M-134, Cedarville / 906-484-2011

AUTO REPAIR

Mackinac Ford, 1052 W US 2 / 906-643-8040

St. Ignace Automotive Supply Inc., 460 North State Street / 906-643-8038

AIR SERVICE

Chippewa County International Airport, Kinross / 906-495-5631

Great Lakes Air, 180 North Airport Road / 906-643-7165

MEDICAL

Mackinac Straits Hospital and Health Center, 220 Burdette / 906-643-8585

West Mackinac Health Clinic, Engadine / 906-477-6066

FOR MORE INFORMATION

St. Ignace Chamber of Commerce
560 North State Street
St. Ignace, MI 49781
906-643-8717

Besides the hunting, there is always beautiful scenery to see in Michigan. (Photo by Chris Zimmerman)

Hunting Guides, Outfitters and Preserves

REGION I

Drummond Island Resort
33494 East Maxton Road
Drummond Island, MI 49726
Chukars, huns, pheasant

EUP Adventures
219 Rapids Drive
Sault Ste. Marie, MI 49783
906-632-6430
Canada goose

Little Munuscong River Resort
3831 East Mills Road
Pickford, MI 49774
906-647-2024
Ruffed grouse, woodcock, ducks

Nine Pines Resort
HC1, Box 99SN
Marenisco, MI 49947
906-842-3361

Jerry Timm hunting on a bluebird day in the Upper Peninsula.

Grouse Hunting Is Exacting But Satisfying

No one was more surprised than I was when my first grouse hit the ground. I was a freshman in college, out with my new roommate Ed Carstens of Pinconning, Michigan, during a wonderful late September afternoon in Michigan's eastern Upper Peninsula. We hadn't been hunting more than 30 minutes and had just moved into a brilliant stand of hardwoods off a rugged two-track road. The light from the yellow maple and poplar leaves was almost neon.

I heard the grouse flush a second or two before I saw it. It presented a straight going-away shot, the only ones I'm really any good at hitting. I snapped

Heavy cover in a Michigan forest. (Photo by Chris Zimmerman)

the gun to my shoulder and touched off a round. I'll never forget the surprise and delight I felt when the bird disappeared from view and how incredulous my voice sounded when I yelled, "I got it!"

I had shot at very few grouse in my life, but I had seen many in my travels and always marveled at their speed. I never expected to hit this bird, yet when it dropped from sight I was sure I had seen it go down dead in the understory. I hurried over to where I had last seen it.

Ed, who has shot more than a few grouse in his days afield, reached the bird at about the same time that I did. He was giving me a look that appeared to say, "Well, sure you got it. That's what we're here for, isn't it?"

I'll never, ever forget the brilliant colors of the forest as I reached down and picked up that warm bird. Nor will I forget the grouse itself: a red phase that seemed extraordinarily large, with tufts of dark black feathers jutting out to form its "shoulders." As I recall, even Ed commented on the size and beauty of the bird.

I still have that bird's tail fanned out on display in my house. And I wasn't exaggerating its size—to this day I have not shot a grouse with a bigger fan.

Jake, a tricolored English setter, with a ruffed grouse.
(Photo by Chris Zimmerman)

For many Michigan hunters, the ruffed grouse is the symbol of the north woods and the glorious Michigan autumn. For me, the sound of a grouse thundering into the sky from underfoot will always take me back to that wonderful day when I brought my first partridge to bag.

Grouse hunters in Michigan experience boom and bust years with the birds. The population increases and decreases in a cycle that bird hunters will argue lasts anywhere from seven to 10 years. During the height of the cycle, the birds seem to be everywhere, even in places that normally wouldn't hold grouse. At the bottom end of the cycle, veteran bird hunters work very hard to find grouse even in their favorite coverts.

This cycle is documented and predictable. The grouse hunting ranks grow during the "up" years, while only the faithful stick with the tough hunting during the low part of the cycle. But veteran hunters, especially those with good dogs as partners, always seem to be able to find a few grouse no matter where they go. Sometimes it's just a matter of putting your time in.

No matter where the cycle is when you find yourself in the grouse woods, you'll find few northern pursuits that are as satisfying as a hunt for the king of game birds on a fine autumn day.

Zack and Chip both want the credit for this grouse. (Photo by Chris Zimmerman)

Region 2

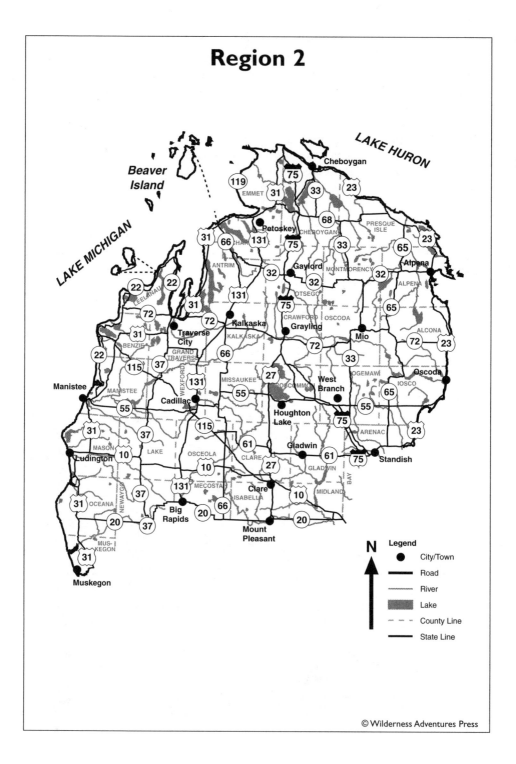

Beaver Island

LAKE HURON

LAKE MICHIGAN

Cheboygan

EMMET

119

75

31

33

23

68

PRESQUE ISLE

Petoskey

CHEBOYGAN

31

66

CHAR

131

75

33

65

23

Atpena

ANTRIM

32

Gaylord

MONTMORENCY

32

ALPENA

32

OTSEGO

131

75

65

CRAWFORD

OSCODA

Kalkaska

Grayling

Mio

ALCONA

72

72

23

Traverse City

KALKASKA

GRAND TRAVERSE

31

BENZIE

72

66

72

33

OGEMAW

Oscoda

22

115

37

WEXFORD

131

MISSAUKEE

27

West Branch

IOSCO

Manistee

MANISTEE

ROSCOMMON

65

55

55

Cadillac

55

Houghton Lake

75

31

37

115

61

Gladwin

ARENAC

23

MASON

LAKE

OSCEOLA

CLARE

Ludington

10

10

27

61

75

Standish

37

GLADWIN

MECOSTA

131

MIDLAND

31

OCEANA

NEWAYGO

37

ISABELLA

Clare

10

BAY

20

66

Big Rapids

20

Mount Pleasant

20

MUS-KEGON

31

Muskegon

N

Legend

● City/Town

—— Road

～～ River

▓ Lake

- - - County Line

—— State Line

© Wilderness Adventures Press

Region 2

Similar to the neighboring Upper Peninsula, Michigan's Region 2 (northern Lower Peninsula) is characterized by an abundance of public land and hunting opportunities. Of this region's 32 counties, only eight of them are home to state game and state wildlife areas. Instead, they're covered by nearly one million acres of public land in the Huron and Manistee National Forests and more than two million acres of the Au Sable, Mackinaw, Pere Marquette, and Pigeon River Country State Forests, plus more than 47,000 acres of commercial forest land.

Many hunters feel that this region of Michigan is the best because of the variety of birds available. Traveling south, the northern Lower Peninsula's woodlands begin to thin out to the point where the southern fringes of Region 2 are interspersed with forest and agricultural land. Generally, but not as a rule, the northern forests are home to more grouse and woodcock, while more waterfowl, pheasant, and turkey are found in and around agricultural land. But it isn't difficult to find a place that will provide opportunities to hunt all of these bird species.

Remote areas of the Pigeon River Country State Forest, Au Sable State Forest, and Huron National Forest have long been favorites among upland bird hunters, but just as they do in the Upper Peninsula, hunters will find grouse and woodcock in all Region 2 counties.

Pockets of pheasant country exist in agricultural land along the western and eastern edges of this region, but the best bets for pheasant in this region are in the southern parts, including Newaygo, Mecosta, Isabella, Midland, and Bay Counties.

Turkeys thrive in Region 2, and a variety of places are available in which to hunt them, from mature forest to agricultural land. In recent years, northern Michigan has been open to fall turkey hunts as well as the spring gobbler season. The state is divided into turkey management units, with each unit having a quota of licenses issued. Hunters must apply in advance for the permits.

Waterfowl hunters have a long list of places to hunt in Region 2. For starters, the shores of Lakes Huron and Michigan provide many places to hunt waterfowl, especially diving ducks. Inland, there are many lakes of varying sizes, along with wildlife floodings and marshland. Houghton Lake in Roscommon County is a longtime favorite among diving duck hunters. Those who prefer mallards and Canada geese usually stick to hunting agricultural land, especially recently cut corn and grain fields adjacent to ponds or lakes that provide roosting areas. However, Michigan produces a good population of locally grown mallards and wood ducks that are available for hunters in any number of small farm ponds, beaver ponds, lakes, rivers, and streams.

With all the opportunities available to bird hunters in Region 2, a good hunting strategy involves hunting waterfowl in the morning, then scouting for new waterfowling places while looking for grouse and woodcock in the afternoons. Unlike many other popular waterfowling states, Michigan allows afternoon and evening hunts for geese, so if you discover a potential goose roost while grouse hunting, you can wait around into the evening to see if a flock of Canada geese returns. Just remember that you can't have any lead shot in your possession while hunting waterfowl!

Similar to the Upper Peninsula, Region 2 offers many places to camp and lots of resorts and cabins that cater to bird hunters.

Duke with a black duck taken at Little Lake George.

Ruffed Grouse

Excellent

Good to Excellent

Fair

Poor

Few to None

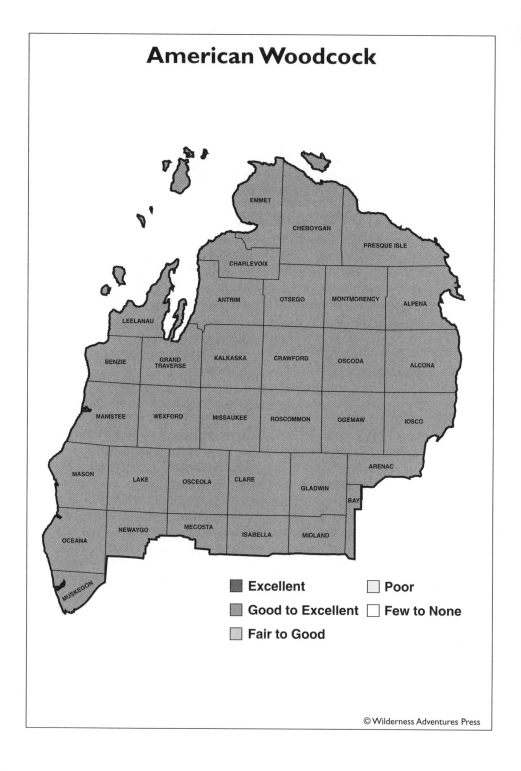

American Woodcock

Excellent
Good to Excellent
Fair to Good
Poor
Few to None

© Wilderness Adventures Press

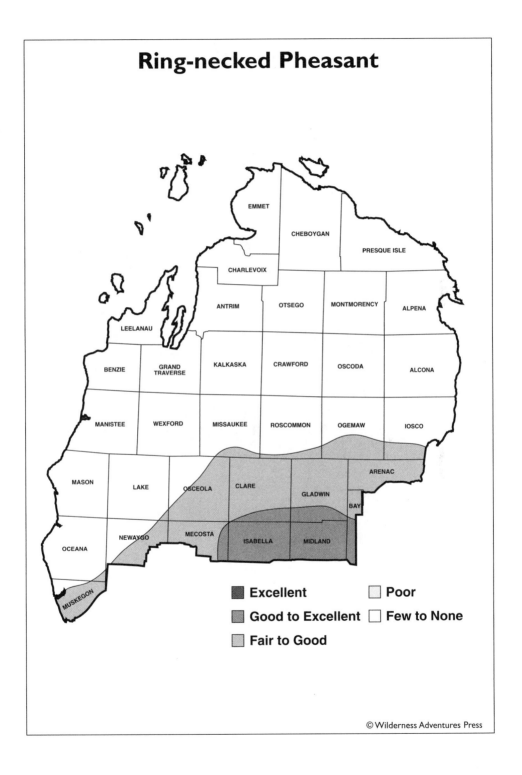

Ring-necked Pheasant

Excellent
Good to Excellent
Fair to Good
Poor
Few to None

© Wilderness Adventures Press

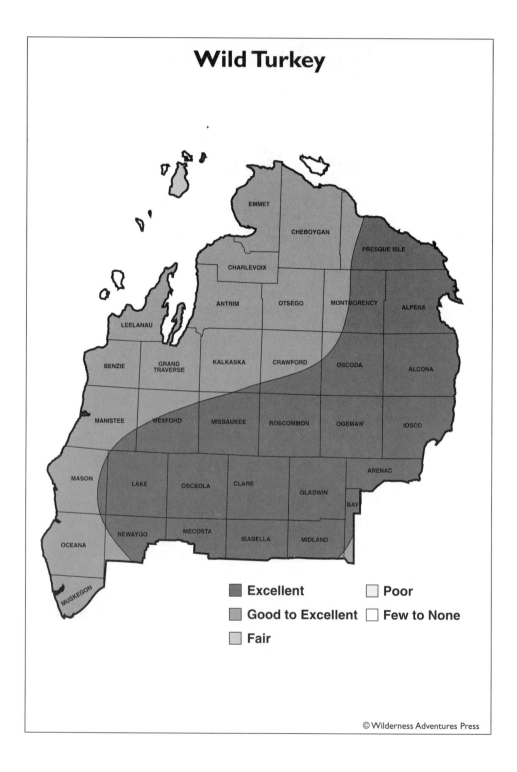

Wild Turkey

Legend	
■ Excellent	□ Poor
■ Good to Excellent	□ Few to None
■ Fair	

Northern Bobwhite

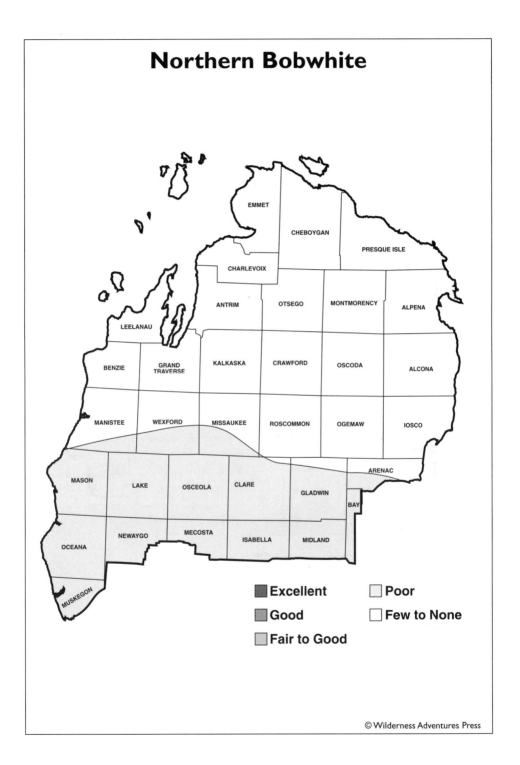

EMMET

CHEBOYGAN

PRESQUE ISLE

CHARLEVOIX

ANTRIM

OTSEGO

MONTMORENCY

ALPENA

LEELANAU

BENZIE

GRAND TRAVERSE

KALKASKA

CRAWFORD

OSCODA

ALCONA

MANISTEE

WEXFORD

MISSAUKEE

ROSCOMMON

OGEMAW

IOSCO

ARENAC

MASON

LAKE

OSCEOLA

CLARE

GLADWIN

BAY

OCEANA

NEWAYGO

MECOSTA

ISABELLA

MIDLAND

MUSKEGON

■ Excellent   □ Poor

■ Good   □ Few to None

■ Fair to Good

Sharp-tailed Grouse

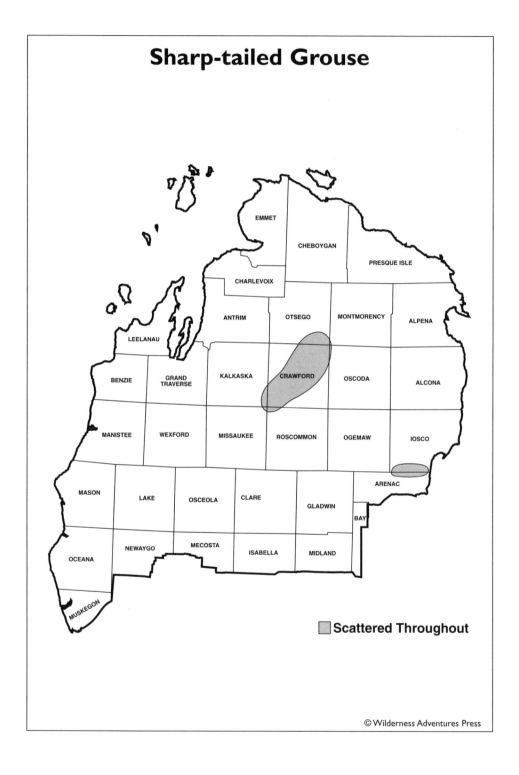

EMMET

CHEBOYGAN

PRESQUE ISLE

CHARLEVOIX

ANTRIM   OTSEGO   MONTMORENCY   ALPENA

LEELANAU

BENZIE   GRAND TRAVERSE   KALKASKA   CRAWFORD   OSCODA   ALCONA

MANISTEE   WEXFORD   MISSAUKEE   ROSCOMMON   OGEMAW   IOSCO

ARENAC

MASON   LAKE   OSCEOLA   CLARE   GLADWIN

BAY

OCEANA   NEWAYGO   MECOSTA   ISABELLA   MIDLAND

MUSKEGON

Scattered Throughout

© Wilderness Adventures Press

Common Snipe

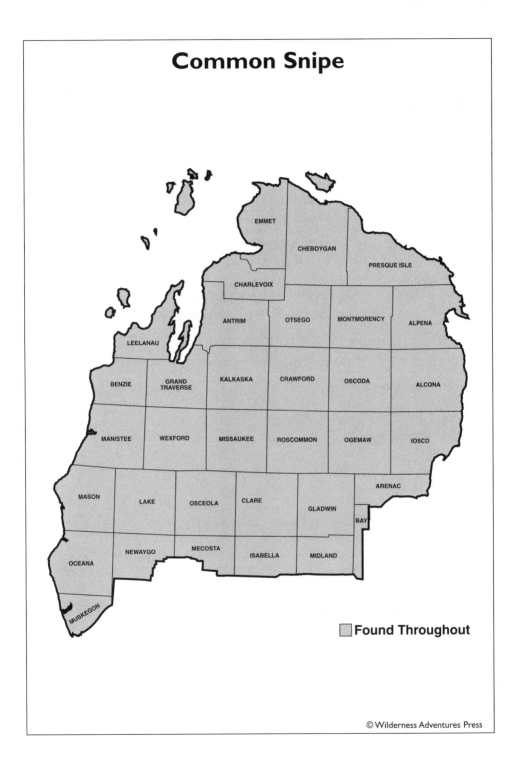

Found Throughout

Petoskey and Emmet / Charlevoix Counties

Population–6,056	October Average Temperature–50°F
County Population:	Elevation–610 ft
Emmet–25,040	Emmet State Land Acres–75,900
Charlevoix–21,468	Charlevoix State Land Acres–58,250
County Area:	
Emmet–468 sq mi	
Charlevoix–417 sq mi	

Petoskey, a name derived from Odawa, means "sun shining through." It is a great place to stay in northwest Michigan, and nearby towns of Charlevoix and Harbor Springs can accommodate bird hunters, too. Sections of Mackinaw State Forest are strung out through both counties, offering good to excellent grouse and woodcock hunting. Turkeys are coming on strong in this region and are a common sight very close to town.

UPLAND BIRDS
Ruffed Grouse, Woodcock, Turkey

WATERFOWL
Ducks, Geese, Snipe

ACCOMMODATIONS
Comfort Inn, 1314 North US-31 / 231-347-3220 / 64 units, in-room whirlpool, cable TV, HBO, continental breakfast / Dogs allowed / $$-$$$
Econo Lodge, 1858 South US-131 / 231-348-3324 / 60 rooms, pool, cable TV, continental breakfast / Dogs allowed / $-$$$
Holiday Inn, 1444 South US-131 / 231-347-6041 / 144 rooms, restaurant, lounge, indoor pool, whirlpool / No dogs / $$$
Petoskey Motel, 722 Spring Street / 231-347-0348 / 38 rooms, in-room jacuzzi, 2-room suites / Dogs allowed / $-$$$

CAMPGROUNDS AND RV PARKS
Crooked River RV Park, 5397 Cheboygan Road, Alanson / 231-548-5534
El Rancho Alanson RV Resort, 6732 Hwy 68, Alanson / 231-548-2600 / 35 tent and trailer sites, electricity, laundry facilities
Fisherman's Island State Park, 4 miles southwest of Charlevoix off US-31 / 231-547-6641 / 90 sites / Hunting nearby
KOA Kampground, 1800 North US-31 / 231-347-0005
Petoskey State Park, Hwy 119 / 231-347-2311 / 90 sites, electricity, water / On Little Traverse Bay

RESTAURANTS
Alan's Northside Restaurant, 1099 US-31 / 231-348-2033 / Breakfast, lunch, dinner / Open 6AM

Big Boy, 751 Spring Street / 231-347-2931 / Burgers, chicken, desserts /
Breakfast, lunch, dinner Darrow's, 301 North Louvingney, Mackinaw City /
231-436-5514 / Breakfast, lunch, dinner

The Grill, 182 Stimpson, Pelston / 231-539-8004 / Breakfast, lunch, dinner /
6:30AM–3PM, Mon–Thurs; 6:30AM–7PM, Fri–Sun

Mitchell Street Pub, 426 East Mitchell Street / 231-347-1801 / Lunch, dinner,
cocktails

Whitney's, 305 Bridge Street, Charlevoix / 231-547-0818 / Oyster bar, fresh
flown-in seafood, beer from around the world

VETERINARIANS

Bay Pines Veterinary Clinic, 8769 M-119, Harbor Springs / 231-347-4552 /
24-hour emergency service

Charlevoix Veterinary Hospital, 05560 US-31, Charlevoix / 231-547-9841

Jensen's Animal Hospital, 4041 US-31 / 231-347-8775 / 24-hour emergency
service

SPORTING GOODS STORES

Kmart, 1401 Spring Street, Petoskey / 231-347-7900 / Licenses
06600 M-66 North, Charlevoix, 616-547-0911 / Licenses

Dunham's Discount Sports, 910 Spring Street, Petoskey / 231-347-9779 / Guns
and ammunition, licenses

Wal-Mart, 1600 Anderson Road, Petoskey / 231-439-0200

AUTO REPAIR

Bill's Auto Clinic, 2175 Howard Road / 231-347-8545 / Major and minor repairs

Lakeshore Tire & Auto Service, 402 West Mitchell Street, Petoskey, 231-347-8144

1405 Bridge Street, Charlevoix, 616-547-1001 / Domestic and foreign

Davis Auto Repair & Wrecker, 3851 Robinson Road, Harbor Springs /
231-526-2098 / 24-hour service

AIR SERVICE

Harbor Springs Airport, 8656 M-119, Petoskey / 231-347-2812

Pellston Regional Airport, US-31, Pellston / 231-539-8441

MEDICAL

Charlevoix Area Hospital, 14700 Lake Shore Drive, Charlevoix / 231-547-4024

Northern Michigan Hospital, 416 Connable Avenue / 231-348-4520

FOR MORE INFORMATION

Charlevoix Chamber of Commerce
408 Bridge Street
Charlevoix, MI 49720
231-547-2101

Petoskey Chamber of Commerce
401 East Mitchell Street
Petoskey, MI 49770
231-347-4150
www.boynecountry.com

Cheboygan and Cheboygan / Presque Isle Counties

Population–4,999	October Average Temperature–49°F
County Population:	Elevation–590 ft
Cheboygan–21,398	Public Land by County (Acres):
Presque Isle–13,743	Presque Isle–State 86,000
County Area:	Cheboygan–State 183,900
Presque Isle–678 sq mi	
Cheboygan–721 sq mi	

Cheboygan and Presque Isle Counties have large tracts of Mackinaw State Forest and Pigeon River Country State Forest available to bird hunters. Adventuresome hunters with a canoe could float the Black or Pigeon rivers for ducks, stopping along the way in likely looking spots for grouse and woodcock. Cheboygan County has more grouse and woodcock, but the entire area is fair to good for upland hunting, including turkeys. Pigeon River Country State Forest is a good bet for upland hunters.

UPLAND BIRDS
Ruffed Grouse, Woodcock, Turkey

WATERFOWL
Ducks, Geese, Snipe

ACCOMMODATIONS
Best Western, 847 South Main Street, Cheboygan / 231-627-5688 / cable TV, pool / No dogs / $$-$$$

Black Lake Hotel, 1712 Black River Road, Cheboygan / 616-625-2625 / On Black Lake / 7 rooms accomodating various size groups, restaurant, lounge / No dogs / $$-$$$

Days Inn, 889 South Main Street, Cheboygan / 231-627-3126 / 42 rooms, continental breakfast, boat slips, on the Cheboygan River / No dogs / $$-$$$

Driftwood Motel, 540 West 3rd Street, Rogers City / 517-734-4777 / On Lake Huron; 43 rooms, restaurant and lounge next door, indoor pool, spa / No dogs / $$$

Manitou Shores Resort, 4521 US-23 North, Rogers City / 517-734-7233 / Cabins and motel rooms on Lake Huron / No dogs

Roger's Ranch & Lodge, 2132 Heythaler Road, Rogers City / 517 734-2178 / Bed and breakfast, kitchen facilities, sauna, steam room, hot tub; game-cleaning facility

CAMPGROUNDS AND RV PARKS
Aloha State Park, 4347 3rd Street, Aloha / 231-625-2522 / On Mullet Lake, 287 sites

Cheboygan State Park, US-23 / 231-627-2811 / 78 sites; sanitation station; hunting nearby
Onaway State Park, Bonz Beach Hwy / 231-733-8279 / 5 miles north of Onaway on southeast end of Black Lake / 101 sites
P.H. Hoeft State Park, US-23 / 231-734-2543 / 144 sites, 4 miles north of Rogers City on Lake Huron / Hunting available
Yogi Bear Jellystone Park, 2201 M-68, Indian River / 231-238-8259 / 173 tent and trailer sites, electricity, laundry facilities

RESTAURANTS
Black Bear Cafe, Business Route 23/68, Rogers City / 517-734-2007
The Brown Trout, M-27, Indian River / 231-238-9441 / Open 7 days after 4PM; cocktails
The Boathouse, 106 Pine Street, Cheboygan / 231-627-4316 /
Chi-Chi's, US-23, Rogers City / 517-734-4454
The Coffee Shop, 116 South Main Street, Cheboygan / 231-627-9525 / Open 6AM, Mon–Sat
Great Lakes Grill, 817 East State Street, Cheboygan / 231-627-8161 / Lunch and dinner; sandwiches, steaks, whitefish; cocktails

VETERINARIANS
Black River Animal Hospital, 10555 North Black River Road, Cheboygan / 231-627-7077
Chalet Veterinary Clinic, 1155 South Main Street, Cheboygan / 231-627-5643
Albert Dobias DVM, 10324 North Straits Hwy, Cheboygan / 231-627-2542
Huron Veterinary Clinic, 3189 South US-23, Rogers City / 517-734-3731
Indian River Veterinary Clinic, 5338 South Straits Hwy, Indian River / 231-238-7022

SPORTING GOODS STORES
Adrian's Sport Shop, 335 North Bradley Hwy, Rogers City / 517-734-2303
Dunham's, 992 South Main Street, Cheboygan / 231-627-1000
Keith's Hunting, Fishing, Camping & Supply, 625 M-33, Aloha / 231-625-9060
Studer's Sporting Goods & Gun Refinishing, 3696 South Straits Hwy, Indian River / 231-238-8125

AUTO REPAIR
The Engine Shop, 3218 US-23, Rogers City / 517-734-4241
LaHaie's Auto Service Center, 11151 North Straits Hwy, Cheboygan / 231-627-3381
Lutz Auto Repair, 4108 US-23 North, Rogers City / 517-734-2140
Vincent's Service, 3567 Sturgeon, Indian River / 231-238-9324
Precision Auto Repair, 10942 North Straits Hwy, Cheboygan / 231-627-6606

AIR SERVICE
Cheboygan City-County Airport, 1520 Levering Road / 231-627-6671
Rogers City Airport, 658 South Bradley / 517-734-7037

MEDICAL

Community Memorial Hospital, 784 South Main Street, Cheboygan /
231-627-5601

Mackinac Straits Hospital & Health Center, 220 Burdette, St. Ignace /
906-643-8585

FOR MORE INFORMATION

Cheboygan Area Chamber of Commerce
124 North Main Street / P.O. Box 60
Cheboygan, MI 49721
231-627-7183
www.cheboygan.com

Presque Isle County Tourism Council
658 South Bradley / P.O. Box 96
Presque Isle, MI 49777
517-595-5095

Rogers City Travelers and Visitors Bureau
292 South Bradley Hwy
Rogers City, MI 49779
517-734-2535

*Turkey near the edge
of a cornfield. (Photo by
Chris Zimmerman)*

Traverse City and Benzie, Grand Traverse, and Leelanau Counties

Population–15,155	October Average Temperature–49°F
County Population:	Elevation–623 ft
Benzie–12,200	Benzie State Land Acres–61,700
Grand Traverse–64,273	Grand Traverse State Land Acres–67,800
Leelanau–16,527	Leelanau State Land Acres–7,500
County Area:	
Benzie–321 sq mi	
Grand Traverse–465 sq mi	
Leelanau–348 sq mi	

The Traverse City area is growing by leaps and bounds and offers many amenities for bird hunters. Hunting for ruffed grouse, woodcock, and turkey is good to excellent in the region's Pere Marquette State Forest and the surrounding agricultural areas. Waterfowl hunters can hunt any number of small inland lakes, marshes, and agricultural fields and, for those who prefer big water, Lake Michigan's Grand Traverse Bay. Traverse City is home to the annual International Cherry Festival.

UPLAND BIRDS
Ruffed Grouse, Woodcock, Turkey

WATERFOWL
Ducks, Geese, Snipe

ACCOMMODATIONS
Baymont Inn & Suites, 2326 North US-31, South / 231-933-4454 / 121 units, cable TV, spa, pool, continental breakfast / No pets / $$-$$$
Economy Inn, 1600 US-31 North / 2331-938-2080 / 10 units / Dogs allowed / $-$$$
Fox Haus Motor Lodge, 704 Munson Avenue / 231-947-4450 / 80 units, cable TV, jacuzzi, kitchenettes, sauna / Dogs allowed / $-$$$
Willow Beach Motel and Cottages, 5795 US-31 North, Box 8, Acme / 231-938-1380 / 8 units, kitchenettes / Dogs allowed / $-$$$

CAMPGROUNDS AND RV PARKS
Grand Traverse Camping & RV Resort, 9700 M-37, Buckley / 231-269-3203 / Full hook-ups, 50 amp service
Holiday Park Campground, 4860 US-31 South / 231-943-4410 / On Silver Lake, one mile west of M-37
Traverse City State Park, US-31 / 231-947-7193 / On Grand Traverse Bay, 343 sites

RESTAURANTS
Mabel's, 8th Street and US 31 North / 231-947-0252 / Homemade meals, in-house bakery; breakfast, lunch, dinner

La Senorita, on US-31 South and at 1245 South / 231 947-8820 or 231-947-4545 / Garfield / Mexican food, beer, wine, cocktails

Gordie Howe's Tavern & Eatery, 851 South Garfield / 231-929-HOWE / Ribs, chicken, pizza, deli

Reflections, US-31 North at 4 Mile Road / 231-938-2321 / Whitefish, steaks, pasta; breakfast, lunch, dinner; cocktails

VETERINARIANS

Acme Veterinary Clinic, 5492 M-72 East, Acme / 231-938-2711

Animal Medical Center of Traverse City, 229 US-31 South / Four veterinarians / 231-943-8500

Cherry Bend Animal Hospital, 10387 East Cherry Bend Road / 231-922-0500

Grand Traverse Veterinary Hospital, 3805 Veterans Drive / 231-946-3770

SPORTING GOODS STORES

Cliff's Rifle Shop, 147 South Airport Road / Shotguns, accessories / 231-947-6881

Fieldsport Ltd, 3313 South Airport Road / Guns, ammunition, gear / 231-933-0767

Grand Traverse Gun, 1218 Garfield Road / 231-935-3100

Northsport Inc., 305 US-31 South / Buy, sell, trade / 231-943-3030

Tackle Town, 13680 SW Bay Shore / 231-941-5420

AUTO REPAIR

A-1 Auto, 1025 Hannah / 231-941-8950 / Major and minor repairs

Auto Service Center Inc., 436 West Front Street, 231-922-2600
116 Gillis, 231-922-2608
2604 South Airport Road West, 231-922-2616
All locations open 7:30AM–4PM Saturday

Auto Tech Mobile Repair, 3037 Cass Road / 231-946-6008 / 24-hour emergency service

Grand Traverse Radiator, 1116 Barlow / 231-947-4220 / Same day service, most repairs

Rog's Garage, 8451 Old M-72, Williamsburg / 231-267-9359 / Open Mon–Fri

AIR SERVICE

Interlochen/Green Lake Township Airport, 5555 Karlin Road, Interlochen / 231-276-9919

Cherry Capital Airport, Airport Access Road / 231-947-2250

MEDICAL

Leelanau Memorial Health Center, 215 South High Street, Northport / 231-386-0000

Munson Medical Center, 1105 6th Street / 616-935-5000 / Emergency: 231-935-6333

Paul Oliver Memorial Hospital, 224 Park, Frankfort / 231-352-9621

FOR MORE INFORMATION

Traverse City Area Chamber of Commerce
202 East Grandview Parkway
Traverse City, MI 49685-0387
231-947-5075
www.tcchamber.org

Frankfort Chamber of Commerce
517 Main Street
Frankfort, MI 49635
231-352-7251

Leelanau County Chamber of Commerce
105 East Phillip
Lake Leelanau, MI 49653
231-256-9895

Benzonia Chamber of Commerce
826 Michigan Avenue
Benzonia, MI 49616
231-882-5801

Not only do dogs make the job easier, they bring extra pleasure to the hunting trip. (Photo by Chris Zimmerman)

Kalkaska and Kalkaska / Antrim Counties

Population–1,952	October Average Temperature–48°F
County Population:	Elevation–1,040 ft
Kalkaska–13,497	Public Land by County (Acres):
Antrim–18,185	Kalkaska–State 155,100
County Area:	Antrim–State 44,700
Kalkaska–561 sq mi	
Antrim–477 sq mi	

Kalkaska may be best known for its annual trout festival held on the last weekend in April when Michigan's regular trout season opens. But the region is also known for its bird hunting, especially when ruffed grouse are in the high point of their cycle. Many acres of Pere Marquette and Mackinaw State Forest are available to hunters.

UPLAND BIRDS
Ruffed Grouse, Woodcock, Turkey

WATERFOWL
Ducks, Geese, Snipe

ACCOMMODATIONS
All Seasons Resort, 760 South Cedar Street, Kalkaska / 231-258-0000 / 61 rooms, pool, continental breakfast, kitchenettes / No dogs / $$$

American Inn North Country, 502 South Cedar Street, Kalkaska / 231-258-9106 / 22 rooms, cable TV, kitchenettes / Dogs allowed / $$

Camelot Inn, 10962 South US-31, Elk Rapids / 231-264-8473 / Cable TV, HBO, kitchenettes, continental breakfast /

Kalkaska Inn Motel, 703 North Cedar Street, Kalkaska / 231-258-9119 / 38 rooms, cable TV, HBO / No dogs / $$$

Mancelona Motel, 8306 US-131, Mancelona / 231-587-8621 / 26 rooms, kitchenettes / Dogs allowed / $-$$

Rapid River Motel, 7530 US-131, Mancelona / 231-258-2604 / 13 units, kitchenettes, continental breakfast, restaurant / Dogs allowed / $-$$

CAMPGROUNDS AND RV PARKS
Black Bear RV Park & Campgrounds, 7390 County Road 612, Kalkaska / 231-258-5593

Kalkaska Campgrounds, 580 M-72 SE, / 231-258-9863

Kalkaska County Campground, Log Lake / 231-258-2940

Rapid River Campground & Cabins, 7182 US-131 NE, Mancelona / 231-258-2042 / 35 sites for tents and trailers; electricity

RESTAURANTS

Avery's Restaurant, 611 North Williams, Mancelona / 231-587-8671
Barnaby's Drive-Thru, 906 North Cedar Street, Kalkaska / 231-258-4701
Country Skillet Cafe, 10945 M-72 NE, Kalkaska / 231-258-8899
Elk River Inn, US-31, Elk Rapids / 231-264-5655
Hole in the Wall Cafe, 105 West State Street, Mancelona / 231-587-8131
Kevin's Olde Time Family Diner, 336 South Cedar, Kalkaska / 231-258-4211

VETERINARIANS

Bellaire Animal Hospital, M-88, Bellaire / 231-533-6522
Elk Rapids Animal Clinic, 402 Bridge Street, Elk Rapids / 231-264-5861
Kalkaska Small Animal Hospital, 110 4th Street, Kalkaska / 231-258-9047
Mancelona Veterinary Hospital, 214 West State Street, Mancelona / 231-587-0520
Village Animal Clinic, 303 North Cedar, Kalkaska / 231-258-4107

SPORTING GOODS STORES

Jack's Sport Shop, 212 North US-131, Kalkaska / Guns and hunting equipment /
231-258-8892
Mancelona Sports & Party Store, US-131, Mancelona / 231-587-9421
Wildfong's Party Store, 528 South Williams, Mancelona / 231-587-5122

AUTO REPAIR

Art's Garage, 103 North Cedar Street, Kalkaska / 231-258-5734
D&S Repair, 424 West State Street, Mancelona / 231-587-0155
Lodi Garage, 4915 State Route 66 SE, Kalkaska / 231-369-2805
Palmer's Service, 111 Dexter, Elk Rapids / 231-264-8931
Village Car Care, 11590 US-31, Elk Rapids / 231-264-9544
Village Garage, 3485 Inwood Circle, Kalkaska / 231-258-8499

AIR SERVICE

Antrim County Airport, 3366-A South Derenzy Road, Bellaire / 231-533-8524
Kalkaska Village Airport / 231-258-9191
Cherry Capital Airport, Traverse City / 231-947-2250

MEDICAL

Kalkaska Memorial Health Center, 419 South Coral / 231-258-7500

FOR MORE INFORMATION

Chamber of Commerce of Kalkaska
353 South Cedar
Kalkaska, MI 49646
231-258-9103

Mancelona Area Chamber of Commerce
431 West Leonard Road
Mancelona, MI 49649
231-587-5500

Gaylord and Otsego / Montmorency Counties

Population–3,256	October Average Temperature–48°F
County Population:	Elevation–1,350 ft
Otsego–17,957	Public Land by County (Acres):
Montmorency–8,936	Otsego–State 97,900
County Area:	Montmorency–State 137,600
Otsego–530 sq mi	
Montmorency–555 sq mi	

Gaylord is a major stopping-off point for northbound golfers, skiers, snow-mobilers, hunters, and fishermen. From here, it is only an hour's drive to the Upper Peninsula or the shores of Lakes Michigan and Huron. The Michigan elk herd, large enough to support a limited hunting season, inhabits the Pigeon River Country State Forest of northern Otsego and Montmorency Counties, and points north. Upland bird hunters should concentrate on the southern fringes of the counties in the Mackinaw State Forest. Turkeys are in good numbers throughout the area.

UPLAND BIRDS
Ruffed Grouse, Woodcock, Turkey

WATERFOWL
Ducks, Geese, Snipe

ACCOMMODATIONS
Atlanta Motel, M-32/33, Atlanta / 517-785-4509 / cable TV, efficiency units / Dogs allowed / $$

Days Inn, 1201 West Main Street, Gaylord / 517-732-2200 / 95 rooms, continental breakfast, pool, jacuzzis / No pets / $$$

Holiday Inn, 833 West Main Street, Gaylord / 517-732-2431 / 140 rooms, pool, whirlpool, sauna, restaurant open at 6 a.m., lounge / Dogs allowed / $$$

Redwood Motor Inn, 4909 Salling Avenue, Lewiston / 517-786-2226 / 50 rooms, continental breakfast, pool, sauna, jacuzzi / No dogs / $$$

Sheridan Valley Motel, 3895 Co Rd 612, Lewiston / 517-786-2655 / 10 rooms, some with refrigerators, microwaves / Dogs allowed / $-$$$

Timber Lodge, 13015 East M-32, Atlanta / 517-785-3339 / Kitchenettes / Dogs allowed / $

Timberly Motel, Old US-27 South, Gaylord / 517-732-5166 / 30 units, cable TV, HBO, continental breakfast / Dogs allowed / $-$$$

CAMPGROUNDS AND RV PARKS
Clear Lake State Park, M-33, 9 miles north of Atlanta / 517-785-4388 / 200 sites, hunting nearby

Gaylord Alpine RV Park & Campground, M-32 West / 517-732-1772 / 135 sites, electricity, water, laundry, showers

Lewiston Shady Acres Campground & Cottages, County Road 489, Lewiston / 517-786-3000

Michaywe Wilderness Resort KOA, Charles Brink Road / 517-939-8723 / On north branch of AuSable River / 120 sites, water, electricity, store, laundry / Open to October 18

Otsego Lake State Park, Old 27 South / 517-732-5485 / 155 sites, showers, electricity

RESTAURANTS

Arlene's Diner, 324 West Main Street, Gaylord / 517-732-5654 / Open at 5AM every day

Big Buck Brewery & Steakhouse, 550 South Wisconsin, Gaylord / 517-732-5781 / Lunch and dinner

Dixie Rose Cafe, 12601 State Street, Atlanta / 517-785-3981

Herman's Restaurant & Lounge, County Road 489, Lewiston / 517-786-2211 / At Garland Golf Course

Jack's Landing Inn & Resort, 20836 Tennis Road, Hillman / 517-742-4370 / Breakfast, lunch, dinner, cocktails, Friday fish fry / View of Fletcher's Floodwaters

La Senorita, 737 West Main Street, Gaylord / 517-732-1771 / Lunch and dinner

VETERINARIANS.

Alpine Animal Hospital, 2202 East M-32, Gaylord / 517-732-6427

Atlanta Veterinary Clinic, 11746 Co. Road 487, Atlanta / 517-785-3521

Gaylord Veterinary Hospital, 1893 North Old US-27, Gaylord / 517-732-4545

SPORTING GOODS STORES

A-1 Woods 'N' Waters, 210 North State Street, / 517-742-3878

Alphorn Sport Shop, 137 West Main Street, Gaylord / 517-732-5616

Discount Firearms Inc, 420 South Otsego Avenue, Gaylord / 517-731-1000

Don-Mar Sport Shop, 3599 Co. Road 612, Lewiston / 517-786-2512

Don's Sport & Marine, 3819 Old US-27 South, Gaylord / 517-732-4157

Sport Stuff, 53 Connie Lane, Gaylord / 517-732-8118

AUTO REPAIR

Bill's Servicenter, 118 North Ohio Avenue / Gaylord / 517-732-4789

Dr. John's Auto Clinic, 819 South Illinois Avenue, Gaylord / 517-732-7720

Fred's Garage, 1035½ West Main Street, Gaylord / 517-732-7333

Otsego Lake Service, 3975 Old US-27 South, Gaylord / 517-732-3627

Ron's Auto & Wrecker Service, 611 West 4th Street, Gaylord / 517-732-3142

AIR SERVICE

Atlanta Municipal Airport, 13251 Airport Road, Atlanta / 517-785-2575

Otsego County Airport, 1185 Van Tyle Road, Gaylord / 517-732-4218

MEDICAL

Andy Schollett Memorial Hospital, 12426 State Street, Atlanta / 517-785-3134

MedCare Walk-In Clinic, 1507 Old 27 South, Gaylord / 517-731-4111
Otsego Memorial Hospital, 825 North Center Street, Gaylord / 517-731-2100

FOR MORE INFORMATION
Gaylord/Otsego County Chamber of Commerce
Gaylord Area Convention and Tourism Bureau
101 West Main Street / P.O. Box 513
Gaylord, MI 49735-0513
517-732-6333
www.gaylord-mi.com

Atlanta Area Chamber of Commerce
263 South Main Street / P.O. Box 410
Atlanta, MI 49709
517-785-3400

Lewiston Chamber of Commerce
2946 Kneeland Street / P.O. Box 656
Lewiston, MI 49756
517-786-2293

Ruffed grouse.
(Photo by Deb Cook)

Alpena and Alpena County

Population–11,354	October Average Temperature–48°F
County Population–30,605	Elevation–689 ft
County Area–574 sq mi	State Land Acres–45,600

While much of Alpena County is privately held among large hunting clubs, the area still has many hundreds of acres of public land available to hunters. Parcels of Mackinaw State Forest are scattered throughout the county, especially in the northern half and along the Lake Huron shore. Waterfowl hunters with small craft should look at Fletcher Pond flooding. Ruffed grouse hunters will do best in the northern half of the county. Hunting for both grouse and woodcock is fair to good.

UPLAND BIRDS
Ruffed Grouse, Woodcock, Turkey

WATERFOWL
Ducks, Geese, Snipe

ACCOMMODATIONS
Amber Motel, 2052 State Street / 517-354-8573 / 22 rooms, kitchen facilities, continental breakfast, cable TV / Dogs allowed / $-$$$
Bay Motel, 2107 South US-23 / 517-356-6137 / 23 rooms, cable TV, kitchen facilities / Dogs allowed / $-$$$
Best Western, 1286 West M-32 / 517-356-9087 / 36 rooms, cable TV, pool, restaurant, lounge / No dogs / $-$$$
Days Inn, 1496 West M-32 / 517-356-6118 / Indoor pool, whirlpool, sauna, cable TV, continental breakfast / No dogs / $$$
Waters Edge Motel, 1000 State Street / 517-354-5495 / 11 rooms, cable TV, kitchen facilities / Dogs allowed / $-$$

CAMPGROUNDS AND RV PARKS
Alpena County Fairgrounds / 517-356-1847
Camper's Cove, 5005 Long Rapids Road / 517-356-3708
Paul Bunyan Kampground, 6969 North Huron Road, Spruce / 471-2921

RESTAURANTS
The Anchorage, 1000 North US-23 / 517-356-2151 / In the Holiday Inn / Breakfast, lunch dinner
Big Boy, 1315 West Chisholm / 517-356-9071
Court Yard, 2024 South US-23 / 517-356-9511 / Italian, Mexican, American; cocktails / Open 4PM, 7 days/week
JJ's Sports Bar & Grill, 411 North 2nd Avenue / 517-354-3854

Veterinarians

Alpena Veterinary Hospital, 5025 North US-23 / 517 354-2925 or 356-1045
Sunrise Veterinary Services, 2565 US-23 / 517-354-2241
Switzer Veterinary Clinic, 3463 West M-32 / 517-356-4880 / Walk-in
  appointments, 4–6PM, Mon–Fri

Sporting Goods Stores

A-1 Woods-n-Water, 210 North State, Hillman / 517-742-3878
Bob's Gun Shop, 3089 West M-32 / 517-356-1777 / More than 1000 guns in
  stock
Clem's Live Bait & Tackle, 304 North 9th Avenue / 517-354-2070 / Open 7 days;
  licenses
Dunham's, 2678 US-23 South / 517-354-3383

Auto Repair

Alpena Transmission Specialists, 3101 South US-23 / 517-356-6341 /
  Front- and four-wheel drive
Andre's Auto & Truck Repair, 930 West Washington Avenue / 517-354-8482
Corey's Auto/Truck Repair, 109 South 9th Avenue / 517-356-1020
J & S Auto Repair, 610 River / 517-354-8918

Air Service

Alpena County Regional Airport, M-32 / 517-354-2907

Medical

Alpena General Hospital, 1501 West Chisholm Street / 517-356-7252

For More Information

Alpena Area Chamber of Commerce
235 West Chisholm / P.O. Box 65
Alpena, Michigan 49707
517-354-4181 / 800-4-Alpena
www.alpena.com

Grayling and Crawford County

Population–1,944	October Average Temperature–48°F
County Population–12,260	Elevation–1,140 ft
County Area–558 sq mi	State Land Acres–78,200
	Federal Land Acres–37,800

Grayling is the home of the Camp Grayling Military Reservation, a training ground for the Michigan National Guard. Crawford County bird hunters, especially those pursuing grouse and woodcock, will find plenty of places to go in the Au Sable State Forest and Huron National Forest. Those who fish as well as hunt might want to bring along fishing gear. The Manistee and Au Sable Rivers provide very good trout fishing. East of Grayling, the Au Sable has an 8-mile stretch of no-kill, flies-only river known as the Holy Waters. It's open all year.

UPLAND BIRDS
Ruffed Grouse, Woodcock, Turkey

WATERFOWL
Ducks, Geese, Snipe

ACCOMMODATIONS

Holiday Inn, Business I-75 South / 517-348-7611 / 151 units, restaurant and lounge, pool, hot tub, sauna / Dogs allowed / $$$

North Country Lodge / 517-348-8471 / 24 units, hot tub, kitchenettes / Dogs allowed / $$

Super 8 Motel, 5828 Nelson Miles Pkwy / 517-348-8888 / 60 units, hot tub / Dogs allowed / $$

Whispering Pines Resort, 5840 Filo Trail, Frederic / 517-348-2044 / 4 cabins / Dogs allowed / $$-$$$

CAMPGROUNDS AND RV PARKS

River Park Campground, 2607 Peters Road / 517-348-9092

Yogi Bear's Jellystone Park, 370 West Four Mile Road / 517-348-2157

Hartwick Pines State Park, M-93 / 517-348-7068 / 6 miles northeast of Grayling / 62 sites, hunting nearby

RESTAURANTS

Big Boy, Business I-75 / 517-348-8822

Bucilli's Pizza, 243 Michigan Avenue / 517-348-4044

Shoppenagon's Inn, 103 East Michigan Avenue / 517-348-6071 / Cocktails

Spike's Keg o'Nails, Business I-75 / 517-348-7113 / Cocktails

VETERINARIANS

Grayling Hospital for Animals, 714 Isenhauer Road / 517-348-8622

Sporting Goods Stores

Caid's Grocery & Sport Shop, 6510 East County Road 612 / 517-348-2283

Skip's Sport Shop, M-72 West / 517-348-7111

Sylvester's, 5610 M-72 West / 517-348-9097

Auto Repair

Fenton's Auto Service, 602 North James Street / 517-348-5242

Grayling Auto Repair, Business I-75 / 517-348-8123

S&B Auto Repair, Frederic / 517-344-9400

Air Service

Oscoda County Airport / 517-848-2446

Otsego County Airport, 1185 Van Tyle Road, Gaylord / 517-732-4218

Roscommon County Airport, 5218 East Houghton Lake Drive, Houghton Lake / 517-366-7660

Medical

Grayling Mercy Hospital, 1100 East Michigan Avenue / 517-348-5461

For More Information

Grayling Area Visitor's Council

213 North James Street

Grayling, MI 49738

517-348-4945

visitor@grayling-mi.com

Grayling Regional Chamber of Commerce

City Park

P.O. Box 406

Grayling, MI 49738

517-348-2921

Mio and Oscoda / Alcona Counties

Population–1,886	October Average Temperature–48°F
County Population:	Elevation–963 ft
Oscoda–7,842	Public by County (Acres):
Alcona–10,145	Oscoda–State 56,300 / Federal 151,600
County Area:	Alcona–State 8,900 / Federal 112,500
Oscoda–565 sq mi	
Alcona–674 sq mi	

Large holdings of Huron National Forest are located in Oscoda and Alcona Counties, as well as small tracts of Au Sable and Mackinaw State Forests, and the area is popular with turkey hunters. Oscoda County's Fairview, site of the reintroduction of turkeys to Michigan in 1964, lays claim to being the Wild Turkey Capital of Michigan. Grouse and woodcock hunting are good throughout the area.

UPLAND BIRDS
Ruffed Grouse, Woodcock, Turkey

WATERFOWL
Ducks, Geese, Snipe

ACCOMMODATIONS
Bavarian Motel, 7985 North M-65, Glennie / 517-735-3174 / 16 units / Store with supplies, licenses / Restaurant, lounge, next door / Dogs allowed / $$
Bear Paw Cabins, 3744 West M-72, Luzerne / 517-826-3313 / 5 cabins, 1 trailer, 1–2 bedrooms, kitchenettes, cable TV / Dogs allowed / $$
Four Seasons Motel, West M-72, Mio / 517-826-6400 / Kitchenettes, by the night or week / Dogs allowed in cages / $$
North Star Resort, 1330 South M-33, Mio / 517-826-3278 / 9 cabins, 16 campsites / kitchens, fireplaces / Dogs allowed / $$-$$$
Pinewood Motel, 142 M-33, Mio / 888-891-7810 / 6 units, kitchenettes, suites / Dogs allowed / $$

CAMPGROUNDS AND RV PARKS
Harrisville State Park, US-23, Harrisville / 517-724-5126 / On Lake Huron / 229 campsites
Mio Pine Acres, 1215 West 8th Street, Mio / 517-826-5590 / Cabins and campsites, electricity, water, store, laundry
Oscoda County Park, 1110 Jay Smith Drive, Mio / 517-826-5114

RESTAURANTS
Aunt Charlotte's, 282 East Miller Road, Mio / 517-848-8222 / Open 7 days / Breakfast, lunch, dinner

Ma Deeters Bar & Restaurant, Luzerne / 517-826-5558

Northwood Gardens, North M-33, Mio / 517-826-6292 / Pizza, Friday fish fry, entertainment, cocktails

Scenic Riverwood Bar & Restaurant, 4700 McKinley Road, McKinley / 517-848-5431 / Cocktails, Friday fish fry

VETERINARIANS

Alcona Animal Clinic, 409 West Millen, Lincoln / 517-736-8890

SPORTING GOODS STORES

Bavarian Motel Store, Glennie / 517-735-3174 / Supplies, licenses, LP gas

D's Bait & Tackle, 590 Lockwood Lane, Mio / Hunting, fishing supplies

The Little Sport Shop, 3744 West M-72, Luzerne / 517-826-3313 / Supplies, licenses, ammunition

Luzerne Hardware, 2244 South Deeter Road, Luzerne / 517-826-8050 / Camping, hunting, fishing supplies

Mio Sport Shop, 406 North Morenci, Mio / 517-826-3758 / Supplies, ammunition, licenses

McKinley Grocery, 4766 McKinley Road, Mio / 517-848-5332 / Food, supplies, licenses

AUTO REPAIR

BCK Repair, 555 North M-33, Mio / 517-826-3850 / 24-hr. road and wrecker service

Blair's Service, 210 South M-33, Mio / 517-826-5033

Gordon's Auto Service, 213 South State Street, Harrisville / 517-724-5275

Mike's Auto & Glass Repair, 525 Morenci Street, Mio / 517-826-6229 / Parts and service

Richardson's Auto Repair, 13775 Hubbard Lake Road, Hubbard Lake / 517-727-3168

AIR SERVICE

Oscoda County Airport / 517-848-2446

MEDICAL

AuSable Valley Health Center, 377 South M-33, Mio / 517-826-8211

FOR MORE INFORMATION

Chamber of Commerce for Oscoda County
P.O. Box 670
Mio, MI 48647
517-826-3331
http://k2.kirtland.cc.mi.us/~oscoda

Harrisville Chamber of Commerce
508 East Main Street
Harrisville, MI 48740
517-724-5107

Manistee and Manistee County

Population–6,968	October Average Temperature–51°F
County Population–21,706	Elevation–670 ft
County Area–544 sq mi	State Land Acres–24,100
	Federal Land Acres–87,500

Perhaps better known for its tremendous salmon and steelhead fishing, Manistee is also located near some great hunting territory. While there is plenty of elbow room to be found in the Pere Marquette State Forest and Manistee National Forest, hunters will be especially interested in Manistee River State Game Area, which stretches for miles along the banks of the Big Manistee. Turkey hunting is fair to good, while grouse and woodcock hunting is good, especially in the south and east sections of the county.

UPLAND BIRDS
Ruffed Grouse, Woodcock, Turkey

WATERFOWL
Ducks, Geese, Snipe

ACCOMMODATIONS
Hillside Motel, 1599 South US-31 / 231-723-2584 / 20 rooms, cable TV / Dogs allowed / $-$$$

Lake Shore Motel, 101 South Lakeshore Drive / 231-723-2667 / On Lake Michigan / Cable TV, in-room coffee, pier fishing, cleaning and freezing facilities available

Riverside Motel, 520 Water Street / 231-723-3554 / On the Manistee River, dock space available / Cable TV, fish cleaning/freezing / Dogs allowed / $$-$$$

Super 8, 220 North US-31 / 231-398-8888 / 44 rooms, jacuzzi suites, cable TV, continental breakfast / No dogs / $-$$$

Sunset Valley Resort, 18726 Burnham Drive, Arcadia / 231-889-5987 / On Lake Michigan / 15 units, 9 kitchenettes, cable TV / Dogs allowed

Travelers Motel, 5606 8 Mile Road, Onekama / 231-889-4342 / 14 rooms, kitchenettes, cable TV / Dogs allowed / $-$$$

CAMPGROUNDS AND RV PARKS
Insta-Launch Campground, 20 Park Avenue / 231-723-3901 / On Big Manistee River / Rustic and full hook-ups, some cottages and trailers with kitchens, boat launch

Orchard Beach State Park, North Lakeshore Road / 231-723-7422 / 175 sites, overlooks Lake Michigan

Pine Lake USFS Campground, Wellston / 231-723-2211 / 12 primitive sites, water / Call for availability after Labor Day

Sand Lake USFS Campground, Dublin / 231-723-2211 / 45 sites, vault and flush toilets, showers, carry-in boat launch / Call for availability after Labor Day

RESTAURANTS
Armedo's, 1569 South US-31 / 231-723-3561 / Steaks, chops, seafood, cocktails
Big Boy, 1525 US-31 / 231-723-8339 / Breakfast, lunch, dinner / Open at 6AM Mon–Sat
Four Forty West, 440 River Street / 231-723-7902 / Lunch, dinner, cocktails
Gregory's, North US-31 / 231-723-4661 / At the Best Western Carriage Inn / Breakfast, lunch, dinner, cocktails

VETERINARIANS
Bear Lake Animal Clinic, 7587 Cody, Bear Lake / 231-864-3692
Manistee Veterinary Hospital, Corner M-22 & US-31 / 231-723-9000
Parkdale Animal Hospital, 420 Parkdale Avenue / 231-723-8998

SPORTING GOODS STORES
Firearms Plus, 1462 Olson Road / 231-723-2715
Northwind Sports, 400 Parkdale Avenue / 231-723-2255
Riley's Tackle & Gun Shop, 289 River Street / 231-723-3354

AUTO REPAIR
Erdmann's Car Care, 1628 Cedar Road / 231-723-5860
Midas, 414 Parkdale Avenue / 231-723-7800
Muffler Man, 245 Arthur Street / 231-723-9921
Northstar Automotive, 12150 7th Street, Bear Lake / 231-864-3139
Schuessler Auto Repair, 421 Tippy Dam Road, Wellston / 231-848-4175

AIR SERVICE
Manistee Blacker Airport, 2323 Airport Road / 231-723-4351

MEDICAL
West Shore Hospital, 1465 North US-31 / 231-398-1000

FOR MORE INFORMATION
Manistee Chamber of Commerce
11 Cypress Street
Manistee, MI 49660
800-288-2286
www.manistee.com

Cadillac and Wexford / Missaukee Counties

Population–10,104	October Average Temperature–47°F
County Population:	Elevation–1,295 ft
Wexford–26,360	Public Lands in County (Acres):
Missaukee–12,147	Wexford–State 50,400 / Federal 96,400
County Area:	Missaukee–State 101,000
Wexford–563 sq mi	
Missaukee–565 sq mi	

Cadillac and nearby Lake City are a good base for bird hunters. Missaukee County has extensive tracts of Pere Marquette State Forest, especially in the north. State land extends into Wexford County, which is also covered in Manistee National Forest, combining for a few hundred thousand acres of public land. Agricultural land adjacent to Wexford County's Hodenpyl Dam Pond in Mesick, as well as around Lakes Cadillac and Mitchell, is good for Canada geese. Wexford County has more grouse and woodcock; and both counties are good bets for turkeys. Make sure to stop in the Carl T. Johnson Hunting and Fishing Center in Mitchell State Park (616-779-1321) for area information.

UPLAND BIRDS
Ruffed Grouse, Woodcock, Turkey

WATERFOWL
Ducks, Geese, Snipe

ACCOMMODATIONS
Bill Oliver's Resort, 5676 West M-55 / 616-775-2458 / 66 rooms, restaurant, lounges, pool / Dogs accepted at managers discretion / $$-$$$
Cadillac Sands Resort, 6319 East M-115 / 616-775-2407 / 55 rooms, cable TV, restaurant, lounge / Dogs allowed / $$-$$$
Days Inn, 6001 M-115 / 616-775-4414 / 60 rooms, cable TV, pool, continental breakfast / No dogs / $$-$$$
Lakeview Motel, 214 Main Street, Lake City / 616-839-4958 / 11 rooms, 3 kitchenettes, in-room coffee / On Lake Missaukee / Dogs allowed / $$
Maple Lane Cottages, 406 North Main Street, Lake City / 616-839-4541
McGuire's Resort, 7880 Mackinaw Trail / 616-775-9947 / 123 rooms, cable TV, pool, sauna, restaurant, lounge / No dogs / $$$
Northcrest Motel, 1341 South Lakeshore Drive, Lake City / 616-839-2075 / 22 units, pool, jacuzzi, cable TV / Small dogs allowed; call first / $$
Pilgrim's Village, 181 South Lake Mitchell Drive / 616-775-5412 / 15 2-bedroom cottages and motel rooms, cable TV, kitchens / On Lake Mitchell / Dogs allowed / $$$

CAMPGROUNDS AND RV PARKS
Birchwood Resort & Campgrounds, 6553 East M-115 / 616-775-9101

William Mitchell State Park, M-115 / 616-775-7911 / 270 sites / On Lakes
   Cadillac and Mitchell
Woodhaven RV Park, 2371 Seeley Road / 616-775-8260

RESTAURANTS
Blue Heron Cafe, 304 North Mitchell Street / 616-775-5461
Country Kitchen, 3728 South Morey Road, Lake City / 616-839-4511
Curly's Up North Bar & Grill, 7880 Mackinaw Trail / 616-775-9947
D & J's Bakery & Pizza, 102 Main Street, Lake City / 616-839-2077
Food Factory & Pub, 118 Main Street, Lake City / 616-839-3663
Hillcrest Family Restaurant, 1250 South Mitchell Street / 616-775-4191
Lakeside Charlie's, 301 South Lake Mitchell Drive / 616-775-5332
Timbers Restaurant, 5535 M-115 / 616-775-6751
Wang's Dynasty, 126 East M-55 / 616-779-3541
Waterfront Restaurant, 2403 Sunnyside Drive / 616-775-7555

VETERINARIANS.
Airport Animal Clinic, 7745 East 34 Mile Road / 616-775-1378
Lake City Animal Clinic, 1455 South Lakeshore Drive, Lake City / 616-839-4936
Meyer Veterinary Clinic, 530 Bell Avenue / 616-775-4104

SPORTING GOODS STORES
Carl's Sport Center, 5415 South Lachonce Road, Lake City / 616-775-2756
Lake City Sport Shop, 110 Main Street, Lake City / 616-839-4875
Laura Lee's Landing, 1749 North Boulevard / 616-775-2648
Pilgrim's Village, 181 South Lake Mitchell Drive / 616-775-5412 / Supplies, licenses
Schafer's Bait & Sporting Goods, 2722 Sunnyside Drive / 616-775-7085

AUTO REPAIR
Budget Transmission, 110 Irma Avenue / 616-775-6055
Don's Auto Clinic, 1110 North Mitchell Street / 616-775-2413
Foster's Northeast Service, 8850 34 Road / 616-779-2891
Kirt's Muffler Shop, 170 Works Avenue / 616-775-8971
R & P Rapid Repair, 6621 34½ Mile Road / 616-779-3196
Westside Auto Service, 6732 West Division Street / 616-775-3323

AIR SERVICE
Wexford County Airport, 8040 East 34 Mile Road / 616-779-9525

MEDICAL
Mercy Hospital, 400 Hobart / 616-876-7200

FOR MORE INFORMATION
Cadillac Area Visitors Bureau
222 Lake Street
Cadillac, MI 49601
616-775-0657
www.cadillacmichigan.com

Lake City Chamber of Commerce
220 Main
Lake City, MI 49651
616-839-4969

Houghton Lake and Roscommon County

Population–3,353	October Average Temperature–48°F
County Population–19,776	Elevation–1,135 ft
County Area–521 sq mi	State Land Acres–202,900

Waterfowl hunters have been coming to Houghton Lake for years to take part in the good diving duck hunting. Layout rigs for scaup and other divers are popular on the lake, which is known for its good walleye fishing, as well. Wood ducks and mallards are another attraction in the surrounding area, including the Backus Creek State Game Area. Grouse, woodcock, and turkeys inhabit the Pere Marquette and Au Sable State Forest land. Hunting for all of these species is good to very good.

UPLAND BIRDS
Ruffed Grouse, Woodcock, Turkey

WATERFOWL
Ducks, Geese, Snipe

ACCOMMODATIONS

Great Escape Motor Lodge, 8097 North Harrison Road, Roscommon / 800-361-8312 / Suites, kitchen units, pool / Dogs allowed / $-$$

Havagooday Resorts, 10911 East Houghton Lake Drive / 517-422-5344 / Cottages in 2 locations / Dogs allowed

Holiday on the Lake, 100 Clearview / 517-422-5195 / Cottages, kitchenettes, cable TV, restaurant, lounge / Dogs allowed / $-$$$

Hutchinson's Airport Motel, 10100 Airport Road, St. Helen / 517-389-7929 /

Lagoon Resort & Motel, 6578 West Houghton Lake Drive / 517-422-5761 / Cottages, kitchenettes, cable TV Dogs allowed / $-$$$

Poplars Resort, 10360 West Shore Drive / 517-422-5132 / 2–3 bedroom housekeeping units on the lake / boats and motors / campground with showers / Dogs allowed

Skaryd's Sportsman Resort, 228 Rapson Avenue / 517-366-5471 / 2–3-bedroom cottages, one mile from boat launch / Dogs allowed with hunters / $$-$$$

CAMPGROUNDS AND RV PARKS

Artesia Beach Campground & Marina, 5941 Poplar, St. Helen / 517-389-4461

Higgins Lake State Park North, Roscommon Road / 517-821-6125 / 8.5 miles north of Roscommon / 218 sites, hunting nearby

Higgins Lake State Park South, Higgins Cut Road / 517-821-6374 / 512 sites / 6.5 miles southwest of Roscommon

Houghton Lake Travel Park, M-55 / 517-422-3931

Poplars Resort, 10360 West Shore Drive / 517-422-5132 / Full hook-ups, showers

RESTAURANTS

Baum's Au Sable Cafe, 802 Lake Street, Roscommon / 517-275-8540 / Breakfast, lunch, dinner / Friday fish fry

Coyle's Restaurant, Old 27 / 517-422-3812 / Buffet, cocktails

Garvin's Spikehorn, Markey Road / 517-366-9698 / Across from the airport on northeast shore of Houghton Lake / Breakfast, lunch, dinner, cocktails / Friday fish fry

The Limberlost, Houghton Lake / 517-366-7242

Maple Valley Restaurant & Lounge, 4995 M-55, St. Helen / 517-389-7005

North Shore Lounge, Corner North & West Shore Drive / 517-422-3031 / Steaks, fish, cocktails

VETERINARIANS

South Shore Animal Hospital, 4258 West Houghton Lake Drive / 517-366-7404

Roscommon Veterinary Clinic, 116 Lake Street, Roscommon / 517-275-5003

SPORTING GOODS STORES

Higgins Lake Sport & Tackle, 10028 West Higgins Lake Drive, Higgins Lake / 517-821-9517 / Licenses, duck stamps, ammunition / Open 7 days

Lenny's Gun Shop & Sporting Goods, M-55 / 517-422-3845

Sports Barn, 9475 North Cut, Higgins Lake / 517-821-9511 / Supplies, licenses

WalMart, 3451 West Houghton Lake Drive / Guns, ammunition, licenses / Open 7 days, 7AM–11PM

AUTO REPAIR

D&L Automotive, 440 South M-76, St. Helen / 517-389-0700

Gibson's Service, Prudenville / 517-366-8216

Jamey's Automotive Service, 1195 North, St. Helen / 517-389-1130

Ray's Automotive, Houghton Lake / 517-366-5411

AIR SERVICE

Roscommon County Airport, 5218 East Houghton Lake Drive / 517-366-7660

MEDICAL

Mercy Hospital, Grayling / 517-348-5461

Northern Michigan Health Services, 9249A M-55 / 517-422-5122

Tolfree Hospital, West Branch / 517-354-3660

FOR MORE INFORMATION

Houghton Lake Chamber of Commerce
1625 West Houghton Lake Drive
Houghton Lake, MI 48629
517-366-5644

St. Helen Chamber of Commerce
2160 M-76
St. Helen, MI 48565
517-389-3725

Higgins Lake/Roscommon Chamber of Commerce
112 South 4th Street
Roscommon, MI
517-275-8760

West Branch and Ogemaw County

Population–2,294	October Average Temperature–48°F
County Population–18,681	Elevation–885 ft
County Area–	State Land Acres–76,500
	Federal Land Acres–20,100

Ogemaw County has a lot to offer a bird hunter. There are thousands of acres of public lands for grouse, woodcock, and turkey hunters. Grouse and woodcock hunting are good throughout, but most public lands are in the northern half of the county. Pheasant hunters won't find as many birds as they will farther south, but there are a few to be found in the agricultural lands. Also, there are many small lakes and beaver ponds for the waterfowler to explore.

UPLAND BIRDS
Ruffed Grouse, Woodcock, Turkey, Pheasant

WATERFOWL
Ducks, Geese, and Snipe

ACCOMMODATIONS
LaHacienda Motel, 9679 West Business I-75 / 517-345-2345 / 13 units, some with kitchens / Dogs allowed / $$

Quality Inn, 2980 Cook Road / 517-345-3503 / Pool, cable TV, 24-hour restaurant, lounge store / No dogs / $$–$$$

Super 8, 2596 Austin Way / 517-345-8488 / 40 rooms, jacuzzi suites, continental breakfast / Dogs allowed / $$–$$$

Tri-Terrace Motel, 2259 South M-76 / 517-345-3121 / Cable TV, refrigerators, microwaves / Dogs allowed / $–$$

CAMPGROUNDS AND RV PARKS
Lake George Campground, 3070 Elm / 517-345-2700 / 97 sites, electricity, laundry

Loon Lake Resort, 5628 Walker Road, Rose City / 517-685-2407

Rifle River State Recreation Area, Rose City Road, Lupton / 517-473-2258 / 181 sites, hunting, trout fishing

RESTAURANTS
Faull Inn, M-33, Rose City / 517-685-2406 / Breakfast, lunch, dinner, cocktails

Jerry's Joint, 2343 South M-76 / 517-345-9837 / Sandwiches, burgers, cocktails

Logger's Depot, 314 West Houghton / 517-345-2656 / Lunch and dinner, cocktails

Wagon Wheel Inn, corner of Lehman & M-30 / 517-345-5570 / Friday fish fry, daily specials

Woods & Waters Restaurant and Lounge, 2355 South M-33 / 517-345-7039 / Grilled steaks, ribs

VETERINARIANS

Eldon Barclay, DVM, 783 East Ogemaw Center / 517-685-2042
Ogemaw Veterinary Clinic, 1866 North M-33, Rose City / 517-685-3941
West Branch Veterinary Services, 3197 West M-55 / 517-345-5363

SPORTING GOODS STORES

Darrel's Live Bait, 5325 South Henderson Lake Road, Prescott / Supplies, ammunition, licenses
Duck Inn, 4349 Baker / 517-345-4581
J&P Sporting Goods, 3275 West M-55 / 517-345-3744 / Guns, ammunition
Jerry's General Store, M-33, Rose City / 517-685-2940
Mill End Store, 205 West Houghton / 517-345-2680 / Clothing, accessories, ammunition

AUTO REPAIR

Maxi Muffler, 930 West Houghton Avenue / 517-345-1970
Sanford Service Center, 2789 South M-76 / 517-345-8761
Village Quik Lube & Auto Service Center, 3149 West Houghton / 517-345-4410
West Branch Tire & Automotive Service, 962 West Houghton / 517-345-5624
West Branch Transmission Service, 2776 South M-76 / 517-345-9799

AIR SERVICE

West Branch Community Airport, Airport Road and South M-76 / 517-345-1453

MEDICAL

Tolfree Memorial Hospital, 335 East Houghton / 517-345-3660

FOR MORE INFORMATION

West Branch Area Chamber of Commerce
West Branch/Ogemaw County Travel & Visitor's Bureau
422 West Houghton Avenue
West Branch, MI 48661
517-345-2821

Oscoda and Iosco County

Population–1,061	October Average Temperature–49°F
County Population–30,209	Elevation–586 ft
County Area–549 sq mi	State Land Acres–24,800
	Federal Land Acres–111,700

The Au Sable River widens and slows through several impoundments in Iosco County, and these areas are of special interest to outdoorsmen as are the hundreds of thousands of acres of Au Sable State Forest and Huron National Forest. Chinook salmon fishing in the Au Sable is worth checking out while you're in the area for an upland hunt. Ruffed grouse and woodcock hunting is fair to good in the north half of the county. It should be noted that some pheasants are available on agricultural land in this area of Michigan, but their numbers improve as one moves farther south.

UPLAND BIRDS
Ruffed Grouse, Woodcock, Turkey, Pheasant

WATERFOWL
Ducks, Geese, Snipe

ACCOMMODATIONS
Aaron's Wooded Acres, 968 North US-23, East Tawas / 517-362-5188 / 14 cottages, fireplaces, overlooking Lake Huron / Dogs allowed
Aspen Motor Inn, 115 North Lake Street / 517-739-9152 / 22 units, HBO, in-room coffee, refrigerators / Dogs allowed / $-$$$
Northern Traveler, 5493 North US-23 / 517-739-9261 / 15 rooms, HBO, in-room coffee, refrigerators / Dogs allowed
Oscoda Resort & Motel, 7418 US-23 / 517-739-2714 / 10 rooms on Lake Huron, kitchens, cable TV, nightly and weekly rates / Dogs allowed / $$$

CAMPGROUNDS AND RV PARKS
Acres & Trails KOA, 3591 Forest Road / 517-739-5115 / 145 sites, 7 Kamping Kabins and furnished cabins / Dogs allowed
Old Orchard Park, 883 River Road / 517-739-7814 / 569 sites (369 primitive) water, showers, electricity / On Au Sable River / Open to November 1

RESTAURANTS
Big Dave's, 5226 North US-23 / 517-739-2069 / Lunch and dinner / Pizza, pasta, grinders
Pier 23, 821 West Bay Street, East Tawas / 517-362-8856 / Fish, seafood, steaks, cocktails
Topsider, 300 North US-23, East Tawas / 517-362-8601 / At the Holiday Inn / Breakfast, lunch dinner / Open 7 days
Wiltse's Brew Pub and Restaurant, 5606 North F-41 / 517-739-2231

VETERINARIANS

Falker Veterinary Clinic, 1790 North US-23, East Tawas / 517-362-5711
Oscoda Veterinary Clinic, 7415 North F-41 / 517-739-8278
Tawas Animal Hospital, 1627 M-55, Tawas City / 517-362-4601

SPORTING GOODS STORES

All-Season Sporting Goods, 1250 South US-23, Tawas City / 517-362-4512 /
Open 7 days, 5AM–9PM
Hale Hardware, downtown Hale / 517-728-9581 / Guns, ammunition, supplies,
licenses
Kmart, 5719 North US-23 / 517-739-9191
Myrick's Autumn Outfitters, 4874 South US-23 / 517-739-0950 / Goods for
camp, kennel, field / Bird dog gear

AUTO REPAIR

Darrell's Maxi Muffler, 5673 North F-41, Oscoda, 517-739-1463 / 1201 South
US-23, Tawas City / 517-362-1463 / Domestic and foreign repairs as well as
exhaust work
Four Seasons Automotive, 2533 North US-23 / 517-739-8888
Northern Truck & Auto Repair, 4262 East River Road / 517-739-4382
Oscoda Transmission Service, 5685 North F-41 / 517-739-9451 / Domestic and
foreign, 4WD

AIR SERVICE

Iosco County Airport, 1131 Aulerich, East Tawas / 517-362-5832
Oscoda-Wurtsmith Airport, 14 WAFB / 517-739-1111

MEDICAL

Oscoda Community Health Center, 5671 Skeel / 517-739-2550
Oscoda Health Park, 5935 North Huron Road / 517-739-1441
St. Joseph Hospital, 200 Hemlock, Tawas City / 517-362-3411

FOR MORE INFORMATION

Oscoda Area Convention and Visitors Bureau
Oscoda/Au Sable Chamber of Commerce
4440 North US-23
Oscoda, MI 48750
1-800-235-4625
www.oscoda.com

Tawas Area Chamber of Commerce
420 Lake Street
Tawas City, MI
517-362-8643

Ludington and Mason / Oceana Counties

Population–8,507	October Average Temperature–50°F
County Population:	Elevation–690 ft
Mason–25,537	Public Land by County (Acres):
Oceana–22,454	Mason–State 6,400 / Federal 60,700
County Area:	Oceana–State 5,700 / Federal 53,200
Mason–495 sq mi	
Oceana–540 sq mi	

Bird hunters need not travel far from where they're staying to find places to hunt here. The Pere Marquette State Game Area is just outside Ludington, and the Pentwater State Game Area and Pere Marquette State Forest are just outside Pentwater. In addition, Ludington State Park and Silver Lake State Park provide hunting opportunities, along with Manistee National Forest land to the east. The Pere Marquette River, designated as a National Wild and Scenic River, is worth exploring. Much of the banks are privately owned, but there are several public access points. Grouse and woodcock hunting, fair to good in this area, are best in northern sections of Mason County. Turkey hunting is fair to good throughout the two counties.

Note: The line that divides Michigan's hunting regions 2 and 3 runs through the southeast corner of Oceana County. This can mean that a season is open in one part of the county and closed in another. Be sure to consult the *Michigan Hunting and Trapping Guide.*

UPLAND BIRDS
Ruffed Grouse, Woodcock, Turkey

WATERFOWL
Ducks, Geese, Snipe

ACCOMMODATIONS
Christie's Log Cabins on Round Lake, 6503 East Sugar Grove / 231-462-3218 / 6 cabins, kitchens / Dogs allowed / $$-$$$

Country Haven Resort, 3263 North Lakshore Drive / 231-845-5882 / On Lower Hamlin Lake / Two 3-bedroom cottages plus six 1–2-bdrm apartments, full kitchens / Next to park with boat launch / No dogs / $$-$$$

Holiday Inn Express, 5323 West US-10 / 231-845-7004 / 102 rooms, pool, sauna, continental breakfast / Dogs allowed / $$$

Lands Inn, 4079 West US-10 / 231-845-7311 / Pool, spa, restaurant, lounge / Dogs allowed / $$-$$$

Nader's Lakeshore Motor Lodge, 612 North Lakeshore Drive / 231-843-8757 / 26 units, kitchenettes, cable TV, hot tub / Dogs allowed / $-$$$

Timberlane Long Lake Resort, 7410 East US-10, Walhalla / 231-757-2142 / Cottages, kitchens, cable TV / Dogs allowed / $-$$$

CAMPGROUNDS AND RV PARKS
Jellystone Park Campground, 8329 West Hazel Road, Mears / 231-873-4502 / 200 sites, full hook-ups, cabin rentals

Ludington State Park, M-116 / 231-843-8671 / On Lake Michigan / 398 sites, water, electricity, hunting nearby

Poncho's Pond, 5335 West Wallace Road / 231-845-6655 / 150 sites, 59 of which are drive-through, full hook-ups, spa, showers

Silver Lake State Park, County Road B-15, Mears / 231-873-3083 / 249 sites, water, electricity, hunting nearby

RESTAURANTS
Gibb's Country House, 3951 West US-10 / 231-845-0311 / Lunch, dinner, cocktails

House of Flavors Restaurant, 402 West Ludington Avenue / 231-845-5785 / Breakfast, lunch, dinner / Open at 6AM daily

Kuntry Kubbard, 5474 West US-10 / 231-845-5217 / Breakfast, lunch, dinner / Open 7AM daily, April–October

Old Hamlin Restaurant, 122 West Ludington Avenue / 231-843-4251 / Breakfast, lunch, dinner, Friday fish fry

Scotty's, 5910 East Ludington Avenue / 231-843-4033 / Lunch and dinner, breakfast on Sunday / Cocktails, perch, steaks, seafood

VETERINARIANS
Animal Hospital of Ludington, 310 South Washington Avenue / 231-845-7719

Hart Animal Clinic, 21 West Main Street Hart / 231-873-5631

Veterinary Medical Center, 243 North Jebavy Drive / 231-845-0585

SPORTING GOODS STORES
Pere Marquette Sports Center, 214 West Ludington Avenue / 231-843-8676

Ruby Creek Store, 8010 East Washington, Branch / 231-898-2425

AUTO REPAIR
Auto Service Center, 5781 West US-10 / 231-845-5161

Avenue Tire & Service, 5797 West US-10 / 231-845-0392

James Tire & Service, 215 North Jebavy Drive / 231-843-3100

AIR SERVICE
Hart-Shelby Airport, Baseline Road, Shelby / 231-861-9910

Mason County Airport, East Ludington Avenue. / 231-843-2049

MEDICAL
Memorial Medical Center, 1 Atkinson Drive / 231-843-2591

FOR MORE INFORMATION
Ludington Area Convention & Visitors Bureau
5827 West US-10
Ludington, MI 49431
231-845-0324
www.ludingtoncvb.com

Big Rapids and Mecosta, Lake, Newaygo, and Osceola Counties

Population–12,603	October Average Temperature–48°F
County Area:	County Populations:
Mecosta–556 sq mi	Mecosta–37,308
Lake–568 sq mi	Lake–8,583
Newaygo–842 sq mi	Newaygo–38,202
Osceola–566 sq mi	Osceola–20,146
Elevation–930 ft (Big Rapids)	Public Land by County (Acres):
	Mecosta–State 14,200 / Federal 2500
	Lake–State 61,300 / Federal 112,400
	Newaygo–State 6825 / Federal 108,800
	Osceola–State 19,400

This four-county area, like so many places around Michigan's midsection, has a mixture of forested and agricultural land. The heavier forested areas are in the state and national forests in the west, giving way to more open land farther east in Osceola and Mecosta. The Muskegon River cuts through this region, and some of its banks are publicly owned in the Pere Marquette State Forest. This region is on the fringe of the more populous southern Michigan, where state game areas become more common and sometimes provide the only opportunity for hunters who have no other access to hunting spots. Haymarsh Lake State Game Area in Mecosta County has thousands of acres available to hunters. Muskegon State Game Area is in the southwest corner of Newaygo and stretches nearly to the Lake Michigan coastline in Muskegon County. Michigan state game areas can be crowded at times, but hunters who go out during the week or who are willing to walk farther from the roads will find less competition and more game. Ruffed grouse and woodcock numbers are fair to good throughout; although hunters will have to do some exploring to find pockets of birds. The best bet for pheasants is Mecosta, but scouting is also required to find the best spots. This entire region is good to very good for turkeys.

NOTE: The line that divides Michigan's hunting regions 2 and 3 runs through Mecosta and Newaygo Counties. This can mean that a season is open in one part of the county and closed in another. Be sure to consult the *Michigan Hunting and Trapping Guide*.

UPLAND BIRDS
Ruffed Grouse, Woodcock, Turkey, Pheasant

WATERFOWL
Ducks, Geese, Snipe

Accommodations

Bob's Villa Mar Motel, 993 South Evergreen Drive, White Cloud / 231-689-1593 / 12 rooms, kitchenettes / Dogs allowed / $$

Cloud Nine, 2733 South M-37, Baldwin / 231-745-3070 / 8 cabins, 1–2 bedrooms, kitchens / Dogs allowed / $-$$

Day Star Motel, 2451 North M-37, Baldwin / 231-745-2111 / 11 rooms, cable TV, kitchenettes / Dogs allowed / $-$$

Ferris Inn, 1010 South State Street / 231-796-6000 / 62 rooms, kitchenettes, pool, continental breakfast / Dogs allowed / $$

Holiday Inn, 1005 Perry Avenue / 231-796-4400 / 118 rooms, restaurant and lounge, refrigerators, pool, hot tub, sauna / No dogs / $$$

Johnson's Pere Marquette Lodge, M-37, Baldwin / 231-745-3972 / 10-room lodge and fully-equipped cabins / Breakfast and dinner served to lodge visitors / Dogs allowed; kennels available / Guide service available / $$$

Miller's Resort, 1932 West Parklane, White Cloud / 231-924-2362 / 4 cottages with fully equipped kitchens / No dogs / $$

Osceola Inn, 110 East Upton Avenue, Reed City / 231-832-5537 / 26 rooms, 11 with baths, daily, weekly rates and packages / Restaurant serving breakfast, lunch, dinner, buffets / Boxed lunches available / Dogs allowed / $$

Reed City Motel, 781 South Chestnut Street, Reed City / 231-832-5373 / 10 rooms, 1 efficiency, cable TV / No dogs / $$

Super 8, 845 Water Tower Road / 231-796-1588 / 52 rooms, pool, whirlpool, cable TV, continental breakfast / No dogs / $$-$$$

Campgrounds and RV Parks

Bluegill Lake Campground, 15854 Pretty Lake Drive, Mecosta / 231-972-7410 / 100 sites, electricity, laundry

Buck's Camping, 21965 8 Mile Road, Stanwood / 231-823-2412 / 24 sites for tents and trailers, electricity

Leisure Time RV Park, 4799 South Spruce Avenue, White Cloud / 231-689-5490 / 45 sites, electricity / On Utley Lake

Newaygo State Park, Oxbow / 231-856-4452 / On Hardy Dam Pond / 99 sites with hunting nearby

Restaurants

Casey Mc Nab's, 1014 South State Street / 231-796-1222

Mancino's Pizza & Grinders, 554 South State Street / 231-796-6666

Peregrine Restaurant, 13120 Northland Drive / 231-796-2613

Ponderosa Steak House, 14321 Northland Drive / 231-796-6445

State Street Grill, 213 South State Street / 231-796-8706

Veterinarians.

Country Veterinary Service, 11770 East US-10, Reed City / 231-832-3680

Newaygo Veterinary Service, 9022 Mason Drive, Newaygo / 231-652-1681

Nineteen Mile Veterinary Clinic, 23531 19 Mile Road / 231-796-0323

Pet Hospital, 931 Rose Avenue / 231-796-5493
Pet Hospital of Newaygo, 53 East 82nd Street, Newaygo / 231-652-7387
Pleasant View Animal Clinic, 20200 Arthur Road / 231-796-9432
Reed City Veterinary Service, 141 West Upton Avenue, Reed City / 231-832-5597
Riversbend Animal Hospital, 10565 Northland Drive / 231-796-3507
Stone Hill Veterinary Clinic, 15906 165th Avenue / 231-796-4499

SPORTING GOODS STORES
Dick's Place, 6604 9 Mile Road, Mecosta / 231-972-2942
Ed's Sport Shop, 712 North Michigan Avenue, Baldwin / 231-745-4974
Pere Marquette River Lodge, RR1 Box 1290, Baldwin / 231-745-3972
Frank's Sporting Goods, 165 South Cass Street, Morley / 231-856-7778
Grunst Brothers Party Store, 624 North State Street / 231-796-7253
Jim's Riverside Sports & Sports, 420 North Chestnut Street, Reed City /
   231-832-5433
Maple Street Sports, 711 Maple Street / 231-796-2007
Newaygo Rod 'n' Gun, 8235 Mason Drive, Newaygo / 231-652-1100
Rustic Sport Shop, 519 Ensley Street, Howard City / 231-937-4372

AUTO REPAIR
Abbott's Alignment & Repair, 18475 16 Mile Road / 231-796-5460
Car Clinic, 827 North State Street / 231-592-0893
County Line Service, 23687 West US-10, Reed City / 231-832-5498
East Town Automotive, 904 Colburn Avenue / 231-796-6845
Height's Garage, 10585 Northland Drive / 231-796-1880
Muffler Man, 700 North State Street / 231-796-4881
Quality Car & Truck Repair, 530 West Avenue / 231-796-8320
Randy's Car Care, 227 North Chestnut Street, Reed City / 231-832-9702

AIR SERVICE
Roben-Hood Airport, 1829 North State Street, Big Rapids / 231-796-5600
White Cloud Airport, 127 North Charles Street, White Cloud / 231-689-5891

MEDICAL
Mecosta County General Hospital, 405 Winter Avenue, Big Rapids / 231-796-8691
Reed City Hospital, 7665 220th Avenue, Reed City / 231-832-3271

FOR MORE INFORMATION
Newaygo Chamber of Commerce
8129 Mason Drive
Newaygo, MI 49337
231-652-3068

Newaygo County Tourist Council
4684 Evergreen Drive
Newaygo, MI 49337
231-652-9298

Reed City Chamber of Commerce
780 North Park Street
Reed City, Michigan 49677
231-832-5431

White Cloud Chamber of Commerce
12 North Charles Street
White Cloud, MI 49349
231-689-6607

Clare and Clare County

Population–3,013	October Average Temperature–48°F
County Population–24,952	Elevation–1,156 ft
County Area–567 sq mi	State Land Acres–52,850

Clare County is part of a line of counties that more or less divides the state between the more open agricultural land of the south and the forests of the north. This doesn't limit hunters; in fact, it provides more opportunities. Grouse and woodcock numbers are good in the northern half of the county, while pheasant numbers are fair to good in the south. Turkey hunting is very good in this midsection of the state.

UPLAND BIRDS
Ruffed Grouse, Woodcock, Turkey, Pheasant

WATERFOWL
Ducks, Geese, Snipe

ACCOMMODATIONS
Budget Host Clare Motel, 1110 North McEwan / 517-386-7201 / 33 rooms, cable TV, jacuzzis / Dogs allowed / $-$$$
Doherty Motor Motel, 604 McEwan Street / 517-386-3441 / 92 rooms, pool, restaurant, lounge / Dogs allowed / $$-$$$
Lone Pine Motel, 1508 McEwan Street / 517-386-7787 / 23 rooms, cable TV, kitchenettes, cabins, restaurant nearby / Dogs allowed / $-$$
Holiday Inn Express, 10218 South Clare Avenue / 517-386-1111 / 96 rooms, pool, hot tubs, breakfast bar / No dogs / $$$
Knight's Inn, 1110 North McEwan Street / 517-386-7201 / 33 rooms, jacuzzi / Dogs allowed / $$
Northgate Motel, 3785 East Colonville Road / 517-386-9004 / 32 rooms, restaurants next door / No dogs / $-$$

CAMPGROUNDS AND RV PARKS
Pettit Park, McEwan Street / 517-386-7541 / 25 sites, electricity, water, vault toilets / On the Tobacco River
Herrick County Park, 6320 East Herrick Road / 517-386-2010 / 69 sites, electricity at each site, water
Hidden Hill Family Campground, 300 North Clare Avenue, Harrison / 517-539-9372 / Open year-round, special rates for hunters
Wilson State Park, 910 North First Street, Harrison / 517-539-3021 / 160 sites, water, electricity

RESTAURANTS
Big Boy, 10240 South Clare Avenue / 517-386-4525 / Breakfast, lunch, dinner

Buccilli's Pizza, 1541 North McEwan Street / 517-386-7231

Town & Country, 1395 North McEwan Street / 517-386-7567 / Breakfast, lunch, dinner

Ponderosa Steak House, 10306 South Clare Avenue / 517-386-7017

VETERINARIANS.

Clare Animal Hospital, 11339 North Mission / 517-386-2481

Surrey Veterinary Clinic, 5957 East Surrey Road / 517-386-2595

SPORTING GOODS STORES

General Jim's Surplus, 8810 South Clare Avenue / 517-386-5425

Jay's Sporting Goods, Old US-27 / 517-386-3475 / Guns, ammunition, supplies, licenses

Meijer's, 1015 East Pickard Road, Mt. Pleasant / 517-772-4700

Mill End Store, 501 North McEwan Street / 517-386-2651

AUTO REPAIR

Don's Maxi Muffler Shop & Auto, 215 West 5th Street / 517-386-9385

Fifth Street Auto Service, 215 East 5th Street / 517-386-1100

Gage Olson Tire & Auto Service, 702 North McEwan Street / 517-386-7167

Kidd's Car Clinic, 103 Schoolcrest Avenue / 517-386-7374

Precision Car Care, 7210 South Clare Avenue / 517-386-4271

AIR SERVICE

Clare Municipal Airport, Corner of Eberhart and Washington Road / 517-386-7541

Mt. Pleasant Airport, 5453 East Airport Road / 517-772-2965

MEDICAL

Mid-Michigan Medical Center / 517-386-9951 / Urgent Care, 517-386-9911

FOR MORE INFORMATION

Clare Chamber of Commerce
609 North McEwan Street
Clare, MI 48617
517-386-2442

Clare County Convention and Visitors Bureau
517-386-6400

Gladwin and Gladwin County

Population–2,682	October Average Temperature–49°
County Population–21,896	Elevation–780 ft
County Area–507 sq mi	State Land Acres–86,650

Gladwin County has a little bit of everything for the bird hunter. There are 85,000 acres of public land in the Au Sable State Forest for grouse and woodcock hunters, agricultural land for pheasant, turkey, and goose hunters, and many rivers, lakes, and streams for duck hunters. The Tittabawassee River, divided into several impoundments, winds through the heart of the county. Best bets are for grouse, woodcock, and turkey hunting, all of which are good to very good. Pheasants are available but not abundant.

UPLAND BIRDS
Ruffed Grouse, Woodcock, Turkey, Pheasant

WATERFOWL
Ducks, Geese, Snipe

ACCOMMODATIONS
All Season Inn, 78 East M-61 / 517-426-5600 / 12 units, 2 kitchenettes, cable TV / Dogs allowed / $$
Cedar Avenue Inn, 2519 West M-61 / 517-426-4534 / 40 rooms, jacuzzis, cable TV, restaurant, lounge / Dogs allowed / $$-$$$
Gladwin Motor Inn, 1003 West Cedar Avenue / 517-426-9661 / 16 rooms, cable TV / Dogs allowed / $-$$
Northwoods Motel, 5800 North M-30 / 517-426-4021 / 15 rooms, refrigerators, restaurant and lounge next door / Dogs allowed / $$
White Star Motel, 100 North M-30 / 517-426-8940 / 10 rooms, cable TV, refrigerators / Dogs allowed / $-$$

CAMPGROUNDS AND RV PARKS
Calhoun Park & Campground, Roehrs Road, Beaverton / 517-435-2100 or 435-9343 / On Ross Lake / 39 sites, electricity, showers
Gladwin City Park, M-18 / 517-426-8126 / 60 sites with electricity, showers
Lost Arrow Resort, 1749 Bomanville Road / 517-345-7774 / Cabins and 20 campsites with electricity, restaurant, lounge, hunting packages
Whiskey Beach Campground, 636 East Highwood / 517-426-4371 / 42 sites with electricity

RESTAURANTS
Hunters Grill & Bar, 2519 West M-61 / 517-426-4536 / At Cedar Avenue Inn
Northern Expresso, 343 West Cedar / 517-426-3386 / Gourmet coffee, bagels, muffins

The Ranch House, 3511 South M-30, Beaverton / 517-435-3214 / Open at 6AM, 7 days per week

Sawmill Restaurant, 350 East M-61 / 517-426-9179 / Open daily at 7AM

Sugar Springs Restaurant, 1930 Sugar River Road / 517-426-9203 / Breakfast, lunch, dinner

VETERINARIANS

Gladwin Veterinary Clinic, 4196 West M-61 / 517-426-6566

SPORTING GOODS STORES

Ace Hardware, 630 North Silverleaf / 517-426-4549 / Hunting licenses, supplies

BLF Sports, 1289 West M-61 / 517-426-4880 / Firearms, ammunition

Mill End, 113 West Cedar Ave / 517-426-7172 / Hunting clothing

Whiskey Beach Bait & Party Store, 1636 East Highwood Road, Beaverton / 517-435-4371

AUTO REPAIR

Auto Tech, 431 South Ross Street, Beaverton / 517-435-9500

Myers for Tires, 801 East Cedar Avenue / 517-426-4261

Wykoff's Auto Repair, M-18 / 517-426-5004 / Between Gladwin and Beaverton

AIR SERVICE

Gladwin Zettel Airport, 517-426-4201

MEDICAL

Mid-Michigan Medical Center, 415 Quarter Street / 517-426-9286

FOR MORE INFORMATION

Gladwin County Chamber of Commerce
608 West Cedar Avenue
Gladwin, MI 48624
517-426-5451

Mt. Pleasant and Isabella / Midland Counties

Population–23,285	October Average Temperature–51°F
County Population:	Elevation–796 ft
Isabella–54,624	Isabella State Land Acres–2,700
Midland–75,651	Midland State Land Acres–42,800
County Area:	
Isabella–574 sq mi	
Midland–521 sq mi	

What Isabella County lacks in public land is made up in opportunities for hunters. Acres of flooded bottomland provide excellent habitat for wood ducks and mallards. Agricultural land in the area is home to an excellent population of pheasants, turkeys, and Canada geese. Midland County has more public land, with thousands of acres of Au Sable State Forest available to hunters. While grouse and woodcock numbers are slightly better in Midland County, pheasant numbers are better in Isabella. Hunting for all species is good to very good in both counties.

Note: The line that divides Michigan's hunting Regions 2 and 3 runs through Isabella and Midland Counties. This can mean that a season is open in one part of the county and closed in another. Be sure to consult the *Michigan Hunting and Trapping Guide*.

UPLAND BIRDS
Ruffed Grouse, Woodcock, Turkey, Pheasant

WATERFOWL
Ducks, Geese, Snipe

ACCOMMODATIONS
Budgetel Inn, 5858 East Pickard / 517-775-5555 / 103 rooms, continental breakfast, pool, close to casino / $$-$$$

Chippewa Motel, 5662 East Pickard / 517-772-1751 / 29 rooms, cable TV, near casino / $-$$

Comfort Inn, 2424 South Mission / 517-772-4000 / 138 rooms, 40 with whirlpools, continental breakfast, lounge, restaurant next door / Dogs allowed / $$-$$$

Fairview Inn, 2200 West Wackerly Street, Midland / 517-631-0070 / 102 rooms, cable TV, pool, restaurant / Dogs allowed / $$-$$$

Holiday Inn, 5665 East Pickard / 517-772-2905 / 184 rooms, kitchenettes, pool, restaurant, lounge / Dogs allowed / $$-$$$

Sleep Inn, 2100 West Wackerly Street, Midland / 517-837-1010 / 82 rooms, cable TV, pool, continental breakfast / Dogs allowed / $$-$$$

CAMPGROUNDS AND RV PARKS
The Flats Condominium Campground, Sanford / 190 sites, electricity
Herrick Recreation Area, 200 North Main Street / 517-386-2010 / 73 sites,
    5 cabins, showers, boat launch
Shardi's Hideaway, 340 North Loomis Road / 517-773-4268 / 102 sites, showers
Valley Plaza RV Park, 5217 Bay City Road, Midland / 517-496-9333

RESTAURANTS
Bennigan's, 2424 South Mission / 517-773-4817
Big Boy Restaurant, 6023 South Mission / 517-772-2476
Corky's Steak House, 5100 Bay City Road, Midland / 517-496-0096
Great North Trading Company, 520 North Mission / 517-773-8030
Pickard Street Grill, 5665 East Pickard / 517-775-3247 / In the Holiday Inn

VETERINARIANS
Animal Clinic, 1500 East Patrick Road, Midland / 517-631-0220
Animal Health Associates, 2039 East Pickard Road / 517-773-3434 / 24-hour
    emergency service
Animal Hospital, 2060 East Remus Road / 517-772-5978
Coleman Veterinary Clinic, 802 East Adams Street, Coleman / 517-465-1127
Eastman Animal Clinic, 5910 Eastman Avenue, Midland / 517-631-5550
Mid-Michigan Veterinary, 2887 Oakhaven Court, Midland / 517-631-2790
Mt. Pleasant Animal Hospital, 1929 South Isabella Road / 517-773-7679

SPORTING GOODS STORES
Ace Hardware, 419 East Main Street Midland / 517-832-8829
Dunham's Sporting Goods, 2129 South Mission Street / 517-772-5464
Hank's Sporting Goods, 35 West Remus Road / 517-773-2776
Jay's Sporting Goods, 8800 South Clare Avenue, Clare / 517-386-3475
Meijer's, 1015 East Pickard Road / 517-772-4700
Meridian Hardware & Sports, 3102 North Meridian Road, Sanford / 517-687-5342
Schafer's Bait & Sporting Goods, 3222 North Woodruff Road, Weidman /
    517-644-3501

AUTO REPAIR
ASAP 24 Hour Towing & Recovery, 825 East Superior Street, Alma / 517-772-7792
Auto-Lab Diagnostic & Tune-Up Center, 402 North Mission Street / 517-772-1720
Souders Service Center, 1035 South Mission / 517-773-5427
T & M Auto Clinic, 2198 South Nottawa Road / 517-773-0029 / 24-hour towing

AIR SERVICE
Mt. Pleasant Airport, 5453 East Airport Road / 517-772-2965
Midland City Airport, 2800 Airport Road, Midland / 517-835-3231

MEDICAL
Central Michigan Community Hospital, 1221 South Drive / 517-772-6700

*Dave Mammel
of Midland with a
limit of roosters.*

Mid-Michigan Medical Center, 4005 Orchard Drive, Midland / 517-839-3000 /
    Ambulance, 517-839-3686
Mid-Michigan Urgent Care, 905 East Pickard / 517-772-9300
ReadyCare, 2124 South Mission / 517-773-1166

FOR MORE INFORMATION
Mt. Pleasant Area Convention & Visitors Bureau
114 East Broadway
Mt. Pleasant, MI 48858
517-772-4433
www.mt-pleasant.net

Midland Chamber of Commerce
300 Rodd Street #101
Midland, Michigan
517-839-9901

Standish and Arenac / Bay Counties

Population–1,377	October Average Temperature–49°F
County Population:	Elevation–645 ft
Arenac–14,931	Arenac State Land Acres–30,600
Bay–111,723	Bay State Land Acres–4,800
County Area	
Arenac–367 sq mi	
Bay–444 sq mi	

Waterfowlers will be particularly interested in this neck of the woods. Arenac and Bay Counties border the west end of Saginaw Bay, a hot spot for generations of duck and goose hunters. Several state game areas and wildlife areas provide opportunities for waterfowlers, including Wigwam Bay near Standish, Nayanquing Point State Wildlife Area near Linwood, and Tobico Marsh and Quanicassee State Game Areas northwest and southeast of Bay City. Farther inland is the Crow Island State Game Area on the Bay-Saginaw County border. The best bet for grouse and woodcock is along the western edge of Bay County, although there isn't a great deal of public land. Pheasant hunting is good to very good in Bay County. We chose Standish as a hub city for this area, but hunters who prefer a bigger city might look into staying at Bay City.

Note: The line that divides Michigan's hunting Regions 2 and 3 runs through Arenac and Bay Counties. This can mean that a season is open in one part of the county and closed in another. Be sure to consult the *Michigan Hunting and Trapping Guide.* In addition, the waterfowl zones differ from the general hunting and fishing zones. Nearly all of Saginaw Bay is included in the southern waterfowl zone. The *Michigan Waterfowl Hunting Guide* gives precise boundaries.

UPLAND BIRDS
Ruffed Grouse, Woodcock, Turkey, Pheasant

WATERFOWL
Ducks, Geese, Snipe

ACCOMMODATIONS
Best Western Pinewood Inn, 510 West Huron, Au Gres / 517-876-4060 / Jacuzzi suites, pool / Dogs allowed / $$$

In Town Inn, 304 North Main Street / 517-846-6247 / 10 rooms, cable TV / No dogs / $-$$

Minard's Hammell Beach Motel & Cottages, 194 North Huron, Au Gres / 517-876-8154 / Kitchen facilities, cable TV / Dogs allowed / $$-$$$

Standish Motel, 525 North Forest / 16 rooms, cable TV / Dogs allowed / $-$$

Campgrounds and RV Parks

Au Gres City Campground, 522 Park Street, Au Gres / 517-876-8310 / 87 sites, water, electricity, boat ramp

Bay City State Park, State Park Road, Bay City / 517-684-3020 / 263 sites / 5 miles north of Bay City on Saginaw Bay and adjacent to Tobico Marsh State Game Area

Big Bend Campground, 513 Conrad / 517-653-2267

Restaurants

A & W Family Restaurant, 302 South Main Street / 517-846-6390

H & H Bakery and Restaurant, 604 East Huron Road, Au Gres / 517-876-7144 / Open at 6:30AM daily, breakfast all day

Subway, 201 South Main Street / 517-846-0219

Wheeler's Restaurant, US-23 / 517-846-6425 / Breakfast, lunch, dinner, beer and wine

White's Beach Tavern & Grocery, 5327 Shady Layne / 517-846-4001 / Friday fish fry

Veterinarians

Abba-Ark Animal Clinics, 5890 North Huron Road, Pinconning / 517-879-2223

Bangor Veterinary Clinic, 3917 North Euclid Avenue, Bay City / 517-686-0802

Linwood Veterinary Clinic, 201 East Center Street, Linwood / 517-697-5248

Tri-City Animal Hospital, 1699 Midland Road, Bay City / 517-684-2625

Vetsmart, 3764 Wilder Road, Bay City / 517-684-4877

Sporting Goods Stores

4-Seasons Bait & Party Store, 427 West Huron Road, Au Gres / 517-876-8801

Dunham's Discount Sports, 4101 Wilder Road, Bay City / 517-667-4100

Frank's Great Outdoors, 1212 North M-13, Linwood / 517-697-5341

Stevens Hunting Supplies, 3876 State Street, Bay City / 517-684-0310

Auto Repair

Au-Tech Automotive Repair, 2101 East Huron Road, Au Gres / 517-876-7736

CarQuest Au Gres Parts & Service, 436 West Huron Road, Au Gres / 517-846-4571

Jim's Repair Service, 3216 Senske Road / 517-846-6909

Philips Auto Repair, 402 South Main Street / 517-846-4241

Air Service

Bay City Airport, 614 River Road, Bay City / 517-895-8991

Gladwin Zettel Airport, 517-426-4201

Midland City Airport, 2800 Airport Road, Midland / 517-835-3231

Medical

Au Gres Medical Clinic, 3210 North Huron Road, Au Gres / 517-876-6080

Bay Medical Center, 1900 Columbus Avenue, Bay City / 517-894-3000

Standish Community Hospital, 805 West Cedar / 517-846-4888

FOR MORE INFORMATION

Arenac Area Chamber of Commerce
263 South Main Street
AuGres, MI 48703
517-876-6688

Standish Area Chamber of Commerce
3233 Grove Road
Standish, MI 48658
517-846-7867

Bay Area Convention and Visitors Bureau
901 Saginaw Street
Bay City, MI 48707
517-893-4567
www.baycityarea.com

John Slack and Zack with pheasant. (Photo by Chris Zimmerman)

Hunting Guides, Outfitters and Preserves

REGION 2

Baldwin Creek Guide Service
Rte. 3, Box 3282
Baldwin, MI 49304
231-745-4410
Ruffed grouse, woodcock, waterfowl

Big Creek Shooting Preserve
P.O. Box 369/269 Zimowske Road
Mio, MI 48647
517-826-3606
Chukars, ruffed grouse, turkey,
    waterfowl, woodcock.

Johnson's Pere Marquette Lodge
M-37, Rt. 1, Box 1290
Baldwin, MI 49304
231-745-3972
www.pmlodge.com
Ruffed grouse, woodcock

Thundering Aspens
4421 North 5½ Mile Road
Mesick, MI 49668
231-885-2420
Chukars, huns, ducks, pheasant, quail,
    ruffed grouse

Wild Wings Game Farm
P.O. Box 1232
Gaylord, MI 49735
616-584-3350
Chukars, huns, pheasant

Wycamp Lake Club
5484 Pleasantview Road
Harbor Springs, MI 49740
231-537-4830
Chukars, ducks, geese, ruffed grouse,
    pheasant, quail, woodcock

Coiled and ready to spring, Chris Zimmerman's Brittanys nail a "reflushed" grouse. (Photo by Chris Zimmerman)

Combined Hunts

One of the great aspects of bird hunting in Michigan is the opportunity to have chances at bagging more than one species of bird in a day's hunt. My partners and I have shot at sharp-tailed grouse that flew over our duck and goose blinds, and we've bagged woodcock and ruffed grouse while stumbling into hidden beaver ponds for ducks, but that's not the kind of combined hunt I'm talking about.

With a little planning, it's quite easy to pursue a variety of species in the same day, whether ducks on a Great Lakes coastal marsh in the morning and woodcock during the afternoon in a nearby aspen forest, or geese in a cut cornfield in the morning and pheasants later in the day, in or near some of the same fields in which you found the geese.

Farther north, especially in the Upper Peninsula, there can be more opportunities for these types of combined hunts than in the south, simply because there are larger tracts of public land available to hunters. However, an industrious hunter can find combined hunt possibilities throughout the state. In fact, no matter where you hunt, it's always a good idea to have waders, upland hunting boots, decoys, birdshot, waterfowl loads, and a variety of other trappings to be sure you're ready for anything.

Years ago, my college roommate and I used to go after deer with our bows in the morning, break for lunch, then pursue grouse and woodcock in the afternoon before exchanging our shotguns for bows again in the evening. There's no reason why you couldn't do the same thing for waterfowl and upland birds, or even turkeys for that matter. With this guide and a county map book to get you started, line up some likely spots and go to it.

Duke brings a mallard to hand. (Photo by Chris Zimmerman)

Region 3

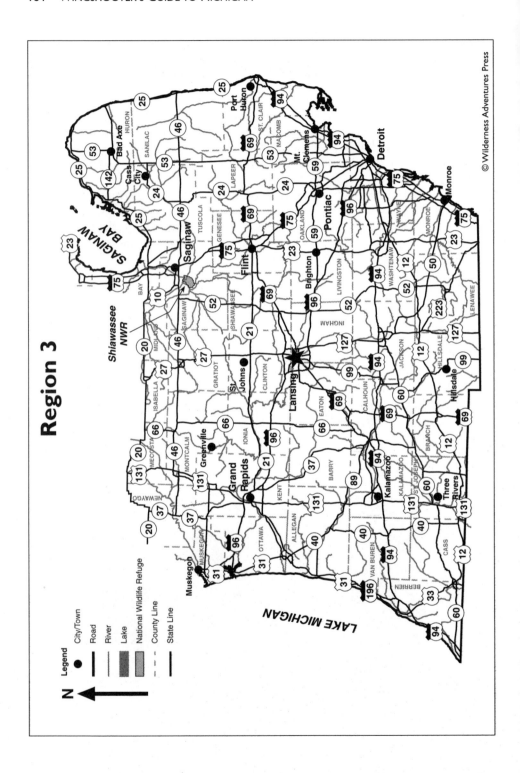

Legend
- City/Town
- Road
- River
- Lake
- National Wildlife Refuge
- County Line
- State Line

Region 3

Michigan's southern Lower Peninsula is home to most of the state's human population. It also holds the most pheasants and offers some of the best waterfowl hunting in the Midwest. It is the only part of the state that offers a bobwhite quail season when the population warrants it.

What Region 3 lacks in state and national forest lands it more than makes up for with a variety of state game areas, state parks, and state recreation areas. Many of the state parks and most of the state recreation areas have acreage open to hunting.

In general, the southern Lower Peninsula does not experience the harsh winters that settle into the northern reaches of the state. Consequently, wildlife flourishes here. Ruffed grouse are available in Region 3, and in many places are abundant, but they can survive just as well in the north, where they burrow into snowdrifts at night to survive the cold and pull aspen buds from tree-tops when the snow is deep. Birds like pheasants and turkeys are "scratchers," relying more on foods that are available on the ground. These birds are more suited for southern Michigan. The turkey population is exploding in southern Michigan, and hunting permits are available in all but two counties, Wayne and Monroe. This will likely change soon, as turkeys were being transplanted in Monroe County as this book was being written.

While many of the state game areas provide good pheasant and turkey hunting, the best places are on private land. The Michigan Department of Natural Resources leases more than 55,000 acres of private land in Region 3 and makes it available to hunters through the Hunting Access Program. You can get a list of the acreage, terrain, and location in a free publication, *Public Hunting on Private Lands*. It's available from DNR field offices, license dealers, Farm Bureau offices, and other places around the state. Another helpful tool for contacting landowners is a county plat book. If you know the county you will be hunting, you can pick up a plat book at the county register of deeds office.

Meanwhile, listed below are some of the state lands that are worth exploring. It is not a complete list, and local opinion varies tremendously over which state game area or recreation area is the best for a particular species in a particular region.

Allegan State Game Area covers a significant portion of Allegan County and is known for its waterfowl hunting, but it also holds some grouse, woodcock, pheasants, and turkey.

Located in Ingham County, Dansville State Game Area is 4700 acres and has some good grouse habitat.

*Gerry Pink with a mallard fetched by Duke during a late season
hunt on Lake St. Clair.*

Deford State Game Area, located in Tuscola County in Michigan's Thumb, is managed for ruffed grouse as well as other small game and holds a good turkey population, as well. Tuscola County is home to several state game areas, including Vassar State Game Area, Murphy Lake State Game Area, Cass City State Game Area, Gagetown State Game Area, and Tuscola State Game Area, along with Fish Point and Quanicassee State Wildlife Areas, which are popular with waterfowl hunters.

Flat River State Game Area has grouse and woodcock available in Ionia and Montcalm Counties.

Fulton State Game Area holds good numbers of pheasants, as does Gourdneck State Game Area, also in Kalamazoo County. Gourdneck also has good habitat for grouse.

Located in Livingston County, Gregory State Game Area is known for its duck hunting, especially in the eastern unit. Other Livingston County public lands include Oak Grove State Game Area, 2000 acres that hold some grouse and waterfowl, and Brighton, Island Lake, and Pinckney State Recreation Areas, which have hunting lands available.

Lake Hudson Recreation Area has waterfowl hunting available on Lake Hudson, and some crops are grown in the area's 4000 acres, making for good pheasant hunting. When bobwhite quail are open, hunters may find some here, too. This recreation area is located in Lenawee County.

Michigan jake out for a stroll. (Photo by Chris Zimmerman)

Lapeer State Game Area has good duck and turkey hunting, along with pockets of grouse and woodcock. Hunters will find good woodcock hunting throughout Region 3, but the hunting can be tremendous in October if you hit the migration.

Lost Nation State Game Area is another area that is popular among pheasant and turkey hunters. It is located in Hillsdale County.

Muskegon State Game Area is comprised of 14,000 acres along the Muskegon River in Muskegon and Newaygo Counties and is interspersed with several other smaller rivers and creeks, making excellent habitat for waterfowl. You'll do best with a small boat or canoe here. Muskegon County also holds large tracts of Manistee National Forest in the north, where there is waterfowl, grouse, woodcock, and turkey hunting.

Petersburg State Game Area, while only 524 acres in size, is the only public land in Monroe County besides the state game areas on the Lake Erie shore that are so popular with waterfowl hunters. Petersburg also has some good pheasant habitat, and watch for woodcock during the migration.

In St. Clair County, Port Huron State Game Area provides 7,000 acres along the Black River and holds some pheasant, grouse, and waterfowl habitat and a growing population of turkeys. Look for woodcock during the migration here, as well.

Shiawassee River State Game Area and nearby Shiawassee National Wildlife Refuge are well known for their waterfowl hunting. Other Saginaw County public

Howard Meyerson of Grand Rapids takes a break with Chip and Zack.
(Photo by Chris Zimmerman)

hunting lands include Gratiot-Saginaw State Game Area and Crow Island State Game Area on the Saginaw River, which are very popular with waterfowlers.

When it comes to waterfowling in Region 3, there is no shortage of public places to hunt, and some of these areas are unparalleled by any other popular waterfowl hunting areas in the state, if not the Midwest. Tens of thousands of migrating ducks and geese stop to rest, feed, and congregate each year in southern Lake Huron, Lake St. Clair, and Lake Erie. Hunters will find an abundance of coastal marsh open to the public. Canada goose hunters will be particularly interested in Goose Management Units, such as Allegan County Goose Management Unit that includes Allegan State Game Area; Saginaw County Goose Management Unit, which includes Shiawassee River State Game Area and Shiawassee National Wildlife Refuge; Tuscola/Huron Goose Management Unit (includes Fish Point Wildlife Area); and Muskegon Wastewater Goose Management Unit, adjacent to Muskegon State Game Area.

Other waterfowling areas that deserve special mention include:

Saginaw Bay: Most of this large Lake Huron bay is included in the state's southern waterfowl zone. Its shoreline is lined with state game areas, state wildlife areas, public access sites, and coastal marshes that are available to duck and goose hunters. State holdings include Wigwam Bay Wildlife Area, Nayanquing Point State Wildlife Area, Tobico Marsh State Game Area, Quanicassee State Wildlife Area, Fish Point State Wildlife Area, and Wildfowl Bay State Wildlife Area.

Even though it is closer to bigger cities, including Detroit, Lake St. Clair is not short on opportunity. Marsh hunters will find plenty of places to hunt in and around the extensive St. Clair Flats Wildlife Area in Anchor Bay. Waterfowlers who go after divers with layout rigs hunt throughout the lake and in the Detroit and St. Clair Rivers.

The west end of Lake Erie and the mouth of the Detroit River are steeped in decades of waterfowling tradition. Pointe Mouillee State Game Area, on the border of Wayne and Monroe Counties, is very popular with duck hunters. Erie State Game Area provides extensive marshes for waterfowlers on the north side of Maumee Bay, and Sterling State Park on the shores of Brest Bay is also open to waterfowlers.

Note: Special rules exist in some parts of the goose management units and in some parts of the above-mentioned wildlife areas and state game areas, where there are daily lotteries for hunters who intend to hunt within the boundaries. The details are available in the *Michigan Waterfowl Hunting Guide*. In most cases, a refuge is set aside with an adjacent hunting area that is available by permit. The remaining acreage is open to public hunting.

Depending on the time of year, wildlife movements, and day of the week, some Region 3 public lands can be crowded. Often, hunters can find more remote areas simply by walking in farther than the next guy. Many hunters do not venture far from roads. If you do, chances are good that you'll find some public places that haven't seen too much hunting activity.

Hunters are also advised to approach landowners about getting permission to hunt their property. Some landowners and farmers welcome hunters, especially if ducks, geese, or turkeys are helping themselves to the farmers' crops.

Another advantage to hunting in Region 3 is the ability to find places to stay, places to eat, places to pick up sporting goods, or repair your firearms. The larger population areas simply have more businesses such as these available to the traveling hunter.

Ruffed Grouse

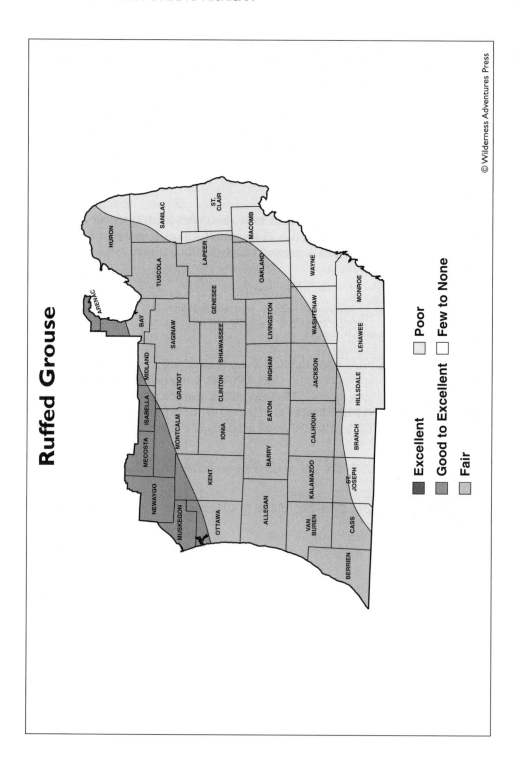

Excellent

Good to Excellent

Fair

Poor

Few to None

American Woodcock

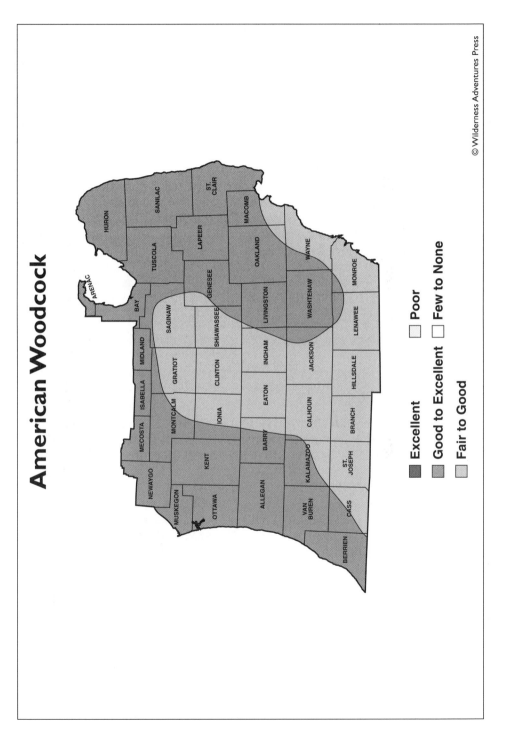

Excellent

Good to Excellent

Fair to Good

Poor

Few to None

Ring-necked Pheasant

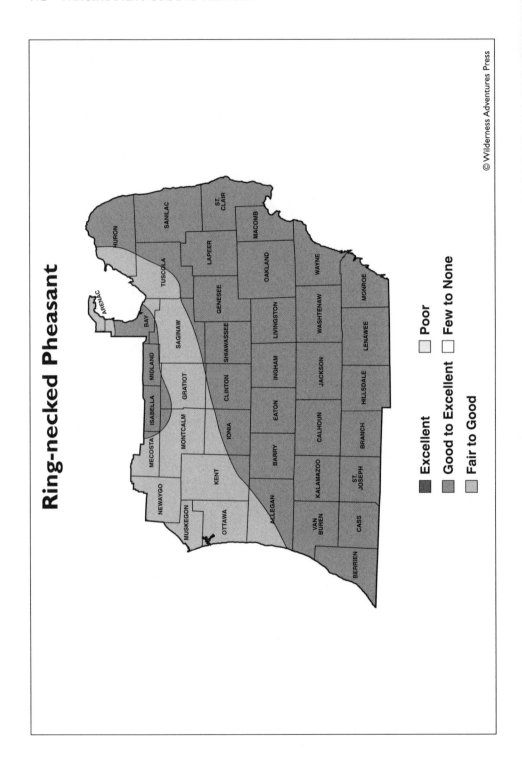

© Wilderness Adventures Press

Excellent

Good to Excellent

Fair to Good

Poor

Few to None

Wild Turkey

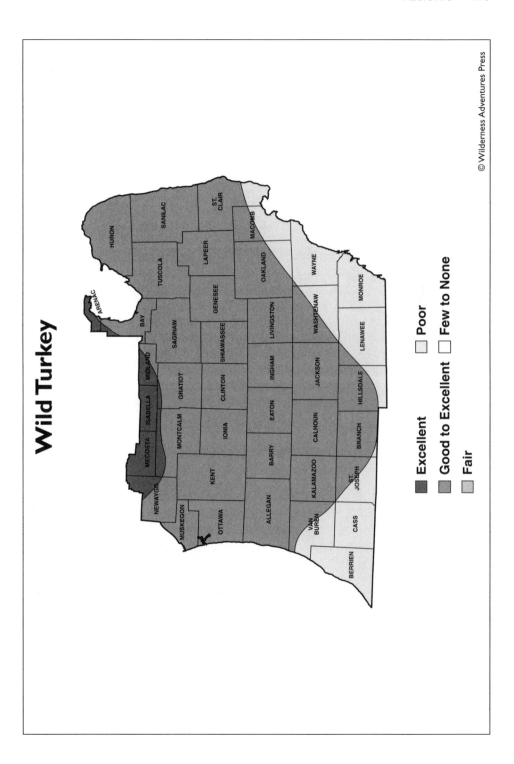

Excellent

Good to Excellent

Fair

Poor

Few to None

Northern Bobwhite

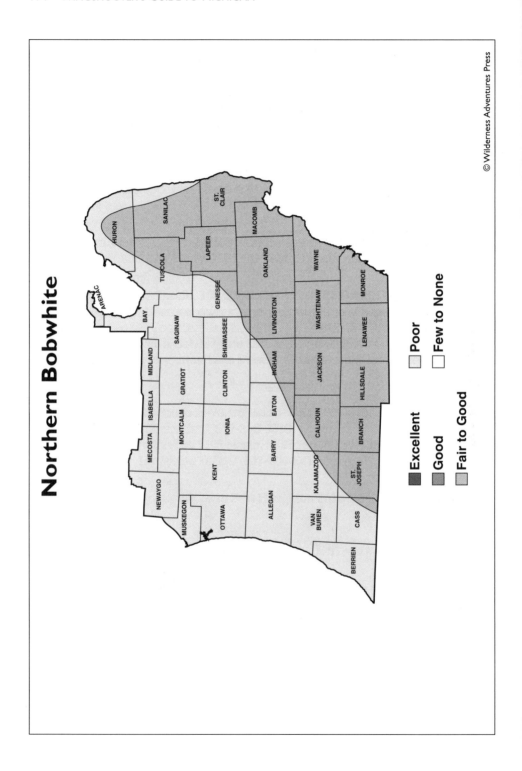

Excellent

Good

Fair to Good

Poor

Few to None

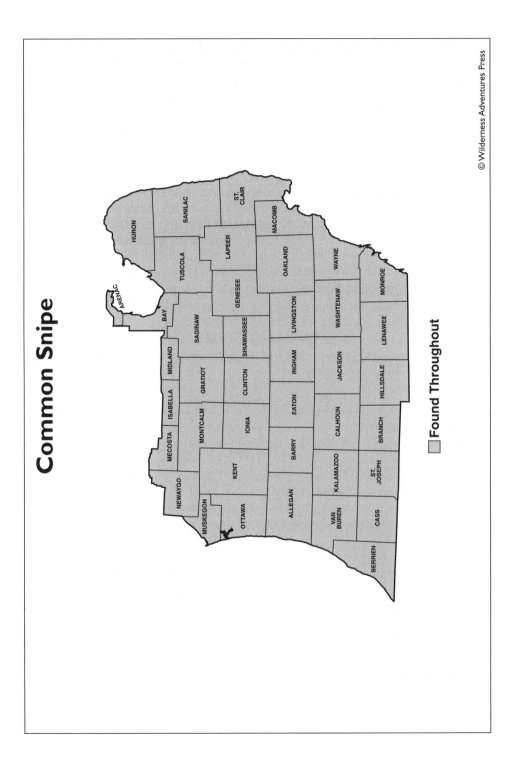

Common Snipe

Found Throughout

Muskegon and Muskegon / Ottawa Counties

Population–40,283	October Average Temperature–51°F
County Population:	Elevation–600 to 900 ft
Muskegon–158,983	Public Land by County (Acres):
Ottawa–187,768	Muskegon–State 12,900 / Federal 12,500
County Area:	Ottawa–State 3,200
Muskegon–510 sq mi	
Ottawa–565 sq mi	

This area bordering Lake Michigan has much to offer the outdoorsman. Many acres of Manistee National Forest stretch across northern Muskegon County. Two state game areas—Grand Haven SGA in Ottawa County and the extensive Muskegon SGA—border large river systems, providing many opportunities for waterfowlers. Grouse and woodcock hunting are fair, while turkey and pheasant hunting in the region are fair to good. Bring along your fishing rod. There are many rivers that offer trout and salmon fishing, and Muskegon is a major port for Lake Michigan salmon charters.

UPLAND BIRDS
Ruffed Grouse, Woodcock, Turkey, Pheasant

WATERFOWL
Ducks, Geese, Snipe

ACCOMMODATIONS
Bear's Den Motel, 2165 Whitehall Road, North Muskegon / 231-744-3835 / Cable TV / Dogs allowed / $-$$
Bel-Aire Motel, 4240 Airline Road / 231-733-2196 / 17 rooms, cable TV, 2-3 bedroom units / Dogs allowed / $$
Holiday Inn, 939 Third Street / 231-722-0100 / 200 rooms, cable TV, restaurant, lounge, pool, sauna / No dogs / $$$
Lakeland Motel, 1002 East Colby Road, Whitehall / 231-894-5644 / 12 rooms, cable TV / Dogs allowed / $
Montgomery Inn, 10233 US-31, Montague / 616-894-4339 / 8 rooms, cable TV / Dogs allowed / $$
Motel Haven, 4344 Airline Road / 616-733-1256 / 19 rooms, cable TV, packages available / Dogs allowed / $$
Seaway Motel, 631 West Norton / 616-733-1220 / 29 rooms, cable TV / Small dogs allowed / $$

CAMPGROUNDS AND RV PARKS
Grand Haven State Park, Harbor Avenue, Grand Haven / 616-842-6020 / 170 sites, pier fishing
Holland State Park, Holland / 616-399-9390 / On Lake Michigan; 368 sites

Muskegon State Park, on Scenic Drive between Muskegon Lake and Lake Michigan / 231-744-3480 / 348 sites

P.J. Hoffmaster State Park, on Muskegon/Ottawa County Line / 231-798-3711 / 333 sites

RESTAURANTS

Bill-Mar Restaurant, 1223 Harbor, Grand Haven / 616-842-5920 / Lunch, dinner, cocktails

Clover Bar & Restaurant, 601 South Beechtree, Grand Haven / 616-846-3580 / Pizza, subs, drinks

Dog House Saloon, 1940 East Laketon / 231-777-3888 / Mon–Sat., 7AM–2AM

The Hearthstone, 3350 Glade / 231-733-1056 / Sandwiches, pasta / Cocktails

House of Chan, 375 Gin Chan Avenue / 231-733-9624 / Chinese and American buffet

Tony's Fine Food & Spirits, Broadway at Henry / 231-739-7196 / Lunch and dinner, cocktails

VETERINARIANS

Animal Clinics of Muskegon, 2007 East Apple Avenue / 231-773-3281 / After hours, call 616-737-2649

Lakeshore Animal Hospital, 896 West Laketon Avenue / 231-759-7387 / After hours, 231-737-3865

Northside Veterinary Hospital, 1416 West Giles Road / 231-744-1787 / After hours, 231-737-4197

Norton Shores Veterinary Clinic, 5216 Grand Haven Road / 231-798-3664 / After hours, 231-737-4199

Robbins Road Animal Clinic, 1000 Robbins Road, Grand Haven / 616-842-7610

SPORTING GOODS STORES

Barnes Hardware, 7170 East Apple Avenue / 231-788-4474

Dunhams Discount Sports, 5313 Harvey Street / 231-798-8255

Felix's Marina & Guns, 14023 Green Street Grand Haven / 616-842-3680

J. Fricano Gunsmith, 15258 Moreland Avenue, Grand Haven / 616-846-4458

Jones Sporting Goods, 699 West Clay Avenue / 231-726-3234

Northwest Shooter's Supply, 4786 Holton Road, Twin Lake / 231-828-6894

Parkside Motel & Sport Shop, 3492 Memorial Drive / 231-744-3440

Riverside Sports Shop, 3473 Maple Island Road, Twin Lake / 231-821-2779

Gander Mountain, Inc., 2890 Acquest Avenue SE, Grand Rapids / 616-975-1000

Meijer's, 4411 Plainfield Avenue, Grand Rapids / 616-361-4398
   2425 Alpine Avenue NW, Grand Rapids / 616-365-6001

Great Lakes Fly Fishing Co., 2775 10 Mile Road, Rockford / 616-866-6060

AUTO REPAIR

Campbell's Automotive & 24-hour Towing, 796 Apple Avenue / 231-722-2796

Dan Cooper Auto Center, 2221 Henry / 231-755-1656 / Domestic and imports

Harold's North Shore Service, 2801 Celery Lane / 231-744-0469

Muskegon Brake, 848 East Broadway Ave / 231-733-0874 / Cars and trucks; foreign and domestic

Thrifty Tire & Wheel, 25 West Apple Avenue / 231-722-6041 / Complete auto and light truck service

AIR SERVICE

Muskegon County Airport, 99 Sinclair Drive / 231-798-4596

Park Township Airport, 1269 Ottawa Beach Road, Holland / 616-399-9333

MEDICAL

Hackley Hospital, 1700 Clinton Street / 231-726-3511

Intensive Hospital of Muskegon, 1700 Clinton Street / 231-728-5800

Mercy Hospital, 1500 East Sherman Boulevard / 231-739-9341

Muskegon General Hospital, 1700 Oak Avenue / 231-773-3311

North Ottawa Community Hospital, 1309 Sheldon Road, Grand Haven / 616-842-3600

FOR MORE INFORMATION

Muskegon County Convention
and Visitors Bureau
610 West Western Avenue
Muskegon, MI 49440
1-800-250 WAVE (9283)
www.visitmuskegon.org

White Lake Chamber of Commerce
124 West Hanston Street
Whitehall, MI 49461
231-893-4585
222.WhiteLake.org

Duck hunters love Michigan. A canvasback, wigeon, mallard, and gadwall are shown here.

Greenville and Montcalm, Kent, and Ionia Counties

Population–8,274 County Population: Montcalm–53,059 Kent–500,621 Ionia–57,024 County Area: Montcalm–708 sq mi Kent–856 sq mi Ionia–573 sq mi	October Average Tempreature–51°F Elevation–600 to 900 ft Montcalm State Land Acres–22,600 Kent State Land Acres–8,700 Iona State Land Acres–11,000

What the southern counties of Michigan lack in extensive state and national forests they make up for in state game areas and state recreation areas. Greenville puts you right in the middle of several SGAs, including Flat River, Rogue River, Cannonsburg, Langston, Edmore, Stanton, Vestaburg, Portland, and Lowell, plus Ionia State Recreation Area. Hunt weekdays and far from roads to find less crowded areas. The northwest corner of Montcalm County has holdings of Manistee National Forest. Grouse and woodcock hunting are fair; pheasant hunting is better. And, as it is in most of southern Michigan, the area's turkey flock is increasing. If you are looking for a bigger place to stay, you might want to consider Grand Rapids (Kent County), a city of 189,000.

UPLAND BIRDS
Ruffed Grouse, Woodcock, Turkey, Pheasant

WATERFOWL
Ducks, Geese, Snipe

ACCOMMODATIONS
Candlestone Inn, 8100 North Storey Road, Belding / 616-794-1580 / 25 rooms, cable TV / Restaurant and lounge / No dogs / $$
Edmore Inn, 1260 East Main, Edmore / 517-427-5163 / 24 rooms, cable TV, microwave, refrigerators / No dogs / $$
Greenville Motor Inn, 1104 West Washington Street / 616-754-3668 / 35 rooms, cable TV / No dogs / $$
Parker's Half Moon Motel, 3094 South Sheridan Road, Sheridan / 517-831-4708 / 16 rooms, cable TV / Dogs allowed / $$-$$$
Tour-In Motel, 601 South Ensley, Howard City / 231-937-4444 / 12 rooms, cable TV / Restaurant next door / Dogs allowed / $
Westwood Inn, 109 Greenville West Drive / 616-754-8734 / 20 rooms, cable TV, jacuzzi suites, in-room coffee / No dogs / $$

Winter Inn, 100 North Lafayette Street / 616-754-3132 / 13 rooms, cable TV, continental breakfast / Restaurant and lounge / No dogs / $$

CAMPGROUNDS AND RV PARKS
Lincoln Pines Resort, 13033 19 Mile Road, Gowen / 616-984-2100 / 384 sites, store / On Lincoln Lake
Snow Lake Kampground, 644 East Snows Lake Road, Fenwick / 517-248-3224 / 200 sites, electricity, water, showers, laundry facilities
Three Seasons RV Park, 6956 West Fuller Road / 616-754-5717

RESTAURANTS
Blue Lake Inn, 12587 Maston Lake Drive, Sand Lake / 616-984-5100 / Breakfast, lunch, dinner; cocktails
The Halfway Restaurant, 10792 M-57 / 616-754-9084 / Breakfast, lunch, dinner / Open at 6AM daily, 7AM on Sunday
Hi-Delite Country Restaurant, 500 North Lafayette / 616-754-8249 / Breakfast, lunch, dinner / Open at 5:30AM daily; 8AM on Sunday
Village Hearth, 135 North Bridge, Belding / 616-794-3150 / Lunch and dinner / American and Mexican, seafood, prime rib; cocktails

VETERINARIANS
Belding Veterinary Hospital, 6899 Belding Road, Belding / 616-794-1260
Lakeview Animal Clinic, 102 2nd Street, Lakeview / 517-352-6684
Orchard View Veterinary Clinic, 5785 South Greenville Road / 616-754-9633
994 North M-60, Stanton / 517-831-5287

SPORTING GOODS STORES
Gander Mountain, 2890 Acquest Avenue SE, Grand Rapids / 616-975-1000
Orvis Thornapple Shop, 1200 East Paris Avenue SE #4, Grand Rapids / 616-975-3800
Great Lakes Fly Fishing Co., 2775 10 Mile Road NE, Rockford / 616-866-6060
Bert's Surplus, 10 Burton SW, Grand Rapids / 616-241-3664
Hilltop Sports, 13700 West M-57 / Guns, gear, ammunition, licenses / Open at 6AM every day
Kmart, 205 South Greenville West Drive / 616-754-1800
Off-Center Ltd., 350 Covered Village, Belding / 616-794-4000

AUTO REPAIR
Auto Clinic, 111 North Lafayette / 616-754-0950
Fred's Auto Service, 6537 South Greenville Road / 616-754-5971 / Foreign and domestic
Lehman's Auto Service, 8418 14 Mile Road, Cedar Springs / 616-866-0064 / Foreign and domestic
Premium Truck & Auto, 6100 East Belding Road, Belding / 616-794-2582
Wittenbach Tire & Auto, 402 North Lafayette / 616-754-9124

AIR SERVICE
Greenville Airport, 10593 South Greenville Road / 616-754-5534

Ionia County Airport, 3148 South State Road / 616-527-9070
Kent County International Airport, 5500 44th Street SE, Grand Rapids /
   616-336-4500

MEDICAL

United Memorial Hospital, 615 South Bower Street / 616-754-4691
Sheridan Community Hospital, 301 North Main Street, Sheridan / 517-291-3261
Ionia County Memorial Hospital, 479 Lafayette Street, Ionia / 616-527-4200
Kent Community Hospital, 750 Fuller Avenue NE, Grand Rapids / 616-336-3373
Blodgett Memorial Medical Center, 1840 Wealthy Street SE, Grand Rapids /
   616-774-7444

FOR MORE INFORMATION

Greenville Area Chamber of Commerce
116 East Washington Street
Greenville, MI 48838
616-754-5697
pathwaynet.com/chamber

Belding Chamber of Commerce
120 Covered Village
Belding, MI 48809
616-794-2210

Ionia Chamber of Commerce
434 West Main Street
Ionia, MI 48846
616-527-2560

Grand Rapids Chamber of Commerce
111 Pearl Street NW
Grand Rapids, MI 49503-2831
616-771-0300

*Chris Zimmerman
with Zack and pheasants.
(Photo by Chris
Zimmerman)*

St. Johns and Clinton / Gratiot Counties

Population–7,414	October Average Temperature–52°F
County Population:	Elevation–600 to 800 ft
Clinton–57,883	Clinton State Land Acres–10,500
Gratiot–38,982	Gratiot State Land Acres–16,600
County Area:	
Clinton–571 sq mi	
Gratiot–570 sq mi	

Clinton and Gratiot Counties are largely made up of privately held agricultural lands, with the exception of some extensive state game areas, including Gratiot-Saginaw and Maple River. Sleepy Hollow State Park and Rose Lake Wildlife Research Area also provide hunting opportunities. Ruffed grouse and woodcock hunting are fair to poor, with pockets of good numbers here and there. Turkeys are found in fair numbers throughout the region. Pheasant hunting is good, especially in Clinton County. Bobwhite are present but few in number.

UPLAND BIRDS
Ruffed Grouse, Woodcock, Turkey, Pheasants, Bobwhite Quail

WATERFOWL
Ducks, Geese, Snipe

ACCOMMODATIONS
Capri Motel, 1203 South US-27 / 517-224-4239 / 12 rooms, pool, hot tub / No dogs / $$

Hub Motel, 2451 North US-27 / 517-224-2324 / 16 rooms, cable TV / No dogs / $$

St. Johns Motel, 1212 North US-27 / 517-224-2321 / 10 rooms, whirlpool suites, cable TV / Dogs allowed / $$-$$$

Sleep Inn, 1101 Commerce Park Drive, DeWitt / 517-669-8823 / 59 rooms, cable TV, continental breakfast / No dogs / $$-$$$

Sunset Motel, 2317 South US-27 / 517-224-4538 / 6 units, cable TV / Dogs allowed / $

CAMPGROUNDS AND RV PARKS
Maple River Campground, 15420 French Road, Pewamo / 517-981-6792 / 50 sites, electricity

Moon Lake Resort, Colby Lake Road, east of Rose Lake Wildlife Research Station, Laingsburg / 54 sites, electricity, laundry facilities

Sleepy Hollow State Park, 7835 East Price Road, Laingsburg / 517-651-6217 / 181 modern sites, hunting allowed

RESTAURANTS

Country Kitchen, 8875 East M-21, Ovid / 517-834-9640
Dershey's Cafe, 111 West High Street / 517-227-2233
Draft House, 12449 North US-27, DeWitt / 517-669-5206
Gram's Kitchen, 13631 Main Street, Bath / 517-641-7117
Main Street Cafe/Pizza, 205 North Clinton / 517-224-9252
Relli's Sports Bar & Pizzeria, 202 East Main Street, DeWitt / 517-669-9243 /
    Homemade pizza and Italian food; cocktails

VETERINARIANS

Animal Care Center, 311 South 7th Street, Carson City / 517-584-3844
Clinton Veterinary Service, 100 South Scott Road / 517-584-3844
DeWitt Veterinary Hospital, 11371 US-27, DeWitt / 517-669-2381
Fowler Veterinary Service, 10684 East M-21, Fowler / 517-593-2500
Ovid-Elsie Animal Clinic, 3900 North Hollister Road, Ovid / 517-834-5333
St. Johns Animal Clinic, 4137 South US-27 / 517-224-6495

SPORTING GOODS STORES

Kmart, 2119 South US-27 / 517-224-8956
Maple River Sportsman Supply, 120 East Main Street, Maple Rapids / 517-682-4693
Sportsman's Tackle, 13630 Main Street, Bath / 517-641-7243
Wal-Mart, 1939 South Scott Road / 517-224-8099

AUTO REPAIR

Accurate Auto Repair, 506½ North Clinton / 517-224-0309 / Will pick-up and
    deliver
DeWitt Service Center, 10890 North US-27, DeWitt / 517-669-1165 / Foreign
    and domestic; towing
Eagle Auto Clinic, 14322 Ohio Street, Eagle / 517-627-2648
Hovey's Service & Towing, 110 South Bridge Street, DeWitt / 517-669-8215
Superior Car Care, 13636 Main Street, Bath / 517-641-6400 / Foreign and
    domestic; open Saturdays only by appointment

AIR SERVICE

Capital City Airport, Lansing / 517-321-6121

MEDICAL

Clinton Memorial Hospital, 805 South Oakland Street / 517-224-6881
Clinton County Medical Center, 1055 South US-27 / 517-224-3000

FOR MORE INFORMATION

St. Johns Area Chamber of Commerce
201 East State Street / P.O. Box 61
St. Johns, MI 48879
517-224-7248

Saginaw and Saginaw, Shiawassee, and Genesee Counties

Population–69,512	October Average Temperature–52°F
County Population:	Elevation–600 to 900 ft
Saginaw–211,946	Saginaw State Land Acres–15,800
Shiawassee–69,770	Shiawassee State Land Acres–918
Genesee–430,459	Genesee State Land Acres–158
County Area:	
Saginaw–809 sq mi	
Shiawassee–539 sq mi	
Genesee–640 sq mi	

Bird hunters will find many opportunities in this region for all species, as well as many places to sleep and eat. The large cities of Saginaw and Flint provide everything a hunter needs. Waterfowl hunters will be especially interested in Shiawassee River State Game Area and Shiawassee National Wildlife Refuge, as well as Crow Island State Game Area, all in Saginaw County. Ruffed grouse and woodcock hunting are fair, with the best bet being in Genesee County. Pheasant hunting is fair to good, especially in Shiawassee. Turkeys are increasing and providing better hunting every year. Bobwhite quail are open in all three counties, although the population is small. State game areas can be crowded—it's best to hunt during the week.

UPLAND BIRDS
Ruffed Grouse, Woodcock, Turkey, Pheasant, Bobwhite Quail

WATERFOWL
Ducks, Geese, Snipe

ACCOMMODATIONS
Baymont Inns, 6460 Dixie Hwy, Bridgeport / 517-777-3000 / 104 rooms, some refrigerators, microwaves, continental breakfast / Dogs allowed in smoking rooms / $$$

Econo Lodge, 2225 Tittabawassee Road / 517-791-1411 / 100+ rooms, hot tub, jacuzzi, continental breakfast / Dogs allowed / $-$$

Four Points Hotel, 4960 Towne Center Road / 517-790-5050 / 156 rooms, indoor pool, hot tub, sauna / Restaurant and lounge / Dogs allowed / $$$

Knights Inn, 1415 South Outer Drive / 517-754-9200 / 108 rooms, jacuzzis, continental breakfast / Dogs allowed / $-$$

Super 8 Motel, 4848 Towne Center Road / 517-791-3003 / 68 rooms, some microfridges, coffee / Dogs allowed / $-$$

CAMPGROUNDS AND RV PARKS
Hickory Lake Campgrounds, off Old 78, west of Perry / 108 sites, electricity

Jellystone Park Camp-Resort, 1339 Weiss Road, Frankenmuth / 517-652-6668 / 224 sites, electricity, LP gas, laundry facilities

Myers Lake Resort, Murray Road, Byron / 126 sites, electricity, LP gas, laundry facilities

Pine Ridge RV Campground, 11700 Gera, Birch Run / 517-624-9029

RESTAURANTS

Bavarian Inn, 713 South Main, Frankenmuth / 517-652-9941 / Famous chicken and German food

Big John Steak & Onion, 3300 East Holland Street / 517-754-5012

El Farolito, 1346 North Washington / 517-771-9460 / Mexican food, cocktails

Gracie's Country House, 12201 M-13, Burt / Steaks, seafood, chicken / Open seven days

Tony's, 2612 State Street / 517-793-1801 / Giant sandwiches / Open at 7AM, seven days

VETERINARIANS

Agawa Companion Animal Hospital, 5880 State Street / 517-799-6859

Bavarian Veterinary Hospital, 141 Churchgrove, Frankenmuth / 517-652-6189

Bridgeport Veterinary Clinic, 5960 Dixie Hwy / 517-777-2131

Freeland Animal Clinic, 7250 Midland Road, Freeland / 517-695-2072

Mid-Michigan Veterinary Hospital, 3304 Davenport / 517-792-8665

PetSmart Veterinary Services, 3431 Tittabawassee Road / 517-793-8478

SPORTING GOODS STORES

Alaskan Gun Trade, 10475 Buck Road, Freeland / 517-695-9165

Dick's Sporting Goods, 3343 Tittabawassee Road / 517-793-3346 / Guns, ammunition, gear

Dick Williams Gun Shop, 4985 Cole Road / 517-777-1240

Gander Mountain, 2270 Tittabawassee Road / 517-791-3500 / Guns, ammunition, gear

Williams Gun Sight & Outfitters, 7389 East Lapeer Road, Davison / 810-742-2120

Meijer's, 2980 Wilder Road, Bay City / 517-667-9506
    7300 Eastman Avenue, Midland / 517-839-5959

AUTO REPAIR

Dale Stroebel's Complete Automotive Service, 100 Campbell Lane / 517-781-4307

Gobeyn's Marathon Service, 6162 Dixie Hwy, Bridgeport / 517-777-3560

Nationwide Service Center, 2725 Bay Street / 517-792-7371 / Specialize in GM; towing

Quality Clutch & Gear, 2951 McCarty / 517-791-8111 / Transmission specialists

Raquepaw's Auto Service, 8099 Main Street, Birch Run / 517-624-0103

Totten Tire Center Northwest, 7410 Gratiot / 517-781-4190

AIR SERVICE
Bishop International Airport, G-3425 West Bristol Road, Flint / 810-235-6560
Harry Browne Airport, 4821 Janes Road / 517-758-2459
MBS International Airport, 8400 Garfield Road, Freeland / 517-695-5555

MEDICAL
Saginaw General Hospital, 1447 North Harrison / 517-771-4000
St. Luke's Hospital, 700 Cooper Avenue / 517-771-6121
St. Mary's Medical Center, 830 South Jefferson Avenue / 517-776-8000

FOR MORE INFORMATION
Saginaw County Chamber of Commerce
901 South Washington Avenue
Saginaw, MI 48601
517-752-7161
www.saginawchamber.org

Saginaw County Convention and Visitors Bureau
517-752-7164

*Young
ruffed grouse.*

Bad Axe and Huron County

Population–3,484	October Average Temperature–51°F
County Population–34,951	Elevation–700 ft
County Area–837 sq mi	State Land Acres–13,300

Huron County advertises itself as being the place where the countryside meets the lakeshore. It is a good description. The county is surrounded by Lake Huron on three sides and makes good use of the shoreline with the establishment of two state parks, both of which allow hunting, and extensive coastal marshes that attract many waterfowlers each year. The west side of the county borders Saginaw Bay, one of the best places in the Midwest to hunt waterfowl. Ruffed grouse and woodcock numbers are fair, while turkey and pheasant populations are good.

UPLAND BIRDS
Ruffed Grouse, Woodcock, Turkey, Pheasant

WATERFOWL
Ducks, Geese, Snipe

ACCOMMODATIONS
Apple Creek Inn, 1151 South VanDyke Road / 517-269-6465 / Cable TV, coffee / No dogs / $-$$
Bayport Inn, 827 Promenade, Bay Port / 517-656-9911 / 4 sleeping rooms with bathroom down the hall / Restaurant and lounge / Dogs allowed / $
Bella Vista Inn, 6024 Port Austin Road, Caseville / 517-856-2650 / Motel rooms, efficiencies, cottages with cable TV / restaurant and lounge / No dogs / $$-$$$
Franklin Inn & Plaza, 160 East Huron Street / 517-269-9951 / 36 rooms, cable TV, restaurant / No dogs / $$
Maple Lane Motel, 958 North VanDyke Road / 517-269-9597 / 16 rooms, cable TV, refrigerators / Dogs allowed, with permission / Hunter's rate / $
Parkside Cottages, 6417 Main Street, Caseville / 517-856-2650 / Cabins with kitchens / Restaurant and lounge / No dogs / $$-$$$

CAMPGROUNDS AND RV PARKS
Albert East Sleeper State Park, 6573 State Park Road, Caseville / 517-856-4411 / 223 sites, minicabins, electricity, showers, boat launch / Adjacent to Rush Lake State Game Area / Open all year
Caseville County Park, 6400 Main Street, Caseville / 517-856-2080 / 214 sites, showers, electricity
Port Crescent State Park, 1775 Port Austin Road, Port Austin / 517-738-8663 / 138 sites, showers, electricity
Wagener County Park, 2671 South Lakeshore Road, Harbor Beach / 517-479-9131 / 96 sites, 8 minicabins, showers, electricity / Open through October 15

RESTAURANTS

Coral Gables Restaurant, 782 South VanDyke Road / 517-269-9666
Cousins Food & Spirits, 113 Pt. Crescent Road / 517-269-2236
Dufty's Blue Water Inn, 6584 Main Street, Caseville / 517-856-3663 / Food & spirits
Main Street Cafe & Bakery, 15 South Main Street, Pigeon / 517-453-3663 /
    Open at 6AM Mon–Sat; 8AM on Sunday / Friday night seafood buffet
Peppermill, 685 North Port Crescent / 517-269-9347 / Breakfast anytime /
    Open at 6AM Mon–Sat; 7AM on Sunday
Sportsman's Inn, 8708 Lake Street, Port Austin / 517-738-7520 / Pizza, steaks,
    sandwiches

VETERINARIANS

Bad Axe Animal Medical Clinic, 1054 North VanDyke Road / 517-269-8502
Caseville Small Animal Clinic, 6970 Main Street, Caseville / 517-856-3525
Harbor Beach Veterinary Services, 8508 Sand Beach Road, Harbor Beach /
    517-479-3377
Miller, East Wayne DVM, 327 South Main Street, Pigeon / 517-453-3411

SPORTING GOODS STORES

Holdwick Gun Shop, 1768 Eppenbrock Road, Harbor Beach / 517-479-6704 Call
    first / Gunsmith, guns, ammunition
Kmart, 760 North VanDyke Road / 517-269-9945
Randy's Hunting & Sport Center, 337 Main Street, Kinde / 517-874-5869 /
    Guns, ammunition, supplies
Wal-Mart, 850 North VanDyke Road / 517-269-9746
Walsh Gun & Tackle, 5020 North Caseville Road, Caseville / 517-856-4465 /
    Guns, ammunition, gear, license

AUTO REPAIR

Dave's Auto, 3640 North VanDyke Road / 517-269-7723 / Nights, 517-874-5979 /
    24-hour towing
Dunk's Garage, 4496 North Washington Street, Ubly / 517-658-2300
Fleet Repair & Service, 6977 Main Street, Caseville / 517-856-4925 / 24-hour
    road service
Oak Beach Auto Repair, 6701 Oak Beach Road, Port Austin / 517-738-5346 /
    24-hour towing, call 517-738-6081
Thumb Auto Repairs & Service, 4509 North VanDyke, Kinde / 517-874-5115

AIR SERVICE

Huron County Memorial Airport, 352 Thompson Road / 517-269-6511
Sebewaing Township Airport, West Sebewaing Street, Sebewaing / 517-883-9964

MEDICAL

Harbor Beach Community Hospital, 210 South First Street, Harbor Beach /
    517-479-3201
Huron Memorial Hospital, 1100 South VanDyke Road / 517-269-9521
Scheurer Hospital, 170 North Caseville Road, Pigeon / 517-453-3223

FOR MORE INFORMATION

Bad Axe Chamber of Commerce
P.O. Box 87
Bad Axe, MI 48413
517-269-6936

Bay Port Chamber of Commerce
P.O. Box 188
Bay Port, MI 48720
517-453-3638

Caseville Chamber of Commerce
P.O. Box 122
Caseville, MI 48725
517-856-3818

Port Austin Chamber of Commerce
P.O. Box 274
Port Austin, MI 48467
517-738-7600
www.huroncounty.com

Scott DeFrain of Mt. Pleasant with a late season grouse. (Photo by Chris Zimmerman)

Cass City and Tuscola / Sanilac Counties

Population–2,276	October Average Temperature–51°F
County Population:	Elevation–600 to 900 ft
Tuscola–55,498	Tuscola State Land Acres–30,700
Sanilac–39,928	Sanilac State Land Acres–8,700
County Area:	
Tuscola–813 sq mi	
Sanilac–964 sq mi	

Tuscola and Sanilac Counties, as well as Huron, to the north, are at the heart of pheasant country in Michigan's Thumb. Most of the land is privately held (some of it enrolled in the Hunting Access Program), but several state game areas hold pheasants, including Minden City, Sanilac, Cass City, Deford, Gagetown, Tuscola, Vassar, and Murphy Lake. Tuscola's Saginaw Bay shoreline is one of the better places to hunt waterfowl in the state. Waterfowlers concentrate their efforts at Fish Point State Wildlife Area and Quanicassee State Wildlife Area. Sanilac State Game Area has recently opened a half-mile asphalt trail for hunters with physical disabilities. Tuscola County is best for grouse and woodcock. The area's turkey flock is growing steadily.

UPLAND BIRDS
Ruffed Grouse, Woodcock, Turkey, Pheasant, Bobwhite Quail

WATERFOWL
Ducks, Geese, Snipe

ACCOMMODATIONS
Charmont Motel, 6138 Cass City Road / 517-872-2270 / 25 rooms, cable TV, restaurant, lounge / Dogs allowed / $$

Fish Point Lodge, 4130 Miller Avenue, Unionville / 517-674-2631 / Cabins, rooms, RV sites, group rates / Boats, blinds, decoys / Guided waterfowl hunts / Dogs allowed / $$-$$$

Highway Host, 7550 South VanDyke Road, Marlette / 517-635-3654 / 12 units, color TV, coffee, restaurant / Dogs allowed / $$

Thumb Heritage Inn, 405 West Sanilac Road, Sandusky / 810-648-4811 / 26 rooms, cable TV, coupons for breakfast nearby / Dogs allowed with permission / $$

CAMPGROUNDS AND RV PARKS
Ber-Wa-Ga-Na Campground, M-46, Vassar / 150 sites, electricity, LP gas, laundry facilities

Lexington RV Resort, 7181 Lexington Boulevard, Lexington / 210 sites, electricity, water, sanitation station, laundry facilities

RESTAURANTS
Bubba's Place, 6234 Main Street / 517-872-1237
Cass Tavern, 6448 Main Street / 517-872-4838
Charmont Restaurant, 6138 Cass City Road / 517-872-4321
Crys Grill, 6487 Main Street / 517-872-5553
Fran's Country Kitchen, 2954 Main Street, Marlette / 517-635-3044
Subway, 6144 East Cass City Road / 517-872-4373

VETERINARIANS
All Pets Veterinary Clinic, 4438 Seeger Street / 517-872-2255
Cass City Veterinary Clinic, 4849 North Seeger Street / 517-872-2935
Community Animal Clinic, 2617 South Van Dyke Road, Marlette / 517-635-7095
Marlette Veterinary Clinic, 6760 West Marlette Road, Marlette / 517-635-2101
South Sanilac Veterinary Hospital, 590 South Sandusky Road, Sandusky /
   810-648-2294
Town & Country Animal Clinic, 93 South Elk Street, Sandusky / 810-648-4281

SPORTING GOODS STORES
Beaver's Sporting Goods, 6616 Bray Road Vassar / 517-871-4568
Wal-Mart, 1121 East Caro Road, Caro / 517-673-7900

AUTO REPAIR
Bartnik Service, 6524 Van Dyke Road / 517-872-3541
Cass City Tire, 6392 Main Street / 517-872-5303
Double D Gas & Diesel Repair, 7923 Cass City Road / 517-872-4540
Hank's Repair, 5549 Cass City Road / 517-872-3851
J & C Service, 6268 Main Street / 517-872-3488

AIR SERVICE
Bay City Airport, 614 River Road, Bay City / 517-895-8991
Harry West Browne Airport, 4821 Janes Road, Saginaw / 517-758-245
Huron County Memorial Airport, 352 Thompson Road, Bad Axe / 517-269-6511
Sandusky City Airport, 1213 North Sandusky Road, Sandusky / 810-648-9894

MEDICAL
Hills & Dales General Hospital, 4675 Hill Street / 517-872-2727
Marlette Community Hospital, 2770 Main Street, Marlette / 517-635-4000

FOR MORE INFORMATION
Cass City Chamber of Commerce
6506 Main Street
Cass City, MI 48726
517-872-4618
www.travel.to/casscitymi

Port Huron and St. Clair / Lapeer Counties

Population–33,694
County Population:
  Lapeer–74,768
  St. Clair–145,607
County Area:
  Lapeer–654 sq mi
  St. Clair–724 sq mi
	October Average Temperature–53°F
	Elevation–700 to 1,000 ft
	St. Clair State Land Acres–13,500
	Lapeer State Land Acres–12,800

Public land is harder to find in this area, but each of the counties holds a large state game area: Lapeer SGA in Lapeer County and Port Huron SGA in St. Clair County. Southern St. Clair County's Algonac State Park provides some public hunting land, too. Consult your Hunting Access Program handbook, which details many acres of private lands available to hunters. Waterfowlers will find plenty of public water in Lake St. Clair, a major migration area. In fact, duck hunters who want to be close to northern Lake St. Clair and St. Clair Flats Wildlife Area on Harsen's Island will probably want to stay south of Port Huron in Algonac or in other towns bordering Lake St. Clair. Ruffed grouse hunting is fair, with Lapeer County being the best of the two. Woodcock flights during the migration can be good, especially in St. Clair, which is also very good for pheasants. The turkey population is coming on strong in this area of Michigan. Although the bobwhite quail population is small, hunting for these birds in St. Clair County is as good as it gets in the state.

UPLAND BIRDS
Ruffed Grouse, Woodcock, Turkey, Pheasant, Bobwhite Quail
WATERFOWL
Ducks, Geese, Snipe

ACCOMMODATIONS
Colony Motel, 6077 Pointe Tremble Road, Algonac / 810-794-5974 / 14 rooms, jacuzzis, cable TV, VCR, refrigerators, freezer, microwave, coffee / No dogs / $$-$$$

Comfort Inn, 1700 Yeager Street / 810-982-5500 / 80 rooms, suites, pool, hot tub, deluxe continental breakfast, laundry facilities / No dogs / $$$

Days Inn, 2908 Pine Grove Avenue / 810-984-1522 / 104 rooms, cable TV, efficiencies / Dogs allowed / $$-$$$

Fairfield Inn, 1635 Yeager Street / 810-982-8500 / 63 rooms, some microwaves, refrigerators, cable TV, continental breakfast / Pool and jacuzzi / No dogs / $$-$$$

Holiday Inn Express, 1720 Hancock Street / 810-987-5999 / 96 rooms, cable TV, pool, continental breakfast / No dogs / $$$

Knights Inn, 2160 Water Street / 810-982-1022 / 104 rooms, cable TV, continental breakfast, pool / Dogs allowed / $-$$

Pine Tree Motel, 3121 Lapeer Road / 810-987-2855 / 15 rooms, cable TV, one efficiency / No dogs / $

CAMPGROUNDS AND RV PARKS

Algonac State Park, M-29, Algonac / 810-765-5605 / 281 sites, water, electricity, hunting nearby

Kings Landing Kampground, 121 Kings Landing Drive, Columbiaville / 810-793-2608 / 84 sites, water, electricity

Lakeport State Park, M-25, north of Port Huron / 810-327-6765 / 300 sites, water electricity

RESTAURANTS

Bob Evans Restaurant, 2190 Water Street / 810-984-4455

Cavis Grill, 401 Quay Street / 810-982-2192

Cheap Charlie's, 3990 24th Avenue / 810-985-3411

Decker's Landing, 9081 Anchor Bay Drive, Algonac / 810-794-4600 / Food and spirits

Fogcutter Restaurant, 511 Fort Street / 810-987-3300

Kay's Restaurant, 5347 Pointe Tremble Road Algonac / 810-794-9075

Loxton's Family Restaurant, 3535 Lapeer Road / 810-982-7771

Main Street Family Dining, 502 Huron Avenue / 810-984-1570

Yorkshires Tavern, 515 Wall Street / 810-987-5732

VETERINARIANS

Animal Hospital of Lakeport, 7269 Lakeshore Road, Fort Gratiot / 810-385-3515

Huron Veterinary Clinic, 2003 Griswold Street / 810-985-8300

Port Huron Veterinary House, 1317 Exmouth Street / 810-987-1550

Veterinary Associates, 3801 Lapeer Road / 810-985-6144

SPORTING GOODS STORES

Ace Hardware, 326 Huron Avenue / 810-987-4200

Bluewater Outdoorsman, 10683 Gratiot Avenue, Casco / 810-727-5060

Dunham's Discount Sports, 4163 24th Avenue, Fort Gratiot / 810-385-3939 / Guns and ammunition, licenses

Lumber Jack Building Center, 3470 Pointe Tremble Road, Algonac / 810-794-4921

Voight's Firearms Archery, 4136 Lapeer Road / 810-985-7733 / Guns, ammunition, supplies, licenses

Au Sable Outfitters, 17005 Kercheval, Grosse Pointe / 313-642-2000

FM Flymart, 1002 North Main Street, Royal Oak / 800-573-6335

Gander Mountain, Inc., 13975 Hall Road, Utica / 810-247-9900

Orvis Fly Fishing & Hunting, 203 East University Drive, Rochester / 248-650-0440
29500 Woodward Avenue, Royal Oak

Meijer's, 27255 23 Mile Road, Chesterfield / 810-598-1118

AUTO REPAIR

Bob's Auto Repair, 9586 Nook Road, Algonac / 810-794-9220
Don's Towing, 2547 Conner Street / 810-982-6673
Honest Engine Automotive Service, 1807 Chestnut Street / 810-987-9614
Mac's Service, 1309 St. Clair River Drive, Algonac / 810-794-4310
Modern Motor Service, 3292 Lapeer Road / 810-985-8196

AIR SERVICE

Berz Macomb Airport, 15801 22 Mile Road, Macomb / 810-247-7400
Macomb Airport, 59819 Indian Trail, Ray / 810-749-9558
Sandusky City Airport, 1213 North Sandusky Road, Sandusky / 810-648-9894
St. Clair County Airport, 250 Airport Drive, Smiths Creek / 810-364-6890

MEDICAL

Emergency Center of Port Huron Hospital, 1221 Pine Grove Avenue /
    810-989-3300
Mercy Hospital, 2601 Electric Avenue / 810-985-1500
Port Huron Hospital, 1221 Pine Grove Avenue / 810-987-5000
River District Hospital, 4100 South River Road, East China / 810-329-7111

FOR MORE INFORMATION

Port Huron Chamber of Commerce
920 Pine Grove Avenue
Port Huron, MI 48061
810-985-7101

St. Clair Chamber of Commerce
505 North Riverside Avenue
St. Clair, MI 48079
810-329-2962

*Gerry Pink with a
mixed bag of redheads
and mallards taken
on Lake St. Clair.*

Kalamazoo and Allegan, Barry, Calhoun, Kalamazoo, and Van Buren Counties

Population–80,277	October Average Temperature–53°F
County Population:	Elevation–600 to 1,100 ft
Allegan–90,509	Allegan State Land Acres–49,900
Barry–50,057	Barry State Land Acres–24,500
Calhoun–135,982	Calhoun State Land Acres–135
Kalamazoo–223,411	Kalamazoo State Land Acres–6,300
Van Buren–70,060	Van Buren State Land Acres–1,790
County Area:	
Allegan–827 sq mi	
Barry–556 sq mi	
Calhoun–709 sq mi	
Kalamazoo–562 sq mi	
Van Buren–611 sq mi	

Public hunting land in Van Buren County is limited to Van Buren State Park and lands enrolled in the Hunting Access Program. Likewise, public hunting opportunities are extremely limited in Calhoun, where there are no state game areas and few acres enrolled in the HAP. However, Allegan and Barry hold two of the larger state game areas in Michigan. Barry SGA borders the large Gun Lake and has several smaller lakes within its boundaries. Allegan SGA, which contains a managed waterfowl area, is well known among Canada goose hunters. Kalamazoo County hunters will want to explore Gourdneck SGA and Fulton SGA, especially for pheasants. Grouse and woodcock hunters will find fair to good hunting throughout the region, as will pheasant and turkey hunters, especially in Barry County.

UPLAND BIRDS
Ruffed Grouse, Woodcock, Turkey, Pheasant

WATERFOWL
Ducks, Geese, Snipe

ACCOMMODATIONS
Allegan Motel, 1509 Lincoln Road, Allegan / 616-673-2977 /

Baymont Inn, 2203 South 11th Street / 616-372-7999 / 87 rooms, cable TV, continental breakfast / Dogs allowed / $$

Budget Host Inn, 1580 Lincoln Road, Allegan / 616-673-6622 / 20 rooms, cable TV, one efficiency / Dogs allowed / $$$

Holiday Inn West, 2747 South 11th Street / 616-375-6000 / 186 rooms, pool, restaurant and lounge / Dogs allowed / $$$

Super 8 Motel, 618 Maple Hill Drive / 616-345-0146 / 62 rooms, cable TV / Dogs allowed / $$

CAMPGROUNDS AND RV PARKS

Fort Custer State Recreation Area, Custer Road, Augusta / 616-731-4200 / 112 sites, water, electricity, hunting nearby

Tri-Ponds Family Camp Resort, 3687 Dumont Road, Allegan / 616-673-4740 / 75 sites, water, electricity

Van Buren State Park, 23960 Ruggles Road, South Haven / 616-637-2788 / 205 sites, water, electricity, hunting nearby

Yankee Springs State Recreation Area, Hwy 430, Orangeville / 616-795-9081 / 345 sites, water, electricity, hunting nearby

RESTAURANTS

Colonial Kitchen, 330 North Drake Road / 616-349-9928 / Home of the six-egg omelet / Breakfast and lunch served all day / Open 6:30AM–2:30PM, Mon–Sat; 8AM-3PM, Sun

Damon's, 3124 South Westnedge Street / 616-342-8186 / Ribs, seafood, cocktails / Lunch and dinner

Main Street Pub, 4514 West Main / 616-342-9710 / Sandwiches, steaks, cocktails / Lunch and dinner

Rykse's Restaurant, 5924 Stadium / 616-372-3838 / Homemade soups, baked goods, daily specials / Open 6:30AM–9PM, Mon–Sat

VETERINARIANS

Allegan Animal Clinic, 1096 32nd Street, Allegan / 616-673-5236

Allegan Veterinary Clinic, 100 Water Street, Allegan / 616-673-6981

Kalamazoo Animal Hospital, 3301 South Burdick Street / 616-381-1570

Oakwood Animal Hospital, 2009 Whites Road / 616-349-1831

Town and Country Veterinary Hospital, 2753 116th Avenue, Allegan / 616-673-5654

West Main Animal Hospital, 7250 West Main Street / 616-375-1114

Woodland Animal Hospital, 7795 Douglas Avenue / 616-381-2127

SPORTING GOODS STORES

Country Guns & Ammo, 11536 Sprinkle Road, Vicksburg / 616-649-4868

D & R Sports Center, 8178 West Main Street / 616-372-2277

J & R Gun Shop, 2048 101st Avenue, Otsego / 616-694-6011

Miner Lake Store, 2607 122nd Avenue, Allegan / 616-673-3624

On Target Guns & Gunsmithing, 6984 West Main Street / 616-375-4570

Shooters Choice, 3738 East Main Street / 616-345-2225

Meijer's, 2177 Columbia Avenue West, Battle Creek / 616-968-2938

AUTO REPAIR

Allegan Car Care Clinic, 1283 M-89 Allegan / 616-673-4700

Discount Muffler, 1298 Lincoln Road Allegan / 616-673-9433

East Main Auto Repair, 3616 East Main Street / 616-343-1617

Goodyear Commercial Tire and Service, 3407 East Cork Street / 616-343-2141

Hunter's Shell, 550 Water Street, Allegan / 616-673-6154

Kalamazoo Motor and Transmission, 912 North Park Street / 616-381-4900
Kelly Radiator and Auto Repair, 534 Gibson Street / 616-343-1533
Ken's Tire Service, 500 Water Street, Allegan / 616-673-6668
Muffler and Hitch, 702 West Michigan Avenue / 616-344-7185

AIR SERVICE
Kalamazoo/Battle Creek International Airport, 5235 Portage Road, Portage /
616-388-3668
W. K. Kellogg Airport, 2712 Territorial Road West, Battle Creek / 616-966-3470
South Haven Regional Airport, 73574 County Road 380, South Haven /
616-637-7343

MEDICAL
Allegan General Hospital, 555 Linn Street, Allegan / 616-673-8424
Borgess Emergency and Trauma Center, 1521 Gull Road / 616-226-4815
Borgess Medical Center, 1521 Gull Road / 616-226-7000
Bronson Methodist Hospital, 252 East Lovell Street / 616-341-7654
Gull Road Immediate Care, 6010 Gull Road / 616-345-4054

FOR MORE INFORMATION
Kalamazoo County Convention and Visitors Bureau
346 West Michigan Avenue
Kalamazoo, MI 49007
616-381-4003

Allegan Chamber of Commerce
402 Trowbridge Street
Allegan, MI 49010
616-673-2479

Brighton and Eaton, Livingston, Ingham, Jackson, and Washtenaw Counties

Population–5,686	October Average Temperature–51°F
County Population:	Elevation–700 to 1,000 ft
Eaton–92,879	Eaton State Land Acres–282
Ingham–281,912	Livingston State Land Acres–17,900
Jackson–149,756	Ingham State Land Acres–5,300
Livingston, 115,645	Jackson State Land Acres–17,400
Washtenaw, 282,939	Washtenaw State Land Acres–16,600
County Area:	
Eaton–577 sq mi	
Ingham–559 sq mi	
Jackson–707 sq mi	
Livingston–568 sq mi	
Washtenaw–710 sq mi	

Situated around the population centers of Lansing, Ann Arbor, and the tri-county metropolitan Detroit area, Brighton is close to the most public land to be found in this four-county region. Public hunting grounds include portions of Waterloo, Pinckney, Island Lake, and Brighton State Recreation Areas, as well as Chelsea, Gregory, Sharonville, Dansville, and Oak Grove State Game Areas. Try Dansville, Gregory, and Oak Grove for grouse and woodcock. Pheasant and turkey numbers are very good in this five-county area—in fact southcentral Michigan rivals the Thumb for top honors as the best pheasant hunting in the state. The state game areas can be crowded on weekends, especially during deer seasons, but weekday hunters and those who move far from roads can find some secluded spots. This region produces some good bobwhite quail hunting, too, although the population is quite small.

UPLAND BIRDS
Ruffed Grouse, Woodcock, Turkey, Pheasant, Bobwhite Quail

WATERFOWL
Ducks, Geese, Snipe

ACCOMMODATIONS
Country Meadow Inn, 26820 Pontiac Trail, South Lyon / 248-437-4421 / 19 rooms, color TV, microwave, refrigerator / Dogs allowed with permission / $
Grand View Motel, 5474 East Grand River Avenue, Howell / 517-546-2690 / 30 units, cable TV, efficiencies / Dogs allowed / $$$
Holiday Inn, 8079 Challis Road / 810-225-9948 / 107 rooms, cable TV, suites / No dogs / $$$

Island Lake Resort Motel, 6269 Academy Drive / 810-229-6723 / 1, 2, 3-bedroom efficiencies, by the weekend, week or season / Dogs allowed with permission / $$-$$$

Smith Motel, 11290 Grand River Road / 810-227-7441 / 19 rooms, 6 efficiencies, cable TV / Dogs allowed / $$

Woodland Lake Motel, 8029 Grand River Avenue / 810-229-7093 / 15 rooms, cable TV / No dogs / $$

CAMPGROUNDS AND RV PARKS

Bright State Recreation Area, 6360 Chilson, Howell / 810-229-6566 / 222 sites, water, electricity, showers, hunting nearby

Haas Lake Park, 25800 Haas Road, New Hudson / 248-437-0900

Highland State Recreation Area, 5200 East Highland Road, White Lake / 248-685-2433 / 30 campsites, water, electricity, showers, hunting nearby

Island Lake State Recreation Area, 12950 East Grand River Avenue / 810-229-7067 / No camping, but rustic cabins available, and hunting nearby

Lake Chemung Outdoor Resort, 320 South Hughes Road, Howell / 517-546-6361

Pontiac Lake Recreation Area, 7800 Gale Road, Waterford / 248-666-1020 / 176 sites, water, electricity, showers, hunting nearby

Proud Lake State Recreation Area, 3500 Wixom Road, Milford / 248-685-2433 / 130 sites, water, electricity, showers, hunting nearby

RESTAURANTS

Border Cantina, 8724 West Grand River Avenue / 810-229-7562

Brighton Bar and Grill, 400 West Main Street / 810-229-4115

Cajun Joe's, 5757 Whitmore Lake Road / 810-227-0707

E.G. Nicks Crab Shack and Barbeque, 11600 Grand River Avenue / 810-227-2131

Lone Star Steakhouse and Saloon, 8075 Challis Road / 810-225-7827

Outback Steakhouse, 7873 Conference Center Drive / 810-225-2109

VETERINARIANS

Alpine Animal Clinic, 10443 Grand River Avenue / 810-229-2300

Brighton Animal Hospital, 695 East Grand River Avenue / 810-227-4351

Towne and Country Animal Hospital, 5445 South Old US-23 / 810-220-1079

Woodland Animal Hospital, 7980 Grand River Avenue / 810-229-5300

SPORTING GOODS STORES

B & J Sporting Goods, 118 East Grand River Avenue / 810-227-1962

Dick's Discount Sport Center, 3600 East Grand River Avenue, Howell / 517-546-8530

Hot Shots Firearms and More, 408 Curzon Road, Howell / 517-548-2879

Hunter's Depot, 9536 Spencer, Whitmore Lake / 734-449-4341

Powder Keg Gun Shop, 2717 East Grand River Avenue, Howell / 517-545-4867

Weimer's Gun Shop, 11820 Highland Road, Hartland / 810-632-6126

Westbank Anglers, 6612 Telegraph Road (Bloomfield Plaza), Bloomfield Hills / 248-538-3474

Cabela's (opening September 2000), intersection of US 23 and MI 50, Dundee

Gander Mountain, Inc., 14100 Pardee Road, Taylor / 734-287-7420

                                    6359 Gander Drive, Swartz Creek / 810-635-7800

                                    2230 Mall Drive East, Waterford / 248-738-9600

Meijer's, 37201 Warren Road, Westland / 734-641-0421

Auto Repair

A-Plus Transmissions, 4355 South Old US-23 / 810-229-7878

AAA Mufflers, 301 West Grand River Avenue / 810-227-2751

Bob's Tire and Auto Service, 7991 Grand River Avenue / 810-229-7005

Brighton Auto Service, 5402 South Old US-23 / 810-227-1324

Chris's Engine Repair, 7975 Kensington Court / 810-227-7999

Conely Engines and Transmissions, 7208 Grand River Road / 810-227-7570

Hag's Radiator Clinic, 9894 Weber Street / 810-227-2530

Huffman Auto Service, 948 North Old US-23 / 810-632-7011

Spartan Tire and Muffler Center, 7100 Grand River Road / 810-220-0050

Air Service

Detroit Metropolitan Airport, 1 Detroit Metro Airport, Detroit / 734-942-3222

Livingston County Airport, 3480 West Grand River Avenue, Howell / 517-546-6675

Oakland County International Airport, 6500 Highland Road, Waterford / 248-666-3900

Price Airport, 618 Silver Lake Road, Linden / 810-735-4406

Medical

Brighton Hospital, 12851 Grand River Road / 810-227-1211

St. Joseph Mercy Hospital, 136 Kissane Avenue / 810-220-0997

For More Information

Brighton Chamber of Commerce
131 Hyne Street
Brighton, MI 48116
810-227-5086

Whitemore Lake Chamber of Commerce
9571 Main Street
Whitmore Lake, MI 48189
734-449-8540

South Lyon Chamber of Commerce
214 South Lafayette Street
South Lyon, MI 48178
248-437-3257

Howell Chamber of Commerce
123 East Washington Street
Howell, MI 48843
517-546-3920

Mt. Clemens and Macomb, Oakland, and Wayne Counties

Population–18,405 County Population: Macomb–717,400 Oakland–1,083,592 Wayne–2,111,687 County Area: Macomb–480 sq mi Oakland–873 sq mi Wayne–614 sq mi	October Average Temperature–52°F Elevation–580 ft Macomb State Land Acres–1,265 Oakland State Land Acres–26,900 Wayne State Land Acres–1,462

Historically, this region was a hotbed for pheasant hunters, but today the three-county area has very limited opportunities for the upland bird hunter because of urban sprawl. Wayne County is almost completely covered by urban development, while Macomb County offers very little public land open to hunting. Wetzel State Park in northern Macomb County offers small numbers of pheasants and some woodcock during the migration. In addition, private lands in Macomb and Oakland Counties have good to very good pheasant hunting and some woodcock. Oakland County has more public land open to hunting in the form of several recreation areas, but again, upland bird opportunities are limited.

While upland hunting may not be fantastic here, any number of Macomb communities along Lake St. Clair, from Fair Haven (St. Clair County) to St. Clair Shores, would be good base camps for waterfowlers interested in big water hunting. Most duck hunters target the St. Clair Flats in the northeast end of the lake as well as Canadian waters in the southeast, but great rafts of diving ducks can be found all along the western shore of the lake, especially in November. In Wayne County, some hunters target the Detroit River for waterfowl, especially late in the season. There are few areas of coastal marsh along the western shore of Lake St. Clair and along the Detroit River, so layout boats or sneak boats in the open lake are the best way to go.

UPLAND BIRDS
Pheasant, Woodcock, Ruffed Grouse

WATERFOWL
Ducks, Geese, Snipe

ACCOMMODATIONS
Baymont Inns, 20675 East 13 Mile Road, Roseville / 810-296-6910 / Continental breakfast / Dogs allowed with $50 deposit / $$$
Comfort Inn, 1 North River Road / 810-465-2185 / Cable TV / No dogs / $$-$$$
Econo Lodge, 31811 Little Mack Avenue, Roseville / 810-294-6140 / Cable TV, continental breakfast / No dogs / $$

Lakecrest Motel, 10451 Dixie Hwy, Fair Haven / 810-725-9693 / 20 units, kitchenettes, by day, week, month / Dogs allowed / $-$$
Lakeview Motel, 10161 Dixie Hwy, Fair Haven / 810-725-0551 / 17 units, kitchenettes, cable TV / No dogs / $-$$
Lodge Keeper Inn, 29101 23 Mile Road, New Baltimore / 810-949-4520 / 38 units, cable TV / Dogs allowed, small fee
Super 8 Motel, 20445 Erin Street, Roseville / 810-296-1730 / Cable TV, continental breakfast / No dogs / $$-$$$

CAMPGROUNDS AND RV PARKS
Pontiac Lake Recreation Area, 7800 Gale Road, Waterford / 248-666-1020 / 176 sites, water, electricity
Riverview Campground/Marina, 4175 Pte.Tremble Road, Clay / 810-794-0182
Yogi Bear's Jellystone Camp, 7072 Grange Hall Road, Holly / 248-634-8621

RESTAURANTS
J. Barleycorn, 112 Macomb Place / 810-465-1830
North Channel Brewing Co., 30400 23 Mile Road, Chesterfield / 810-948-2337 / Microbrewery
Paul's Riverhouse, 24240 North River Road / 810-465-5111
Pizza Hut, 1180 South Gratiot Avenue, Clinton Twp / 810-468-4343 / Pizza, beer, wine
Surf North, 10069 Dixie Hwy, Fair Haven / 810-725-7888 / Cocktails
Tubby's Submarine, 37594 South Gratiot Avenue, Clinton Twp / 810-469-0700
Vernier's, 8822 Vernier Road, Fair Haven / 810-725-0361 / Breakfast, lunch, dinner, cocktails

VETERINARIANS
Elm Animal Hospital, 29160 Gratiot Avenue, Roseville / 810-777-0110
Mt. Clemens Veterinary Hospital, 21384 Cass Avenue, Clinton Twp / 810-463-4561
North Gratiot Veterinary Hospital, 46808 Gratiot Avenue, Chesterfield / 810-949-3200
Patterson Vet Hospital, 35115 Harper Avenue, Clinton Twp / 810-791-6260
Snyder Veterinary Clinic, 29950 23 Mile Road, New Baltimore / 810-949-1505

SPORTING GOODS STORES
Ark Surplus, 1351 South Gratiot Avenue, Clinton Twp / 810-463-5873
Bass Pro Shops, 4500 Baldwin Road, Auburn Hills / 248-209-4200
B & R Sporting Goods, 41851 Garfield Road, Clinton Twp / 810-263-7941
Convenient Sportsman, 43682 North Gratiot Avenue, Clinton Twp / 810-469-7545
Dean's Gun Shop, 51088 Seaton Drive, Chesterfield / 810-783-3186
Gander Mountain, 13975 Hall Road, Utica / 810-247-9900
2230 East Mall Drive, Waterford / 248- 738-9600
14100 Pardee Road, Taylor / 734-287-7420
Michi-Gun, 31516 Harper Avenue, St. Clair Shores / 810-296-2360
Miller Sport Shop, 273 North Groesbeck Hwy, Mt. Clemens / 810-954-1320

Dick's Sporting Goods, 21061 Haggerty Road, Novi / 248-735-8180
                     400 John R. Road, Troy / 248-577-2879
                     1290 South Rochester Road, Rochester Hills / 248-608-9696
                     23349 Eureka Road, Taylor / 734-374-0429
                     45230 Northpointe Boulevard, Utica / 810-254-2653
                     35500 Central City Parkway, Westland / 734-523-0984
Au Sable Outfitters, 17005 Kercheval, Grosse Pointe / 313-642-2000
FM Flymart, 1002 North Main Street, Royal Oak / 800-573-6335
              29229 Northeastern Hwy, Southfield / 248-350-8484
              31009 Jefferson Avenue, St. Clair Shores / 810-415-5650
Westbank Anglers, 6612 Telegraph Road, Bloomfield Hills / 248-538-3474
Orvis Fly Fishing & Hunting, 203 East University Drive, Rochester / 248-650-0440
                     29500 Woodward Avenue, Royal Oak

AUTO REPAIR

A-1 Quality Car Care, 265 North Gratiot Avenue / 810-954-0258
Gerry's Towing & Garage, 74 Dickinson Street / 810-954-1004
Mr. Muffler, 171 North Groesbeck Hwy / 810-469-1030
Repairs Unlimited, 185 Madison Avenue / 810-469-0430

AIR SERVICE

Berz Macomb Airport, 15801 22 Mile Road, Macomb / 810-247-7400
Detroit Metropolitan Airport, 9000 Middlebelt Road, Detroit / 734-942-3550
Marine City Aviation, 7115 Marine City Hwy, Marine City / 810-765-8289
Oakland County International Airport, 6500 Highland Road, Waterford /
   248-666-3900

MEDICAL

Harbor Oaks Hospital, 35031 23 Mile Road, New Baltimore / 810-725-5777
Mt. Clemens General Hospital, 1000 Harrington Street / 810-493-8000
St Joseph's Mercy Hospital, 900 Woodward Avenue, Pontiac / 248-858-3000
St. Joseph's Mercy-East, 215 North Avenue / 810-466-9300

FOR MORE INFORMATION

Central Macomb County C of C
58 South Gratiot Avenue
Mt. Clemens, MI 48043
810-463-1528

Anchor Bay Chamber of Commerce
34475 23 Mile Road
Chesterfield, MI 48047
810-725-5148

Wayne County Chamber of Commerce
19132 Huron River Drive
New Boston, MI 48164
734-753-4220

Metro Detroit Visitors Bureau
39843 Wales Street
Canton, MI 48188
734-397-9313

Pontiac Chamber of Commerce
30 North Saginaw Street
Pontiac, MI 48342
248-335-9600

Three Rivers and Berrien, Cass, and St. Joseph Counties

Population–7,413	October Average Temperature–52°F
County Population:	Elevation–600 to 1,000 ft
Berrien–161,378	Berrien State Land Acres–2,300
Cass–49,477	Cass State Land Acres–4,000
St. Joseph–58,913	St. Joseph State Land Acres–2,300
County Area:	
Berrien–571 sq mi	
Cass–492 sq mi	
St. Joseph–504 sq mi	

Three Rivers is named for the three rivers that come together in this location: the St. Joseph, Portage, and Rocky. The entire area is known as River Country because St. Joseph County holds more navigable rivers, creeks, and streams than any of Michigan's counties. You may want to bring along your fishing rod. Bird hunters will want to explore Three Rivers State Game Area along the Cass-St. Joseph county line, as well as Crane Pond State Game Area, which is interspersed throughout the eastern side of Cass County. Berrien County's only state game area is also Michigan's newest — Boyle Lake SGA, nearly 350 acres, was established in 1997. Hunting for grouse, woodcock, and pheasant is fair to good, with Berrien County being the best for all three species. Turkeys are found throughout the region.

UPLAND BIRDS
Ruffed Grouse, Woodcock, Turkey, Pheasant

WATERFOWL
Ducks, Geese, Snipe

ACCOMMODATIONS
Hampton Inn, 71451 South Centerville Road, Sturgis / 616-651-4210 / 60 rooms, cable TV, pool and spa, continental breakfast / No dogs / $$$
Greystone Motel, 59271 US-131 / 616-278-1695 / 60 rooms, cable TV, refrigerators / Dogs allowed / $$
Holiday Inn Express, 1207 West Broadway / 616-278-7766 / 56 rooms, cable TV, pool and spa, continental breakfast / No dogs / $$$
Redwood Motel, 59389 US 131 / 616-278-1945 / 15 rooms, cable TV / No dogs / $-$$
Three Rivers Inn, 1200 West Broadway / 800-553-4626 / 100 rooms, cable TV, complimentary hot breakfast, pool and whirlpool / Restaurant and lounge / Dogs allowed / $$

CAMPGROUNDS AND RV PARKS
Green Valley Campgrounds, 25499 West Fawn River Road, Sturgis / 616-651-8760 / 220 sites, showers, LP gas
Corey Roberts Lake Campground, 10705 Corey Lake Road / 616-244-8214
Kline's Resort, 22460 Klines Resort Road / 616-649-2514
Rocky's Hideaway, 10838 Born Street / 616-244-5603

RESTAURANTS
The Country Table, 15174 US-12, White Pigeon / 616-483-9567 / Breakfast, lunch, dinner
Fisher Lake Inn, 19984 East M-60 / 616-279-7984 / Seafood, steaks / Lunch and dinner
The Seasons, 601 West Hoffman Road / 616-279-5144 / Lunch and dinner; brunch, 10AM–2PM on Sunday / Cocktails
Paisano's, 16 North Main Street / 616-278-8525 / Pizza, subs / Lunch and dinner
Short Stop Restaurant, 618 South Main Street / 616-273-8867
Turfside Restaurant & Lounge, 52065 Pulver Road / 616-279-5131

VETERINARIANS
Colon Animal Clinic, 490 North Burr Oak Road, Colon / 616-432-3610
Country Garden Veterinary Clinic, 62183 North M-66, Sturgis / 616-651-6750
Crossroads Veterinary Clinic, 15275 M-60 / 616-278-1345
Hedges Veterinary Hospital, 1100 North Main Street / 616-273-1056
Sturgis Veterinary Hospital, 67161 North M-66, Sturgis / 616-651-6010

SPORTING GOODS STORES
Charlie's Gun Shop, 27519 Marvin Road, Centreville / 616-432-2712
D & R Sports, 238 South Front Street, Dowagiac / 616-782-8989
Happy Landing Grocery, 59640 County Line Road / 616-244-1120 / Licenses, boat rental
Lacy's Grocery & Bait, 69130 Klinger Lake Road, Sturgis / Licenses, supplies
Sonny & Sons, Inc., 25024 West US-12, Sturgis / Licenses, supplies, LP gas

AUTO REPAIR
Bob's Auto Machine Shop, 53266 Wilbur Road / 616-279-6285
Bone's Garage, 20097 M-60 / 616-467-6237
Brownie's Radiator Service, 400 South Main Street / 616-273-8950
C & G Garage, 262 East Michigan Avenue / 616-273-1360
Guaranteed Muffler & Tire Center, 59108 South US-131 / 616-273-9198
Motor Car Specialist, 1218 5th / 616-273-6004
P.M. Auto Clinic, 706 Webber Avenue / 616-279-7172

AIR SERVICE
City of Dowagiac Airport, 710 West Prairie Ronde Street, Dowagiac / 616-782-8530 Kalamazoo/Battle Creek International Airport, 5235 Portage Road, Portage / 616-388-3668

MEDICAL

Sturgis Hospital, 916 Myrtle Street, Sturgis / 616-651-7824
Three Rivers Area Hospital, 1111 West Broadway Street, Three Rivers /
   616-278-1145

FOR MORE INFORMATION

River Country Tourism Council
P.O. Box 186
Centreville, MI 49032
1-800-447-2821
www.rivercountry.com

Three Rivers Area Chamber of Commerce
103 Portage Avenue
Three Rivers, MI 49093
616-278-8193
www.tronline.com/chamber

Sturgis Area Chamber of Commerce
113 North Monroe
Sturgis, MI 49091
616-651-5758
www.2mm.com/chamber

*Dan Zeneberg
of Mt. Pleasant with
Sheena, his German
shorthaired pointer.
(Photo by Chris
Zimmerman)*

Hillsdale and Hillsdale, Branch, and Lenawee Counties

Population–8,170	October Average Temperature–51°F
County Population:	Elevation–700 to 1,200 ft
Branch–41,502	Hillsdale State Land Acres–3,400
Hillsdale–43,431	Branch State Land Acres–447
Lenawee–91,476	Lenawee State Land Acres–4,300
County Area:	
Branch–507 sq mi	
Hillsdale–597 sq mi	
Lenawee–751 sq mi	

Though public land is scarce in these counties of Michigan's southern border, a few places provide some good opportunities. Hunters will want to explore Lost Nation State Game Area, which is fair for ruffed grouse and woodcock, along with Lake Hudson State Park (fair numbers of pheasants) and Onsted State Game Area, which has turkeys available. All three counties have lands enrolled in the Hunting Access Program, but Branch and Hillsdale have the most of the three. Hillsdale and Lenawee Counties have good to very good hunting for pheasants. Waterfowl hunting is fair, and a few bobwhite quail are available in the three-county area.

UPLAND BIRDS
Ruffed Grouse, Woodcock, Turkey, Pheasant, Bobwhite Quail

WATERFOWL
Ducks, Geese, Snipe

ACCOMMODATIONS
Days Inn, 3241 Carleton Road / 517-439-3297 / 41 rooms, jacuzzis, continental breakfast / No dogs / $$-$$$

Econolodge, 884 West Chicago, Coldwater / 517-278-4501 / 48 rooms, some refrigerators, microwaves, continental breakfast / Dogs allowed / $$

Pinecrest Motel, 516 West Chicago Street / 517-849-2137 / 23 rooms, one efficiency, cable TV / Restaurant next door / Dogs allowed / $$

Quality Inn, 1000 Orleans Boulevard, Coldwater / 517-278-2017 / 130 rooms, cable TV, suites, kitchenettes, pool, hot tub / Restaurant and lounge / Dogs allowed / $$$

CAMPGROUNDS AND RV PARKS
Gateway Park Campground, 4111 West Hallet Road / 517-437-7005 / 90 sites (40 available), electricity, water, showers

W.J. Hayes State Park, M-124, 1220 Wampler's Lake Road, Onsted / 517-467-7401 / 185 sites, water, electricity, mini-cabins
Historic Marble Springs, 9411 West US-12, Allen / 517-869-2522 / 60 sites, water, electricity, showers, store
Lake Hudson State Recreation Area, M-156, Hudson / 517-467-7401 / 50 sites, water, electricity, hunting nearby

RESTAURANTS
Big Boy, 390 West Carleton Road / 517-439-9110 / Breakfast, lunch, dinner
Fillmore's Steak & Spirits, 394 West Chicago, Jonesville / 517-849-2542 / Steak, cocktails
Finish Line, 75 West Carleton / 517-437-3470 / Breakfast, lunch, dinner
The Hunt Club, 24 North Howell Street / 517-427-7356
Linda Lou's Coffee Cup, 73 North Broad Street / 517-439-0140
Savarino's Next Door, 171 East South Street / 517-439-1100
Sigman's, 268 West Carleton / 517-439-9862 / Eat in or carry out

VETERINARIANS
Countryside Veterinary Service, 14247 East US-12, Somerset / 517-547-3096
Hillsdale Veterinary Hospital, 280 South Broad Street / 517-437-4431 / Open Mon–Sat
Litchfield Veterinary Clinic, 142 West St. Joe, Litchfield / 800-694-8713
Northside Veterinary Hospital, 1091 West Moore Road / 517-437-5544
Walden II Veterinary Clinic, 116 South Centennial Road, Coldwater / 517-278-2839

SPORTING GOODS STORES
Al's Gun Shop, 2991 South Lake Wilson Road / 517-437-4650
Jake's Place, 8760 East US-12, Moscow / 517-688-9106 / Guns and ammunition
WalMart, 4623 Carleton Road, Jonesville / 517-849-7000
Meijer's, 2777 Airport Road, Jackson / 517-787-3467
3333 East Michigan Avenue, Jackson / 517-787-3356

AUTO REPAIR
Gene's Shell Service, 17 Hillsdale Avenue / 517-439-1221 / Open 7AM Mon–Sat
Glory to God Towing & Repair, 196 West Carleton Road / 517-439-1323 / Foreign and domestic
Hawkins Sales & Service, 3351 Carleton Road / 517-439-5147
Performance Automotive, 490 South M-99, Jonesville / 517-849-7500
Scott's Auto World, 3300 Beck Road / 517-437-5900 / Automatic transmission specialists

AIR SERVICE
Hillsdale Aero, Inc., 3998 State Road / 517-437-4755
Riley Aviation, 400 Airport Road, Coldwater / 517-278-6516

MEDICAL

Community Health Center of Branch County, 274 East Chicago Street,
  Coldwater / 517-279-5400
Hillsdale Community Health Center, 168 South Howell Street / 517-437-4451

FOR MORE INFORMATION

Hillsdale County Chamber of Commerce
3203 Beck Road
Hillsdale, MI 49242
517-439-4341
www.hillsdalecountychamber.com

Coldwater/Branch County Chamber of Commerce
20 Division Street
Coldwater, MI 49036
517-278-5985

The walk back is always more pleasant with a bird in hand. (Photo by Chris Zimmerman)

Monroe and Monroe County

Population–22,902	October Average Temperature–53°F
County Population–133,600	Elevation–600 to 700 ft
County Area–551 sq mi	State Land Acres–7,100

Most bird hunters who come to this part of Michigan are looking for ducks. They find plenty of opportunity on this western end of Lake Erie, specifically in the Erie State Game Area and Point Mouille State Game Area. This is one of the best places for waterfowl in the Midwest and has long been a favorite of duck hunters. The town of Rockwood is the site of the annual Michigan Duck Hunters Tournament and Wildlife Show in September. Woodcock hunting is good during the migration, and pheasant hunting is good. Try Petersburg State Game Area for pheasants. Bobwhite quail are available, too. Turkey hunting was not permitted in Monroe County as this book was going to press. Lake Erie is also famous for its walleye fishery. Bring your fishing rod or book an area charter boat.

UPLAND BIRDS
Woodcock, Pheasant, Bobwhite Quail

WATERFOWL
Ducks, Geese, Snipe

ACCOMMODATIONS
Amerihost Inn, 14774 LaPlaisance Road / 734-384-1600 / 63 rooms, whirpools, pool and sauna, continental breakfast, in-room coffee / No dogs / $$$

Comfort Inn, 6500 East Albain Road / 734-384-9094 / 64 rooms, deluxe continental breakfast, pool, hot tub, kitchenettes / Dogs allowed in smoking rooms / $$-$$$

EconoLodge, 1440 North Dixie Hwy / 734-289-4000 / 115 rooms, pool, sauna, whirlpool / Restaurant and lounge / Dogs allowed / $$$

Holiday Inn, 1225 North Dixie Hwy / 734-242-6000 / 127 rooms, pool, sauna / Restaurant and lounge / No dogs / $$$

Hollywood Motel, 1028 North Telegraph Road / 734-241-7333 / 13 units, cable TV, weekly rates / No dogs / $

Knights Inn, 1250 North Dixie Hwy / 734-243-0597 / 110 rooms, cable TV / Dogs allowed / $$

Motel 7, 15390 South Dixie / 734-384-1100 / 30 units, cable TV, hot tub, weekly rates / 10% off for first-time customers / No dogs / $$

CAMPGROUNDS AND RV PARKS
Camp Lord Willing, 1600 Stumpmier Road / 734-243-2052 / Tents, trailers or RVs / Open year-round

Monroe County KOA, US-23 at Summerfield Road, Petersburg / 734-856-4972 / Tent and trailer camping, water, electricity, showers, store / Open to October 19

Sterling State Park, North Dixie Hwy / 734-289-2715 / 289 sites, water, electricity, showers, boat launch

RESTAURANTS

Country Pride Restaurant, 1255 North Dixie Hwy / 734-242-1133 / All-you-can-eat steak, breakfast anytime

Detroit Beach Restaurant, 2630 North Dixie Hwy / 734-289-3122 / Lunch and dinner, Italian and American, beer and wine / Closed Monday

Erie Restaurant and Bar, 9788 South Dixie Hwy, Erie / 734-848-4935

Michigan Bar and Grill, 1140 South Monroe Street / 734-243-6690

Ranch Steak and Seafood, 1395 North Telegraph / 734-457-6520

Restaurant Italia and Lounge, 1110 North Telegraph Road / 734-241-7151

Trapper's, 13780 South Dixie Hwy, LaSalle / 734-241-2222

VETERINARIANS

John M. Colby, DVM -Veterinary Clinic, 905 North Telegraph Road / 734-241-5023

Mason Veterinary Clinic, 124 North Monroe Street / 734-243-4222

Monroe Veterinary Clinic, 15161 South Dixie Hwy / 734-241-2525

SPORTING GOODS STORES

Archery & Gun Center of Monroe, 15610 South Telegraph Road / 734-243-0090

Cook's Sportland, 6363 North Monroe Street / 734-242-0774

Don's Gun Shop, 24509 Telegraph Road, Flat Rock / 734-782-3362

Magnum Force, 17 East 2nd Street / 734-457-4242

Meijer's, 9701 Belleville Road, Belleville / 734-699-0401

Cabela's, Intersection of US 23 and Hwy 50, Dundee

AUTO REPAIR

Cottman Transmission Center, 1445 North Monroe Street / 734-457-1720

Dick's Mobile Repair, 4658 South Custer Road / 734-242-1132

Joe Lake Tire & Auto Repair, 1986 North Telegraph Road / 734-241-6686 / Parts and service

Paul's Automotive Service, 425 North Dixie Hwy / 734-243-2188

Penske Auto Center, 1290 North Monroe Street / 734-242-1431

Precision Tune, 1986 North Telegraph Road / 734-457-2777

AIR SERVICE

Custer Airport, 2800 North Custer Road / 734-241-7110

MEDICAL

Mercy Memorial Hospital, 740 North Macomb Street / 734-241-1700

FOR MORE INFORMATION

Monroe County Convention and Tourism Bureau
P.O. Box 1094
Monroe, MI 48161
734-457-1030
www.monroeinfo.com

Hunting Guides, Outfitters and Preserves

REGION 3

Fish Point Lodge
4130 Miller Avenue
Unionville, MI 48767
517-674-2631
Waterfowl

Fowler Farms Shooting Preserve
RR 2, Box 298
South Haven, MI 49090
616-637-4381
Goose, pheasant, quail

Harsens Island Hunt Club
2238 Columbia
Harsens Island, MI 48028
810-748-0000
Pheasant

Lucky Feather Game Farm
2040 North Pittsford Road
Hillsdale, MI 49242
517-523-2050
Huns, pheasant, quail, waterfowl

Paradise Shooting Preserve
1300 State Street
Carsonville, MI 48419
810-622-9800
Chukars, pheasant, quail

Rips Pheasant & Chukar Farm
5997 Burtch Road
Jeddo, MI 48032
810-327-2035
Chukars, pheasant

Smith Creek Hunt Club
8669 Lashbrook
Goodells, MI 48027
810-325-1135
Chukars, ducks, pheasant, quail

Wild About Pheasants

As long as I live, I'll never forget the heart-pounding thrill I had the first time I was able to carry a gun on a hunt for wild pheasants. We were on a farm in Caro, Michigan, where a friend of my father's had secured permission for us to hunt on the opening day of the season. The farm had wonderful pheasant country: croplands, especially corn and soybeans, divided by brushy fencerows and small marshes that were surrounded by thick brush. It was pheasant heaven, and I understood that fact even though I was only 12 years old.

I was one of a couple blockers posted on the end of an 80-acre cornfield. Most of the corn was still standing, but a few rows had been harvested. Standing at the end on a little rise, I had a good view to either side of me.

Shortly after the drivers started walking into the rows of corn, pheasants began moving out of the end of the field near me. As they so often do when they're eluding predators, most of the roosters were running, not flying. But the few that burst cackling from the cornstalks near the drivers were greeted with booms from shotguns down the line. Cottontail rabbits were zipping through the corn, too, and I saw more than a few zoom out the end and into the thick cover before I could make a shot.

Most dyed-in-the-wool pheasant hunters would laugh, but the dog doing the work for us on this opening day was a mutt—a cockapoo, to be exact. One of my father's hunting partners had tried the dog on a whim and found her to be a rabid pheasant dog. She was true to form on this day. The first rooster that ran out of the end of the cornfield was followed closely by Scruffy. Had the bird been flying, I couldn't have shot if I wanted to—she was that close.

Finally, a rooster came out of the end of the corn about 75 yards away and started running straight at me. I remembered what my father had told me, to remain absolutely still, so the bird wouldn't see me. It was moving very quickly up the small rise where I was standing and shaking with excitement. Finally, when I figured it was close enough to shoot, I stepped out of the brush and watched the rooster put on the brakes and turn around to launch itself down the hill.

I wish I could say I took the bird with a picture-perfect shot that tumbled it stone dead from the air, but it wasn't so. It came down with a broken wing, and I watched my first wild rooster disappear into the brush. I was crushed.

When the drivers made it to my end of the field, I babbled and sputtered my story to my dad and brother. My dad did his best to assure me that the dog would find the bird. I took him to the spot where I had last seen the rooster, and sure enough, there were some feathers in the grass.

Scruffy was pressed into action, and after a few minutes that seemed more like hours, my first pheasant was brought to bag. I couldn't have been more proud if that bird had been a 10-point, 200-pound Michigan whitetail. It was a gorgeous rooster, and I was pleased to have it. Even more gratifying was that the dog had been able to make up for my lack of shooting skill. I don't believe I have had a more exciting upland bird hunt since that day. It became plain to me why so many Michigan hunters are wild over pheasants.

It used to be that schools in southern Michigan, especially those in the rural areas of the Thumb, would have to cancel classes on October 20, the traditional opening day of the pheasant season in most of the state. Large numbers of children joined their parents for a day in the fields on the pheasant opener, and truth be told, many of the schoolteachers were just as happy to join them. In some classrooms, there were so many students missing that it just made more sense to close the school for the day.

A cock pheasant takes to the air over a Michigan field. (Photo by Chris Zimmerman)

These days, pheasant season in Michigan takes a backseat to deer hunting, although there are still many faithful followers. Fewer pheasants live in Michigan compared to the heydays of the 1950s and early 1960s, but since there are fewer pheasant hunters as well, the harvest rate per hunter is not much different than it was in the past.

The Conservation Reserve Program, although more popular in states west of Michigan, has helped the pheasant population. Hunters can still find plenty of places that hold good numbers of birds, but more often than not the best places are on private land, so not only is scouting in order, the hunter must secure permission to hunt, also. This is not to say there isn't any good public pheasant hunting country. On the contrary, ambitious hunters can find many public places to pursue ringnecks, and the more diligent of the hunters can even find some places that they will have pretty much to themselves and their partners. But the wise ringneck fanatic will have a few private land spots in his bag of tricks.

Pheasant hunting is still alive and well in Michigan. Opening day still finds kids playing hooky from school and beating the brush with dad or mom. And the family mutt still finds the birds for them.

Cock pheasant. (Photo by Chris Zimmerman)

Hunting Access Program
Participating Counties

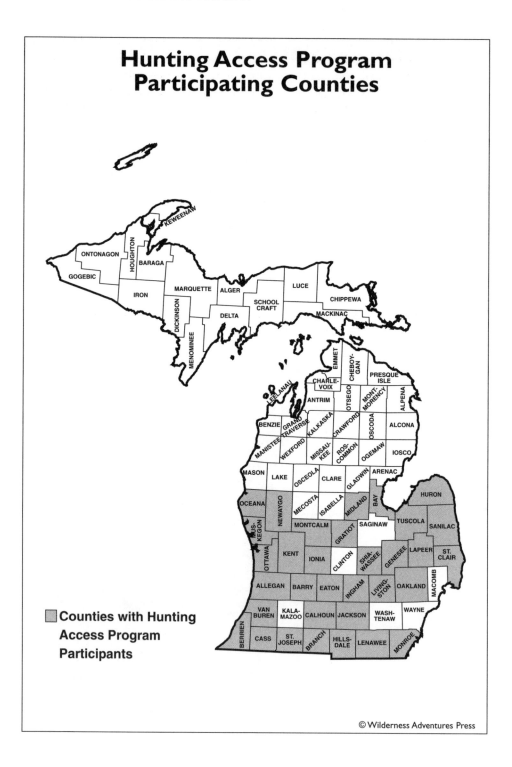

Counties with Hunting
Access Program
Participants

© Wilderness Adventures Press

Hunting Access Program

Michigan's Hunting Access Program (HAP) is comprised of lands leased in the southern part of the state through the Department of Natural Resources' Wildlife Division. These lands are all open to public hunting. Currently, over 55,000 acres are enrolled in the program. The DNR issues a guide, *Public Hunting on Private Lands*, which lists all HAP lands available to hunters. The guide lists township and section numbers where the land is located. A county map book is a good guide to use along with the HAP listing. *Public Hunting on Private Lands* is available from license dealers or by writing:

> Michigan Department of Natural Resources
> P.O. Box 30444
> Lansing, MI, 48909
> 517-373-1263
> www.dnr.state.mi.us

For the most part, properties are open on a first-come, first-served basis, but the DNR cautions hunters to make reservations early, especially for the opening days of the pheasant season. Hunters pick up permits from the farm headquarters on each day they are hunting the property. Each member of the hunting party is required to have a hunter tag in his possession while on the property, and he must return the tag at the end of the hunt. The management offices and the counties in their district are:

DNR Management Unit Office	Counties Where Farm Is Located		
Saginaw Bay 503 North Euclid Avenue, Ste 1 Bay City, MI 48706 517-684-9141	Arenac Bay Clare Gladwin	Huron Isabella Midland Saginaw	Sanilac Tuscola
Northwestern 8015 Mackinaw Trail Cadillac, MI 49601 616-775-9727	Mecosta Newaygo Oceana		
Southeastern 38980 Seven Mile Road Livonia, MI 48152 734-953-0241	Genesee Lapeer Macomb Monroe	Oakland St. Clair Wayne	
Southcentral 10650 South Bennett Road Morrice, MI 48857 571-625-4600	Clinton Eaton Gratiot Hillsdale	Ingham Ionia Jackson Lenawee	Livingston Montcalm Shiawassee Washtenaw
Southwestern 621 North 10th Street Plainwell, MI 49080 616-685-6851	Allegan Barry Berrien Branch	Calhoun Cass Kalamazoo Kent	Muskegon Ottawa St. Joseph Van Buren

Commercial Forest Lands

Other private lands that are open to hunting in Michigan include Commercial Forest (CF) lands. Commercial forest landowners allow the public to hunt and fish on their properties, but other activities such as camping, target shooting, and use of offroad vehicles when the property is fenced or gated are not allowed. Permission is not needed, as it is through the HAP program.

The Lower Peninsula contains approximately 47,500 acres of commercial forest land. A booklet showing the location of these lands can be purchased for $10.00 from the DNR. The Upper Peninsula contains the vast majority of this land at just over 2 million acres. Booklets showing the location of these lands can be purchased for individual UP counties for $3.00 or $30.00 for a set of 15 UP counties. Hunters can obtain a complete listing from:

> DNR Forest Management Division
> P.O. Box 30452
> Lansing, MI, 48909
> 517-373-1275

Aerial photographs are also available, and both the listings and photos are often available in county and township offices, as well as DNR field offices and U.S. Department of Agriculture offices.

Hunters should note that some counties are closed to hunting on Sundays. Closures include: Hillsdale and Lenawee Counties, where there is no hunting with firearms or dogs, except on state lands; Macomb and St. Clair Counties, where there is no hunting with firearms or dogs except on state lands and for waterfowl in off-shore border waters of the Great Lakes and Lake St. Clair; and Tuscola and Washtenaw Counties, where there is no hunting on lands of another person. However, state lands in these two counties are open to hunting.

Counties with Commercial Forest Lands

Counties with Commercial Forest Lands

© Wilderness Adventures Press

Michigan National Forests and Wildlife Refuges

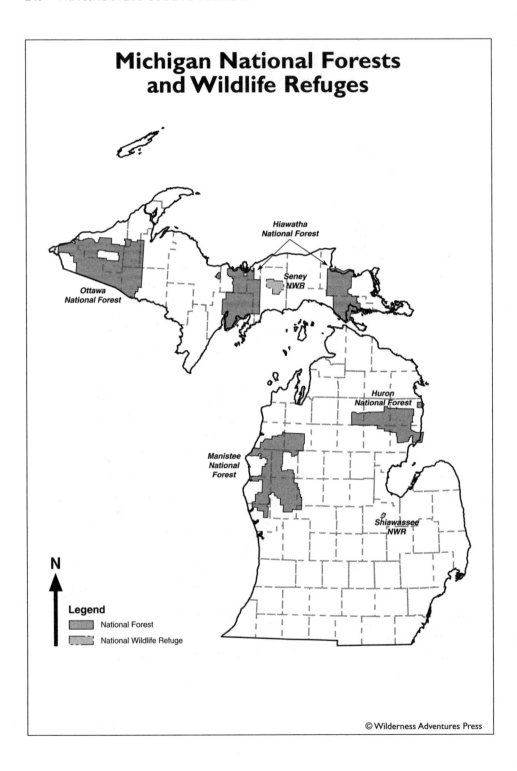

Hiawatha
National Forest

Seney
NWR

Ottawa
National Forest

Huron
National Forest

Manistee
National
Forest

Shiawassee
NWR

N

Legend

National Forest

National Wildlife Refuge

© Wilderness Adventures Press

National Forests

Hiawatha National Forest
2727 North Lincoln Road
Escanaba, MI 49829
906-786-4062

Rapid River Ranger District
8181 US-2
Rapid River, MI 49878
906-474-6442

Manistique Ranger District
499 East Lake Shore Drive
Manistique, MI 49854
906-341-5666

Munising Ranger District
400 East Munising Avenue
Munising, MI 49862
906-387-2512

Sault Ste. Marie Ranger District
4000 I-75 Business Spur
Sault St. Marie, MI 49783
906-635-5311

St. Ignace Ranger District
1798 West US-2
St. Ignace, MI 49781
906-643-7900

Huron-Manistee National Forest
1755 South Mitchell Street
Cadillac, MI 49601
231-775-2421

Baldwin/White Cloud Ranger District
650 North Michigan Avenue
Baldwin, MI 49304
231-745-4631

Cadillac/Manistee Ranger District
412 Red Apple Road
Manistee, MI 49660
231-723-2211

Huron Shores Ranger District
5761 North Skeels Road
Oscoda, MI 48750
517-739-0728

Mio Ranger District
401 North Court Street
Mio, MI 48647
517- 826-3252

Ottawa National Forest
E6248 US-2
Ironwood, MI 49938
906-932-1330

Bessemer Ranger District
500 North Moore Street
Bessemer, MI 49911
906-667-0261

Bergland Ranger District
M-28
Bergland, MI 49910
906-575-3441

Iron River Ranger District
990 Lalley Road
Iron River, MI 49935
906-265-5139

Kenton Ranger District
M-28
Kenton, MI 49943
906-852-3501

Ontonagon Ranger District
1209 Rockland Road
Ontonagon, MI 49953
906-884-2411

Watersmeet Ranger District
Old US 2, P.O. Box 276
Watersmeet, MI 49969
906-358-4551

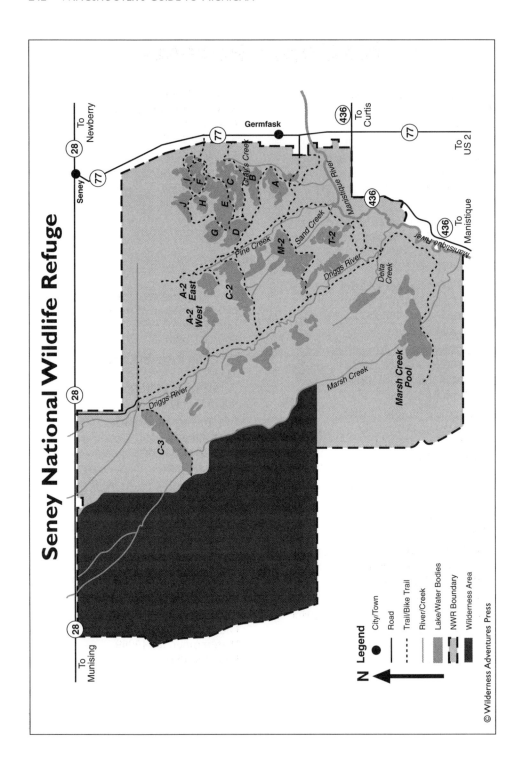

Seney National Wildlife Refuge

Legend

- City/Town
- Road
- Trail/Bike Trail
- River/Creek
- Lake/Water Bodies
- NWR Boundary
- Wilderness Area

© Wilderness Adventures Press

Seney National Wildlife Refuge

Seney National Wildlife Refuge, located in Schoolcraft County, was established in 1935. Much of the 95,000-acre refuge is open to grouse and woodcock hunting; however, waterfowl hunting is not allowed. Populations of grouse and woodcock are good to very good, especially during the peak of the grouse cycle. Maps of open hunting areas are available at the refuge headquarters off M-77.

Seney is also headquarters for several other smaller satellite refuges in the Upper Peninsula and northern Lower Peninsula. For the most part, these satellite refuges are closed to hunting. They include:

Kirtland's Warbler National Wildlife Refuge

This refuge includes 6,543 acres spread in a patchwork fashion over eight northern Lower Peninsula counties. These federal lands are managed to provide habitat for the endangered Kirtland's warbler, which favors young jackpine stands for nesting.

Harbor Island National Wildlife Refuge

This picturesque 695-acre island in Potagannissing Bay north of Drummond Island is open to hunting, however, it is difficult to reach. Game birds found on the island include some ruffed grouse and ducks and geese along the shorelines.

Huron Islands National Wildlife Refuge

An eight-island, 147-acre system located three miles out in Lake Superior near the Keweenaw Peninsula. Closed to hunting.

Michigan Islands National Wildlife Refuge

A four-island, 245-acre system in northern Lake Michigan near Beaver Island that is closed to hunting.

Whitefish Point National Wildlife Refuge

At the writing of this book, this small refuge in Chippewa County near Whitefish Point Bird Observatory was newly established and not open to hunting, if it ever will be.

For More Information

Write or call: Seney National Wildlife Refuge
HCR #2, Box 1
Seney, MI 49883
906-586-9851

Shiawassee National Wildlife Refuge

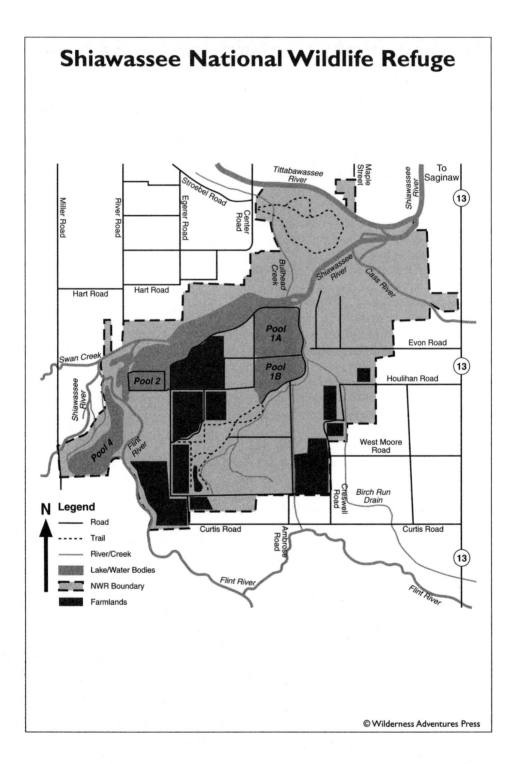

© Wilderness Adventures Press

Shiawassee National Wildlife Refuge

Shiawassee National Wildlife Refuge, established in 1953, is well known among Michigan goose hunters. The 9,104-acre refuge and surrounding area hosts tens of thousands of migrating Canada geese every year. It is located near Saginaw, on what is known as the Shiawassee Flats in the Saginaw Bay watershed. The refuge is open to goose hunting and features 30 dryland blinds that are distributed by lottery every day for morning goose hunts. The refuge also has some of the best hunting for white-tailed deer in the state. While the refuge is good for geese, some of the surrounding private lands and state game areas are very good, too. For example, Shiawassee River State Game Area, which offers managed hunts for ducks and geese, is very popular with waterfowl hunters. Blinds are issued each day on a lottery system.

Shiawassee National Wildlife Refuge is the base for two smaller satellite refuges in the Lower Peninsula. They include:

Michigan Island National Wildlife Refuge

This remote, 128-acre refuge in northern Lake Huron includes Scarecrow and Thunder Bay Islands. It is closed to hunting.

Wyandotte (Grassy Island) National Wildlife Refuge

Although waterfowl hunters in floating blinds and layout boats do hunt near the edges of this refuge in the Detroit River, the 304-acre island itself is closed to hunting.

For more information

Write or call: Shiawassee National Wildlife Refuge
6975 Mower Road
Saginaw, MI 48601
517-777-5930

Michigan State Forests

Michigan State Forests

Spanning 3.9 million acres, Michigan has the largest dedicated state forest system in the nation—three forests in the Upper Peninsula and three forests in the Lower Peninsula.

DNR Forest Management Division Office
P.O. Box 30452
Lansing, MI 48909-7952
517-373-1275

Upper Peninsula

Baraga Forest Management Unit
427 US 41 North
Baraga, MI 49908
906-353-6641

Escanaba Forest Management Unit
6833 Hwy 2, 41 & M-35
Gladstone, MI 49837
906-785-2354

Gwinn Forest Management Unit
410 West M-35
Gwinn, MI 49841
906-346-9201

Newberry Forest Mangaement Unit
Box 428, 5666 M-123 South
Newberry, MI 49868
906-293-3293

Sault Ste. Marie Forest Management Unit
Box 798, 2001 Ashmun
Sault Ste. Marie, MI 49783
906-635-5281

Shingleton Forest Management Unit
M-28 West, P.O. Box 67
Shingleton, MI 49844
906-452-6277

Northern Lower Peninsula

Atlanta Forest Management Unit
13501 M-33
Atlanta, MI 49709
517-785-4251

Gaylord Forest Management Unit
1732 West M-32, Box 667
Gaylord, MI 49734
517-732-3541

Cadillac Forest Management Unit
8015 Mackinaw Trail
Cadillac, MI 49601
231-775-9727

Traverse City Forest Management Unit
970 Emerson
Traverse City, MI 49686
231-922-5280

Gladwin Forest Management Unit
801 North Silverleaf, P.O. Box 337
Gladwin, MI 48624
517-426-9205

Grayling Forest Management Unit
1955 North I-75 BL
Grayling, MI 49738
517-348-6371

Roscommon Forest Management Unit
Box 218
Roscommon, MI 48653
517-275-4622

Southern Lower Peninsula
P.O. Box 30028
Lansing, MI 48909-7928
517-241-9048

Michigan State Game Areas and Wildlife Areas

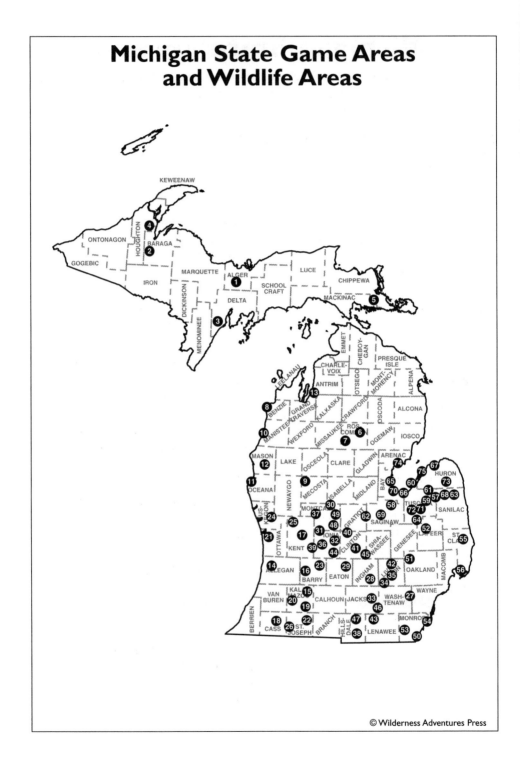

© Wilderness Adventures Press

State Game Areas and Wildlife Areas

Michigan has approximately four million acres of state forest lands and almost three million acres of national forest lands, located primarily in the Upper Peninsula and northern Lower Peninsula. In the southern Lower Peninsula, the most populous area of the state, most of the public hunting lands are comprised of state game and wildlife areas. A complete listing of these areas is provided below with information on what species can be found in each area. Maps are also provided for state game areas of 5,000 acres or more. More maps can be viewed at the Department of Natural Resources website: www.dnr.state.mi.us.

DNR Western Upper Peninsula Management Unit

Area	County	Acreage	Species
1 AuTrain Basin WA	Alger	22,400	gr, wdck,wf
2 Baraga Plains WA	Baraga	13,000	gr, wdck, wf
3 Portage Marsh WA	Delta	350	wf
4 Sturgeon River Sloughs WA	Baraga/Houghton	5400	wf

DNR Eastern Upper Peninsula Management Unit

Area	County	Acreage	Species
5 Munuscong WA	Chippewa	11,000	gr, wdck, wf

DNR Northeast Management Unit

Area	County	Acreage	Species
6 Backus Creek SGA	Roscommon	1800	gr, tu, wf, wdck
7 Houghton Lake WRA	Missaukee/Roscommon	3400	gr, tu, wf, wdck

DNR Northwestern Management Unit

Area	County	Acreage	Species
8 Betsie River SGA	Benzie	3000	wf
9 Haymarsh Lake SGA	Mecosta	6000	gr, tu, wf, wdck
10 Manistee River SGA	Manistee	2400	wf
11 Pentwater River SGA	Oceana	2000	gr, tu, wf, wdck
12 Pere Marquette SGA	Mason	1700	wf
13 Petobago SGA	Antrim	1500	wf, lmt gr, wdck

DNR Southwestern Management Unit

Area	County	Acreage	Species
14 Allegan SGA	Allegan	45,000	gr, ph, tu, wf, wdck
15 Augusta Creek WA	Kalamazoo	300	tu
16 Barry SGA	Barry	15,000	gr, tu, wf, wdck
17 Cannonsburg SGA	Kent	1335	gr, tu, wdck
18 Crane Pond SGA	Cass	3300	gr, tu, wf, wdck
19 Fulton SGA	Kalamazoo	675	ph, tu
20 Gourdneck SGA	Kalamazoo	1950	gr, ph, tu, wf, wdck
21 Grand Haven SGA	Ottawa	1110	tu, waterfowl
22 Leidy Lake SGA	St. Joseph	110	tu, wf
23 Middleville SGA	Barry	3400	gr, ph, tu, wdck
24 Muskegon SGA	Muskegon	9500	gr, tu, wf, wdck
25 Rogue River SGA	Kent	5800	gr, tu, wf, wdck
26 Three Rivers SGA	Cass/St Joseph	2075	tu, wf, wdck

DNR Southcentral Management Unit

Area	County	Acreage	Species
27 Chelsea SGA	Washtenaw	650	ph, tu, wf
28 Dansville SGA	Ingham	4740	gr, ph, tu, wf, wdck
29 Eaton Cty Complex SGA	Eaton	235	ph, tu
30 Edmore SGA	Montcalm	3585	gr, tu, wf, wdck
31 Flat River SGA	Ionia/Montcalm	11,050	gr, tu, wf, wdck
32 Grand River SGA	Ionia	815	tu
33 Grass Lake WA	Jackson	125	Lmt ph, tu
34 Gregory SGA	Livingston	3520	gr, tu, wf, wdck
35 Hillcrest SGA	Livingston	260	Lmt tu
36 Ionia SGA	Ionia	4280	Lmt ph, tu, wdck
37 Langston SGA	Montcalm	3200	gr, tu, wf, wdck
38 Lost Nation SGA	Hillsdale	2440	ph, tu, wf, wdck
39 Lowell SGA	Ionia/Kent	1880	tu, wf
40 Maple River SGA	Clinton/Gratiot	9450	tu, wf, wdck
41 Muskrat Lake SGA	Clinton	200	tu, wf
42 Oak Grove SGA	Livingston	2015	ph, tu, wf
43 Onsted SGA	Lenawee	700	ph, tu, wf
44 Portland SGA	Ionia	1990	gr, tu, wf, wdck

Area	County	Acreage	Species
45 Rose Lake WRA	Clinton	3770	gr, tu, wf, wdck
46 Sharonville SGA	Jackson/Washtenaw	4300	gr, ph, tu, wf, wdck
47 Somerset SGA	Hillsdale	770	ph, tu
48 Stanton SGA	Montcalm	4720	gr, tu, wf, wdck
49 Vestaburg SGA	Montcalm	2760	gr, tu, wf, wdck

Note: Although bobwhite quail are few in number and not always open to hunting (consult the current *Hunting and Trapping Guide* and *Waterfowl Hunting Guide*) all but two of the Southcentral Management Unit counties (Montcalm and Ionia) are open to quail hunting. Private lands offer the best quail hunting, but some can be found in state game areas that hold pheasants.

DNR Southeastern Management Unit

Area	County	Acreage	Species
50 Erie SGA	Monroe	2000	wf
51 Holly SGA	Oakland	340	gr, wdck, tu, lmt ph
52 Lapeer SGA	Lapeer	8350	Lmt gr, ph, wf, wdck, good tu
53 Petersburg SGA	Monroe	435	ph
54 Pointe Mouillee SGA	Monroe	3875	Good wf, lmt ph, wdck
55 Port Huron SGA	St. Clair	6700	Good tu, lmt gr, ph, wf
56 St. Clair Flats WA	St. Clair	3450	Lmt ph and wdck, good wf

Several state recreation areas are worth mentioning in this area of the state. These areas are multipurpose, having picnic grounds, camping facilities, and other areas for a variety of uses. Bald Mountain, Pontiac Lake, and Proud Lake, all in Oakland County, have fair amounts of grouse and woodcock, as well as pheasants at Bald Mountain and Proud Lake. Ortonville Recreation Area, on the Lapeer/Oakland County line, has grouse, woodcock, and turkeys.

Note: Although bobwhite quail are few in number and not always open to hunting (consult the current *Hunting and Trapping Guide* and *Waterfowl Hunting Guide*), all of the Southeastern Management Unit counties are open to quail hunting. Private lands offer the best quail hunting, but some can be found in state game areas that hold pheasants.

DNR Saginaw Bay Management Unit

Area	County	Acreage	Species
57 Cass City SGA	Sanilac/Tuscola	1200	Gr, ph, tu, wdck
58 Crow Island SGA	Saginaw	3000	Wf, lmt ph
59 Deford SGA	Tuscola	9800	Gr, lmt ph, tu, wdck
60 Fish Point WA	Tuscola	3000	Wf
61 Gagetown SGA	Huron/Tuscola	875	Gr, ph, tu, wf
62 Gratiot-Saginaw SGA	Gratiot/Saginaw	15,425	Gr, ph, tu, wf, wdck
63 Minden City SGA	Sanilac	6475	Gr, lmt ph, tu, wdck
64 Murphy Lake SGA	Tuscola	2625	Gr, ph, tu, wf, wdck
65 Nayanquing Pt WMA	Bay	1150	Ph, wf
66 Quanicassee WMA	Bay/Tuscola	488	Ph, wf
67 Rush Lake SGA	Huron	730	Ph, tu, wf
68 Sanilac SGA	Sanilac	1380	Gr, tu, wf, wdck
69 Shiawassee Rvr SGA	Saginaw	8700	Ph, qu, tu, wf
70 *Tobico Marsh SGA	Bay	1900	Lmt ph, tu, wf, wdck
71 Tuscola SGA	Tuscola	8380	Gr, ph, tu, wf, wdck
72 Vassar SGA	Tuscola	3190	Lmt gr, ph, tu, wdck
73 Verona SGA	Huron	6890	Gr, ph, tu, wf, wdck
74 Wigwam Bay SGA	Arenac	300	Gr, wf, wdck
75 Wildfowl Bay WA	Huron	1910	Wf

Note: Saginaw, Sanilac, and Tuscola Counties in this management unit are open to hunting of bobwhite quail. Look for them in areas where you find pheasants.

*This area is difficult to gain access, especially for upland bird hunting.

Legend

gr = grouse	ph = pheasant	tu = turkey
wdck = woodcock	wf = waterfowl	qu = quail
lmt = limited		

Allegan State Game Area

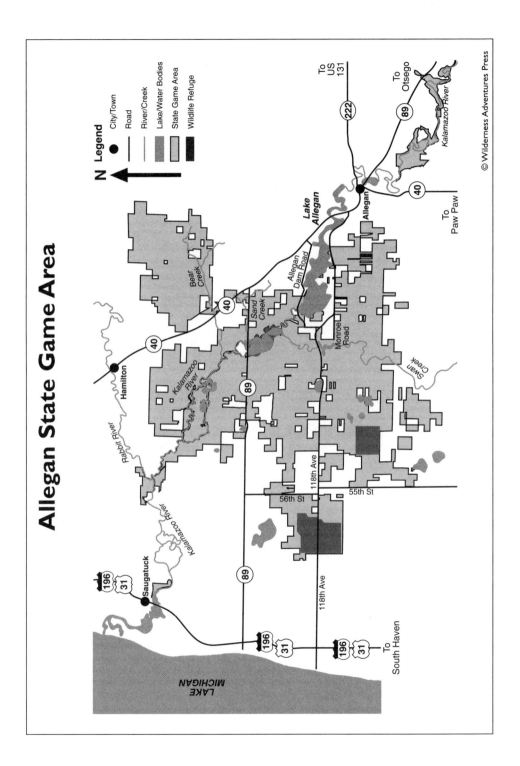

© Wilderness Adventures Press

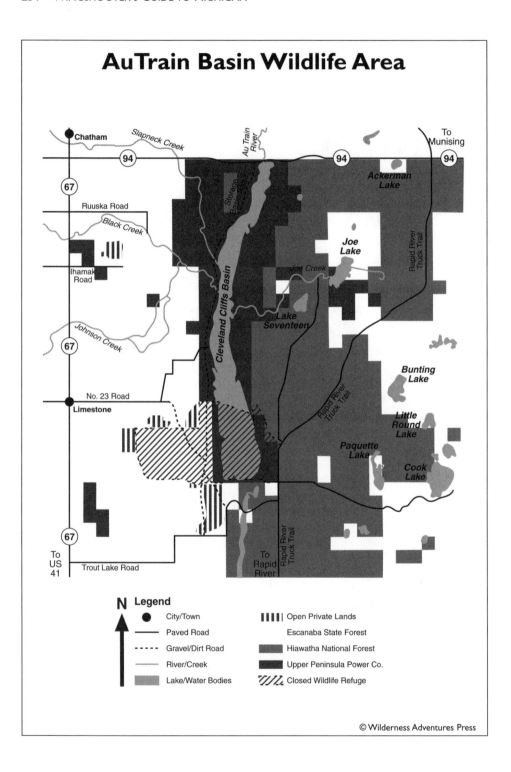

AuTrain Basin Wildlife Area

Chatham
Slapneck Creek
Au Train River
To Munising
94
94
94
Ackerman Lake
67
Ruuska Road
Storage Basin Cliffs
Black Creek
Joe Lake
Rapid River Truck Trail
Ihamak Road
Joe Creek
Johnson Creek
67
Cleveland Cliffs Basin
Lake Seventeen
Bunting Lake
No. 23 Road
Limestone
Little Round Lake
Rapid River Truck Trail
Paquette Lake
Cook Lake
67
To US 41
Trout Lake Road
To Rapid River
Rapid River Truck Trail

N Legend

- ● City/Town
- —— Paved Road
- ---- Gravel/Dirt Road
- —— River/Creek
- Lake/Water Bodies

- |||| Open Private Lands
- Escanaba State Forest
- Hiawatha National Forest
- Upper Peninsula Power Co.
- ///// Closed Wildlife Refuge

© Wilderness Adventures Press

Baraga Plains Wildlife Area

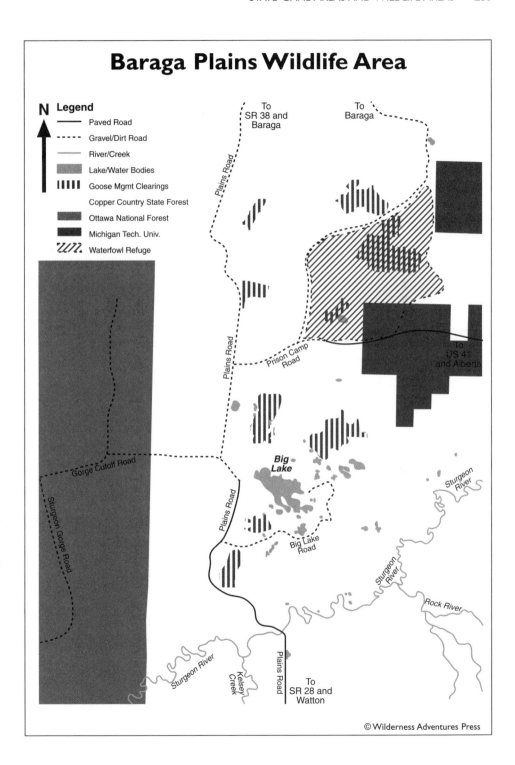

N

Legend

— Paved Road

---- Gravel/Dirt Road

〜 River/Creek

Lake/Water Bodies

||||| Goose Mgmt Clearings

Copper Country State Forest

Ottawa National Forest

Michigan Tech. Univ.

⁄⁄⁄⁄ Waterfowl Refuge

To SR 38 and Baraga

To Baraga

Plains Road

Prison Camp Road

To US 41 and Alberta

Gorge Cutoff Road

Sturgeon Gorge Road

Big Lake

Plains Road

Big Lake Road

Sturgeon River

Sturgeon River

Rock River

Sturgeon River

Kelsey Creek

Plains Road

To SR 28 and Watton

© Wilderness Adventures Press

Barry State Game Area

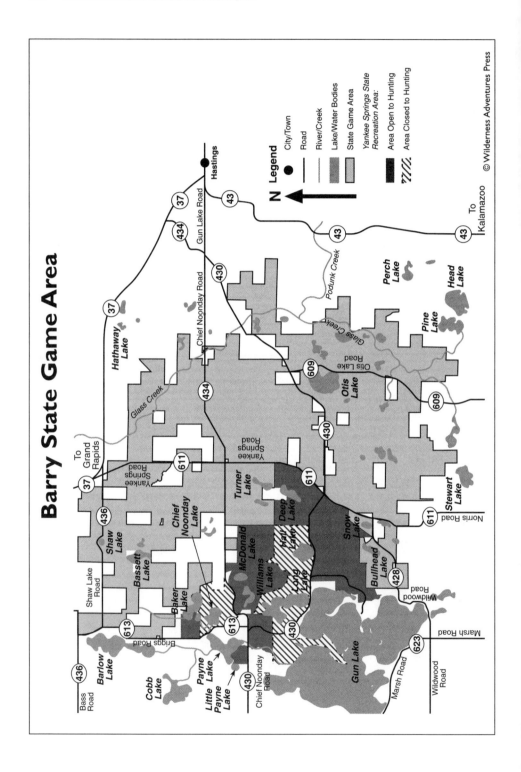

Legend

N

- City/Town
- Road
- River/Creek
- Lake/Water Bodies
- State Game Area

Yankee Springs State
Recreation Area:

- Area Open to Hunting
- Area Closed to Hunting

© Wilderness Adventures Press

Deford State Game Area

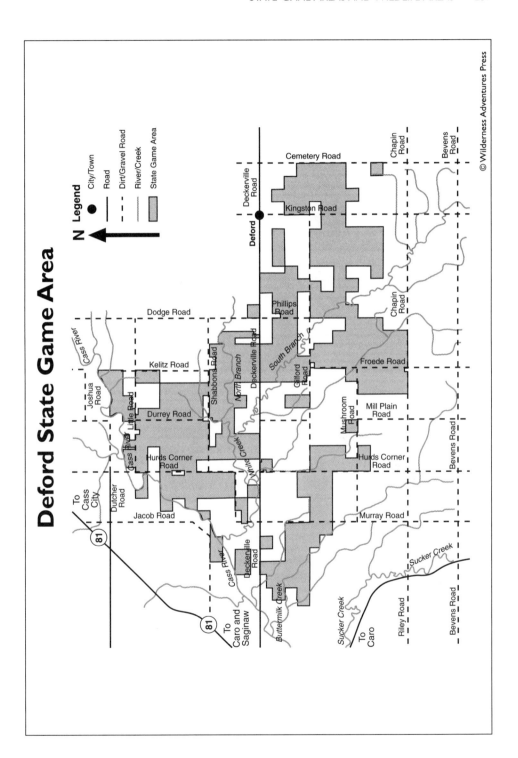

© Wilderness Adventures Press

Flat River State Game Area

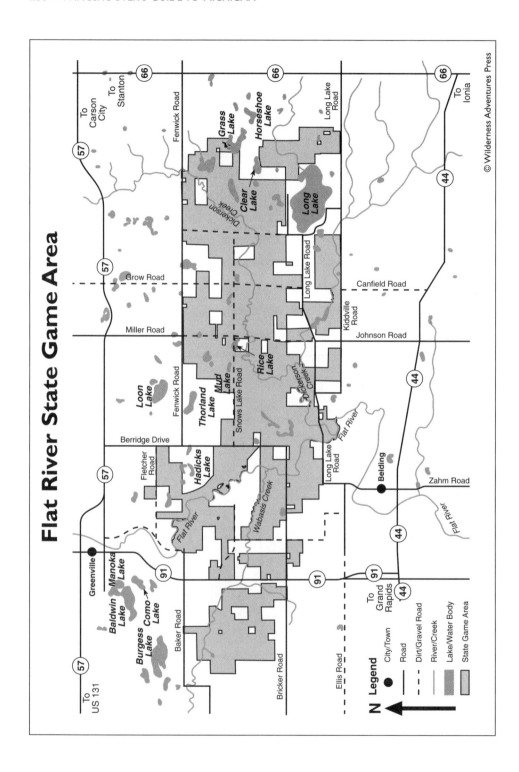

© Wilderness Adventures Press

Legend

● City/Town

── Road

--- Dirt/Gravel Road

River/Creek

Lake/Water Body

State Game Area

N

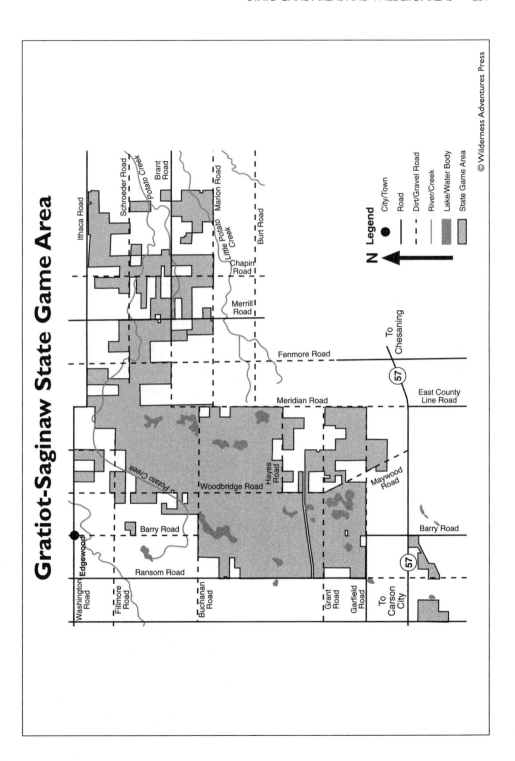

Gratiot-Saginaw State Game Area

Haymarsh Lake State Game Area

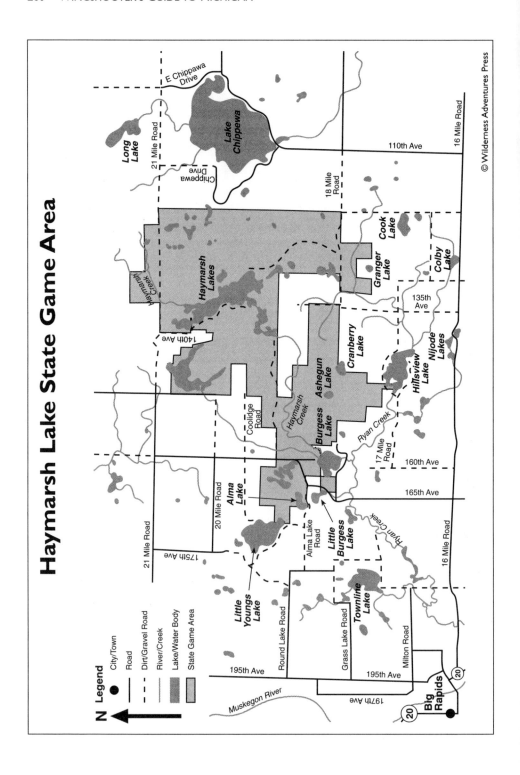

© Wilderness Adventures Press

Legend

● City/Town

— Road

-- Dirt/Gravel Road

River/Creek

Lake/Water Body

State Game Area

N

Lapeer State Game Area

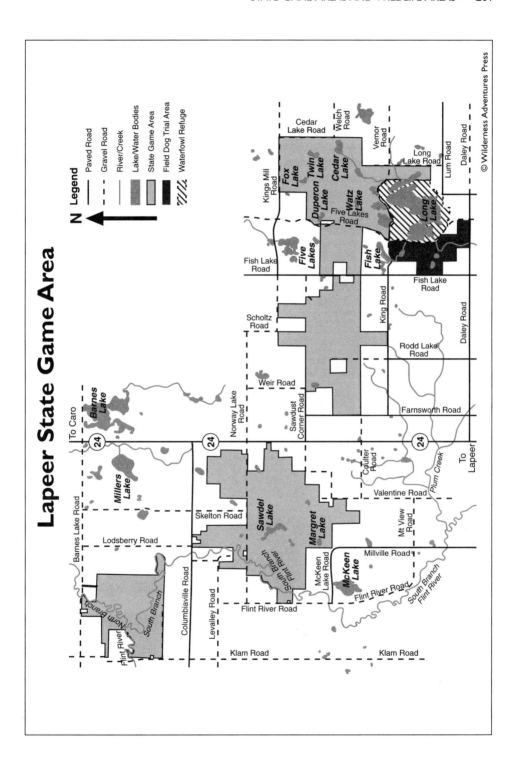

Legend

Paved Road
Gravel Road
River/Creek
Lake/Water Bodies
State Game Area
Field Dog Trial Area
Waterfowl Refuge

© Wilderness Adventures Press

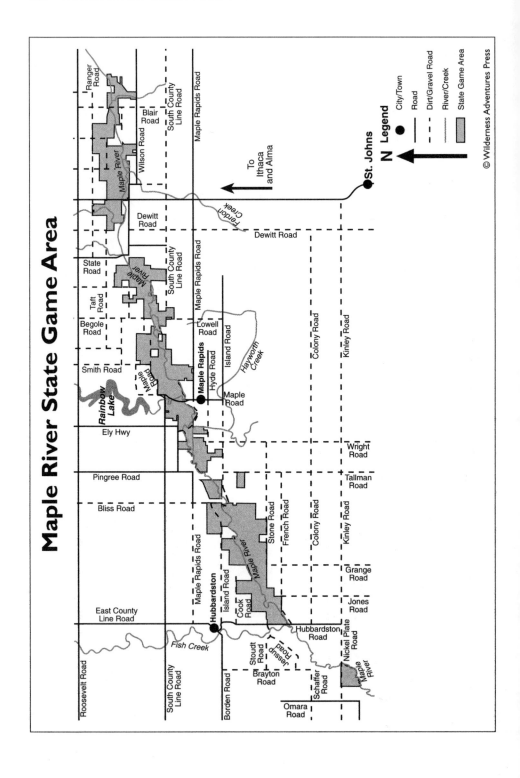

Maple River State Game Area

Legend

- ● City/Town
- —— Road
- ---- Dirt/Gravel Road
- River/Creek
- State Game Area

© Wilderness Adventures Press

Minden City State Game Area

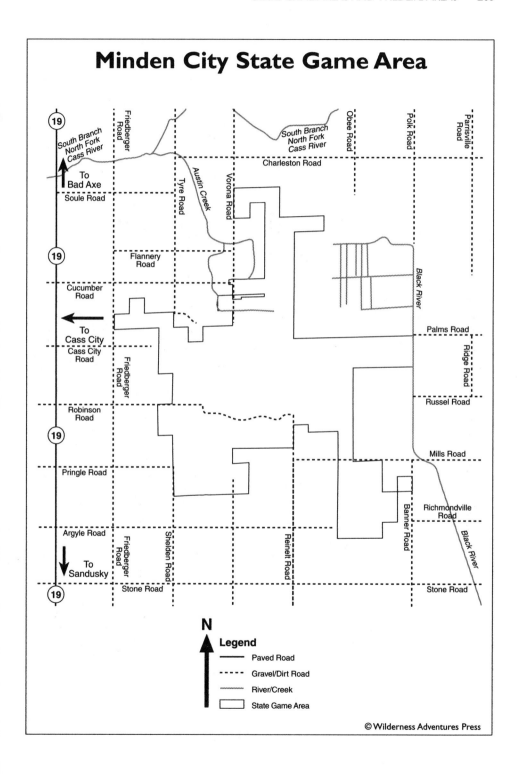

N

Legend

— Paved Road

---- Gravel/Dirt Road

～ River/Creek

☐ State Game Area

© Wilderness Adventures Press

Munuscong Wildlife Area

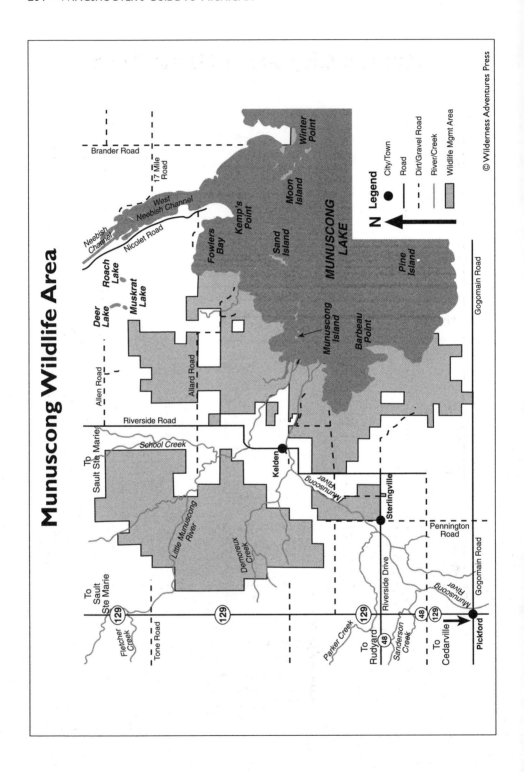

Legend

N

- City/Town
- Road
- Dirt/Gravel Road
- River/Creek
- Wildlife Mgmt Area

© Wilderness Adventures Press

Muskegon State Game Area

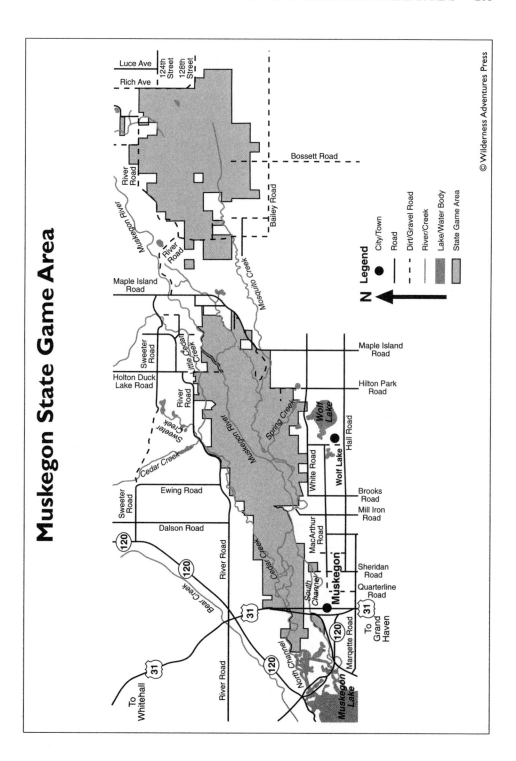

© Wilderness Adventures Press

Legend
- City/Town
- Road
- Dirt/Gravel Road
- River/Creek
- Lake/Water Body
- State Game Area

Port Huron State Game Area

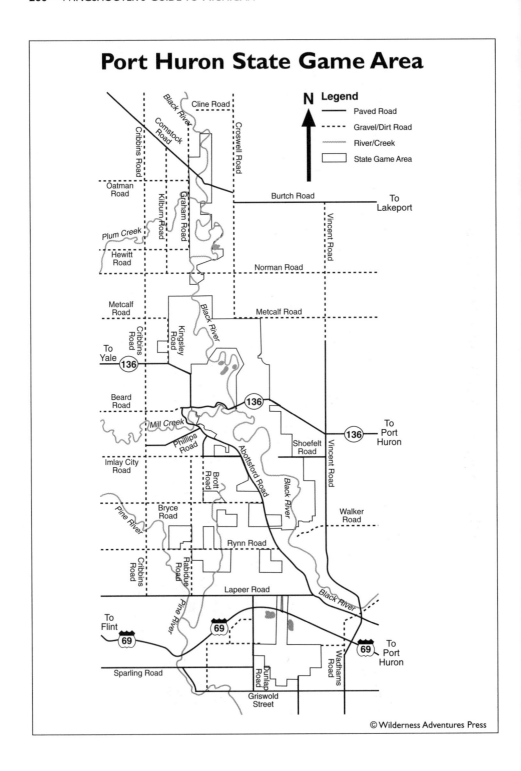

N

Legend
— Paved Road
---- Gravel/Dirt Road
—— River/Creek
☐ State Game Area

© Wilderness Adventures Press

Rogue River State Game Area

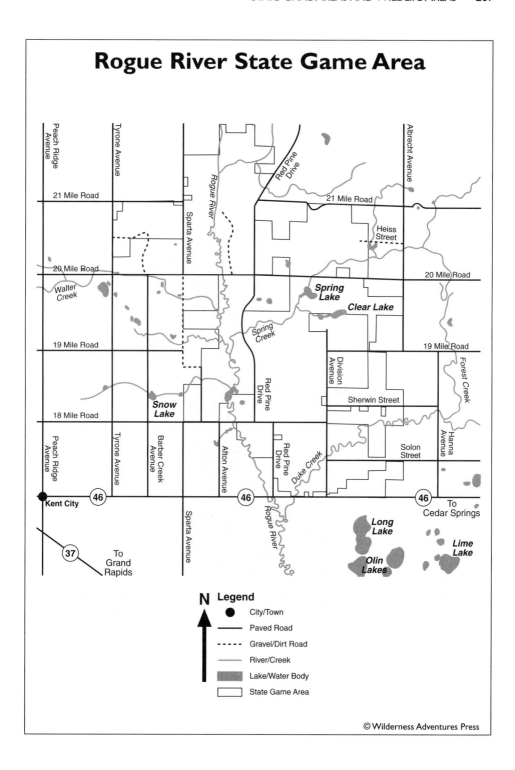

N Legend
- ● City/Town
- —— Paved Road
- - - - Gravel/Dirt Road
- —— River/Creek
- ▨ Lake/Water Body
- ▢ State Game Area

© Wilderness Adventures Press

Shiawassee River State Game Area

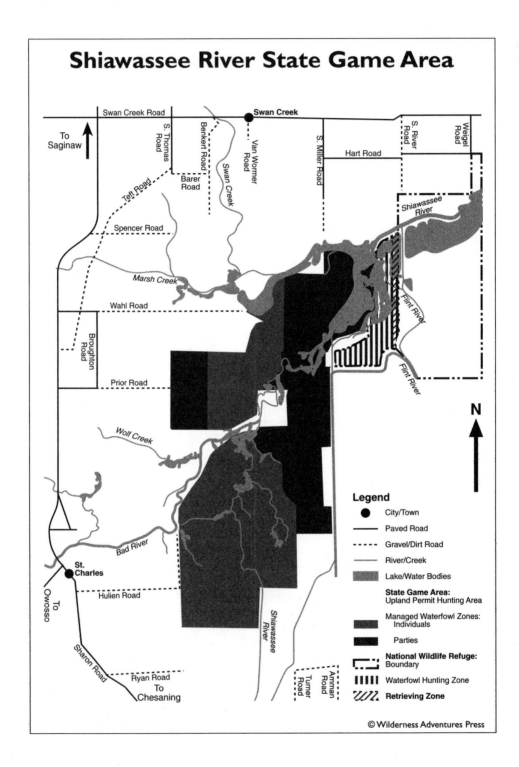

Legend

● City/Town

— Paved Road

--- Gravel/Dirt Road

— River/Creek

Lake/Water Bodies

State Game Area:
Upland Permit Hunting Area

Managed Waterfowl Zones:
Individuals

Parties

National Wildlife Refuge:
Boundary

‖‖‖ Waterfowl Hunting Zone

⧄⧄⧄ **Retrieving Zone**

© Wilderness Adventures Press

Sturgeon River Sloughs Wildlife Area

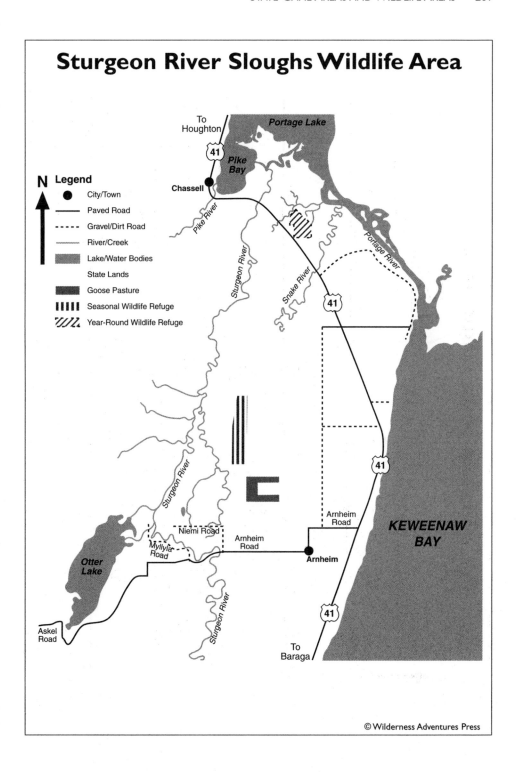

N

Legend
● City/Town
— Paved Road
- - - Gravel/Dirt Road
— River/Creek
▨ Lake/Water Bodies
State Lands
Goose Pasture
‖‖‖‖‖ Seasonal Wildlife Refuge
▨▨▨ Year-Round Wildlife Refuge

To Houghton

Portage Lake

41

Pike Bay

Chassell

Pike River

Sturgeon River

Snake River

Portage River

41

41

41

Sturgeon River

Niemi Road

Arnheim Road

Myllyla Road

Arnheim Road

Arnheim

KEEWEENAW BAY

Otter Lake

Sturgeon River

Askel Road

To Baraga

© Wilderness Adventures Press

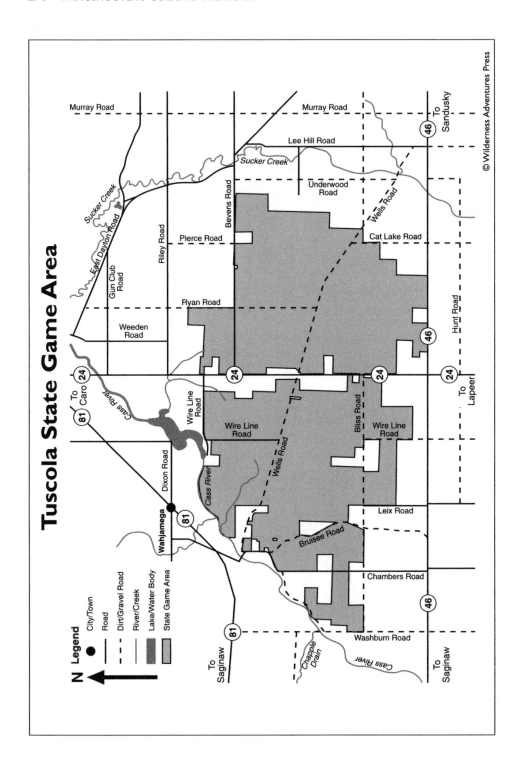

Tuscola State Game Area

© Wilderness Adventures Press

Legend
- City/Town
- Road
- Dirt/Gravel Road
- River/Creek
- Lake/Water Body
- State Game Area

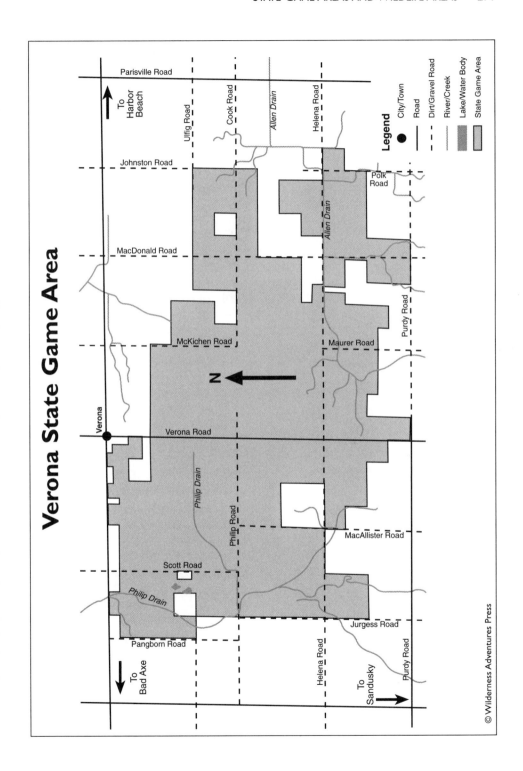

Verona State Game Area

Other Public Hunting Areas

State Parks and State Recreation Areas
with Portions Open to Hunting

State Park	County
Albert E. Sleeper State Park	Huron County
Algonac State Park	St. Clair County
Bald Mountain State Recreation Area	Oakland County
Brighton State Recreation Area	Livingston County
Cheboygan State Park	Cheboygan County
Clear Lake State Park	Montmorency County
Craig Lake State Park	Baraga County
Fisherman's Island State Park	Charlevoix County
Fort Custer State Recreation Area	Kalamazoo County
Hartwick Pines State Park	Crawford County
Higgins Lake State Park, North	Crawford/Roscommon Counties
Highland State Recreation Area	Oakland County
Holly State Recreation Area	Oakland County
Indian Lake State Park	Schoolcraft County
Indian Lake State Park, West Unit	Schoolcraft County
Ionia State Recreation Area	Ionia County
Island Lake State Recreation Area	Livingston County
J.W. Wells State Park	Menominee County
Lake Hudson State Recreation Area	Lenawee County
Leelanau State Park	Leelanau County
Ludington State Park	Mason County
Metamora Hadley State Recreation Area	Lapeer County
Newaygo State Park	Newaygo County
Ortonville State Recreation Area	Lapeer/Oakland Counties
P.H. Hoeft State Park	Presque Isle County
Pictured Rocks National Lakeshore	Alger County
Pinckney State Recreation Area	Livingston/Washtenaw Counties
Pontiac Lake State Recreation Area	Oakland County

State Park	County
Porcupine Mountains State Park	Gogebic/Ontonagon Counties
Port Crescent State Park	Huron County
Proud Lake State Recreation Area	Oakland County
Rifle River State Recreation Area	Ogemaw County
Seven Lakes State Park	Oakland County
Silver Lake State Park	Oceana County
Sleeping Bear Dunes National Lakeshore	Benzie County
Sleepy Hollow State Park	Clinton County
Tahquamenon Falls State Park	Chippewa County
Van Buren State Park	Van Buren County
Van Riper State Park	Marquette County
Waterloo State Recreation Area	Washtenaw County
Wetzel State Park	Macomb County
Wilderness State Park	Emmet County
Yankee Springs State Recreation Area	Barry County

NATIONAL PARKS AND RECREATION AREAS OPEN TO HUNTING

The Upper Peninsula's remote Grand Island National Recreation Area and Pictured Rocks National Lakeshore, both located in Alger County, are open to hunters. Access to Grand Island is by private boat or ferry at Munising. Species available include some ruffed grouse and waterfowl. For more information:

USFS Munising Ranger District Office
400 East Munising Avenue
Munising, MI 49862
906-387-2512

The 72,000-acre Pictured Rocks National Lakeshore is better known among hunters, who enjoy it for its good populations of ruffed grouse and woodcock, and opportunities for waterfowl. Pictured Rocks has some back-country acreage where dogs are not allowed. Call the office for more information:

Pictured Rocks National Lakeshore
P.O. Box 40
Munising, MI 49862
906-387-3700 (information)
906-387-2607 (park headquarters)

In the Lower Peninsula, Sleeping Bear Dunes National Lakeshore, stretching 35 miles along the Lake Michigan shore, is open to hunting. The park is located in the Leelanau Peninsula, approximately 25 miles west of Traverse City. More information is available at:

Sleeping Bear Dunes National Lakeshore
9922 Front Street
Empire, MI 49630
231-326-5134

Important Addresses and Phone Numbers

Department of Natural Resources
Box 30444
Lansing, MI 48909
517-373-1263
www.dnr.state.mi.us

DNR Wildlife Division
Mason Building, 4th Floor
P.O. Box 30444
Lansing, MI 48909-7944
517-373-1263

Upper Peninsula Field Headquarters
1990 US 41 South
Marquette, MI 49855
906-228-6561

DNR Western UP Management Unit
1420 US-2 West
Crystal Falls, MI 49920
906-875-6622

Baraga Field Office
427 US 41 North
Baraga, MI 49908
906-353-6651

Gladstone Headquarters
6833 Hwy 2, 41 & M-35
Gladstone, MI 49837
906-786-2351

Gwinn Field Office
410 West M-35
Gwinn, MI 49841
906-346-9201

Norway Field Office
P.O. Box 126
Norway, MI 49870
906-563-9247

Stephenson Field Office
Rt. 1, Box 31-B
Stephenson, MI 49887
906-753-6317

DNR East UP Management Unit
M-123, Rt. 4
Newberry, MI 49868
906-293-5131

Cusino Wildlife Research Station & Field Office
Department of Natural Resources
Shingleton, MI 49884
906-452-6236

Naubinway Field Office
US 2
Naubinway,MI 49762
906-477-6048

Newberry Field Office
P.O. Box 428
Newberry, MI 49868-0428
906-293-5024

Sault Ste. Marie Field Office
P.O. Box 798
Sault Ste. Marie, MI 49783
906-635-6161

Lower Peninsula Field Headquarters
P.O. Box 128
8717 North Roscommon
Roscommon, MI 48653
517-275-5151

DNR Northeast LP Management Unit
1732 M-32 West
Gaylord, MI 49735
517-732-3541

Atlanta Field Office
13501 M-33
Atlanta, MI 49709-9605
517-785-4252

Grayling Field Office
Rt. 3, 1955 North I-75 BL
Grayling, MI 49738
517-348-6371

Mio Field Office
Box 939, 191 South Mt. Tom Road
Mio, MI 48647
517-826-3211

Northwestern LP Management Unit
8015 Mackinaw Trail
Cadillac, MI 49601
231-775-9727

Baldwin Field Office
Rt. 2, P.O. Box 2810
2374 South M-37
Baldwin, MI 49304
231-745-4651

Paris Field Office
222t0 Northland Drive
Paris, MI 49338
231-832-5520

Traverse City Field Office
970 Emerson Road
Traverse City, MI 49686
231-922-5280

Saginaw Bay Management Unit
503 North Euclid Avenue
Bay City, MI 48706
517-684-9141

Cass City Field Office
4017 East Caro Road (M-81)
Cass City, MI 48726
517-972-5300

Southeastern Management Unit
38980 7 Mile Road
Livonia, MI 48152
734-953-0241

Southcentral Management Unit
10650 South Bennett
Morrice, MI 48857
517-625-4600

Southwestern Management Unit
621 North 10th Street
Plainwell, MI 49080
616-685-6851

**Michigan United Conservation
Clubs Map Center**
P.O. Box 30235
Lansing, MI 48909
1-800-777-6720

Report All Poaching
800-292-7800

**Upper Peninsula Travel
and Recreation Association**
P.O. Box 400
Iron Mountain, MI 49801
800-562-7134
906-774-5480

Hunting Dog Conditioning

Your dog's conditioning should be considered nearly as important as your own, and, like your own exercise program, your dog's should be an all-year affair.

Whenever I cross-country ski, snowshoe, or go for a walk, I take my Labrador along most of the time. He needs the exercise just as much as I do. Your dog should get exercise daily, or at least five times per week.

As the seasons change, the workouts change. In the spring, we run and walk and start working on retrieves. In the summer, it's much the same, but the dog does more swimming. In the winter, we don't work with dummies much. We stick to skiing and snowshoeing. The dog gets plenty of exercise plowing through the two to three feet of snow we have on the ground. Fall workouts are mostly in the field, but we get out for walks during weeks when we can't hunt as much as we'd like.

Make sure your dog sees the veterinarian at least once per year, if not twice. It's good to go before the hunting season to make sure your dog is doing all right.

Feeding

Ask six different hunters how to feed your dog during the hunting season, and you'll likely get six different answers. My dog eats the same food during hunting season that he eats during the rest of the year. The difference is that he eats more of it. During most of the year, my dog eats twice a day. When we're hunting, he'll eat three times a day.

We spend a lot of time duck hunting, so that means hours of shivering in a boat or blind. I make sure the dog eats two hours before we're in the blind, and I bring along dog biscuits to give him during the day or after a retrieve. I give him a small meal when I'm eating my lunch, mostly to keep him away from my sandwich. He eats again in the evening.

My theory is that my dog will perform better and stay warmer if he has a little food in his belly. As long as the dog is working, there's no reason to worry about him packing on extra fat, and as long as you don't overdo it in the field, he can eat a little without affecting his performance.

I also believe in keeping my dog as comfortable as possible in the boat or duck blind. Some of my buddies laugh at me for it, but again I feel the dog will perform better if he is relatively warm and dry. If you're hunting out of a boat, keep your dog off the floor, if you can. You can do it by putting a piece of plywood down or piling up your burlap decoy bags for him. I stuff a burlap bag full of styrofoam packing peanuts for my dog. Bring along some towels on tough days so you can dry your beast off a little bit when he gets out of the water. He'll be able to hunt longer.

Duke, the author's chocolate Lab, does his job during a late season hunt.
(Photo by Chris Smith)

Dog Equipment Check List

In the Field

_____ Water

_____ Collapsible water bowl

_____ Honey

_____ Hemostat

_____ *Field Guide to Dog First Aid*

In the Truck

_____ Dog food

_____ Dog bowls

_____ Dog leads

_____ Check cords

_____ First Aid Kit

_____ Dog boots, pad toughener

_____ Training dummies

_____ Beeper Collars

_____ Extra dog whistle

_____ Extra dog collars

_____ Five gallons of water

Hunter Conditioning and Equipment

The type of terrain you will encounter during a Michigan bird hunt largely depends on the species you are seeking. Ruffed grouse and woodcock hunters will see some of Michigan's thickest, toughest cover. Pheasant hunters will face long walks in grass or croplands with occasional forays into brushy draws or wooded edges. Turkey hunters will be on the edges, too, and in forest that is a bit more open and mature than forests where the grouse are found. Waterfowlers won't bust much brush unless it is on the way into a beaver pond or hidden creek, but they'll muck around in swamp and marshland.

No matter what type of bird hunting you pursue, it will all be easier and more enjoyable if you are in good physical shape. If hunters are not physically active all year, many begin a training program at least a month or two or three before the hunting seasons roll around. But as more and more people become aware of the advantages of regular exercise and proper diet, more hunters are involved in daily training and need only intensify their program in the months before hunting season.

The best thing you can do is to make exercise a regular part of your life. If you are in good shape, you can cover more ground and stay out longer. I have a program that includes weight training five or six days per week and cardiovascular or aerobic conditioning three to five days per week. I try to exercise outside as much as possible. In the winter, I walk, snowshoe, and cross-country ski. In the summer, I walk, bike, and sometimes run. My dog joins me in most of these activities (except the weight training).

Clothing

A Michigan hunting outfit varies with the terrain and weather. Wise hunters are prepared for all sorts of weather, and dressing in layers is the norm. I still remember my father advising my brother and me when we were putting together our clothes for a trip: "You can always take some of it off," he'd say, making sure we had enough to keep us warm.

When you're bird hunting, you don't want to lug around extra clothes if you don't have to. Hauling a lightweight jacket or rain parka is easy enough, though. Dress so that you are uncomfortably cool when you step from the truck and you'll feel comfortable while you're walking.

For pheasant, grouse and woodcock hunting, you will want a game vest or game bag, along with brush pants or chaps. It's a good idea to wear some sort of thin gloves (thicker in colder weather) to protect your hands, and you should wear shooting or safety glasses to protect your eyes. Of course, a hunter orange cap or vest is necessary. Comfortable hiking boots with a Gortex lining are ideal.

Turkey hunters should wear enough clothing to keep them warm in the cool morning hours of the spring. You can wear a wool sweater and long underwear if you

*Time to take a break
and cool down.*

are a 'freeze-easy' like me, but you will probably wish you weren't wearing it by noon. Cover everything with camouflaged coveralls and wear camo gloves, hat, and face mask. You can wear the same boots that you wear for other upland bird hunting.

Waterfowl hunters will want neoprene chest waders or, at the least, hip boots. Neoprene waders are wonderful for keeping the duck hunter warm in the blind. They work much better than the old rubber waders, and you won't have to pile as much clothing underneath. Once again, wear layers with a heavier wool sweater underneath. I like to wear cotton sweatpants under my waders because you will sweat in neoprene, no matter how cold the weather. I wear a pair of thick wool socks over a pair of thinner cotton socks. A waterproof, camouflaged coat with a hood, waterproof (neoprene or Goretex) gloves, and a camo Jones cap will top off your outfit.

There are days when the conditions are just too rough to go out.

Equipment

A Michigan bird hunter had better take a compass unless he intends to stay on a trail or logging road. It is very easy to get lost, especially when hunting grouse and woodcock in thick cover. These days, more and more hunters are carrying global positioning systems. Bring waterproof matches or a lighter, and a whistle. It's a good idea to keep a first aid kit in the truck for you and your dog. Include hemostats in the kit, because encounters with porcupines are common. Many upland hunters carry a small amount of water for their dogs, but often it is available along the way during the hunt. It doesn't hurt to carry water for you and your dog in a small jug or goatskin, just in case.

Equipment Checklist

CLOTHING

_____ Polypropylene underwear

_____ Inner socks

_____ Wool socks

_____ Long sleeve canvas/chamois shirts

_____ Pants, double-faced

_____ Hunting boots

_____ Billed hat

_____ Bandana

_____ Shooting gloves

_____ Shooting glasses

_____ Ear protectors

_____ Hunting vest/coat

_____ Down vest/coat

_____ Raingear

_____ Hip boots/waders
for waterfowl hunting

_____ Chaps

DOG SUPPLIES

_____ Food, bowls

_____ Beeper collar

_____ Lead

_____ Dog boots, pad toughener

_____ Hemostat

_____ Whistle

_____ Water bottles

_____ _Field Guide to Dog 1st Aid_

_____ Dog first aid kit

_____ Record of dog vaccinations

_____ Scissors

_____ Toenail clippers

HUNTING SUPPLIES

_____ _Wingshooter's Guide to Michigan_

_____ Shotgun/shells

_____ Cleaning kit

_____ Maps

_____ Knife

_____ Fanny pack

_____ Water bottle

_____ Camera, film

_____ Binoculars

_____ Game shears

_____ Ice chest

_____ Notebook, pen

_____ License

_____ Matches

_____ Axe, shovel

_____ Sunscreen

_____ Twine

_____ Decoys, decoy anchor

_____ Compass

_____ Flashlight

_____ Bird calls

_____ Spare choke tubes

_____ Magnifying glass for maps

Preserving Game Birds for Mounting

by John and Laurel Berger, Berger's Taxidermy

Exploding into the sky with a cackle and brilliant color, the rooster pheasant flushed and I momentarily lost my mind. Regaining my composure, I pulled the trigger and with the crack of my shotgun, the bird fell. That pheasant was a memory well worth preserving, and it now glides across our living room wall in a graceful, open-winged mount.

When deciding if you should mount a game bird, there are a few things to consider. The bird should be mature and have good plumage—we recommend saving birds that have been shot late in the season, ideally after the first of November. However, this doesn't apply to all game birds. Look for pinfeathers on the head and neck, and check the beak, feet, tail, and wings for shot damage. Since most taxidermists use the bird's skull, a bird that has been head-shot may be too damaged or disfigured to be mountable. All of these factors will affect the quality of a finished mount.

If a downed bird is wounded and in good enough condition to mount, do not ring the neck because it will cause skin damage and hemorrhaging. We feel the best method is to grasp the bird from the back just behind wings and then, with your thumb on one side of the rib cage and your fingers on the other, squeeze firmly. This will kill the bird in a humane and timely manner without causing damage to the feathers.

Keep the birds that you plan to have mounted separate from the others in your bag. Carrying them from the field by the feet saves them from damage and allows some cooling. We do not recommend carrying the bird in your game vest because feathers may become damaged, broken, or bloodstained.

After you've chosen the best bird or birds to mount, stop any bleeding by placing tissue or a cotton ball in the wounds. Wipe off any blood that may have run onto the feathers with a dabbing motion. Try not to push the blood down into the feathers. Also, place a cotton ball in the mouth to catch any body fluids that may potentially leak out onto the feathers.

Although some washing may be necessary before mounting, a taxidermist prefers that the bird be blood and dirt free upon delivery. Gently smooth the feathers into place, tuck the head to the chest, and wrap in clean paper towels. Place the bird head first into a plastic bag and store in a cool, protected place until the bird can be frozen.

Another popular method for preserving a bird is using a nylon stocking or cheesecloth. After caring for the bird, place the bird, with its head tucked, chest first into the nylon or cheesecloth. If you choose this method, remember that the only

John and Michael Gierke at Portage Canal—another youngster to carry on the tradition of hunting.

way to get the bird back out is to cut a hole in front of the chest and head and then push it through. If you pull it out by the feet, there will be feather damage.

Once the bird is securely in the nylon or cheesecloth, put the bird in a plastic bag to prevent dehydration or freezer burn. It is best to freeze the bird as soon as possible, and it can be stored in the freezer until you are able to get it to a taxidermist. Make sure that the bag is labeled with the type of bird, date harvested, as well as your name and license number. Taxidermists are required to have this information while the bird is in their possession.

When possible, take two birds to the taxidermist for determining which bird has the best plumage and is in the best shape for mounting.

With just a little care, you can preserve the memory of your hunt through the art of taxidermy. Bird mounts are easy to care for and will provide you with years of enjoyment.

Tip: To clean a mounted bird, use a cottonball dampened with rubbing alcohol. Start from the head using a sweeping motion in the direction of the feathers and work down the bird. Dust is lifted onto the cottonball, and the alcohol will evaporate. Make sure to change the cottonball regularly because they become soiled quickly.

Index

NOTES

WAITED LONG ENOUGH FOR A BETTER VEST?

QUILOMENE ®

Well...wait no longer!!! The Quilomene All Day Vest is far and away the most functional, practical upland bird vest available. This is not a one size fits all vest. They are custom made in Montana to fit each individual hunter. You won't believe the difference until you try one yourself. Check out these features and compare yourself.

WATER
- So important for keeping both you and your dog hydrated.
- 50 to 190 oz. optional water capacity in soft insulated water reservoir.
- Dispense water easily through a tube with valve control.
- Easy fill with an optional siphon tube.
- Allows you to hunt places you wouldn't dare try before.

WAIST BELT
- Carries the load more comfortably on your waist.
- Avoids shoulder fatigue.
- Doesn't allow the load to shift from front to back.

CARGO CAPACITY
- Ten pockets to carry all your gear.
- Unique large zippered clothing pocket – center back.
- Easy to load rear gamebag – not an arm breaker.
- Put nothing in the gamebag except game.
- Large gamebag will easily accommodate three roosters.

CUSTOM FEATURES
- Colors: Tan/Sage, Tan/Blaze, Blaze. Fabric – cordura-supplex.
- Even waist sizes from 30″ – smaller upon request.
- Interchangeable shelloops for different gauges.

OPTIONS
- Hydration systems in 70 oz. and 50 oz. models.
- Pad for carrying small rectangular electric collar transmitters.
- Trigger guard gun carrier for break open guns.
- Sling Thing for carrying shotgun hands free.

All Day Vest	$125.00
Guide's Vest	$135.00
San Carlos Vest	$ 90.00
• Optional Accessories	
Hydration systems	$ 30.00
Transmitter Pad	$ 5.00
Trigger Guard Gun Carrier	$ 5.00
Sling Thing	$ 10.00
Additional Shelloops	$ 10.00

Order Today!
Call 1-800-585-8804
or order Online at
www.quilomene.com

VISA

MasterCard

WILDERNESS ADVENTURES GUIDE SERIES

If you would like to order additional copies of this book or our other Wilderness Adventures Press guidebooks, please fill out the order form below or call **1-800-925-3339** or **fax 800-390-7558.** Visit our website for a listing of over 2000 sporting books—the largest online: **www.wildadv.com**

Mail to: Wilderness Adventures Press, 45 Buckskin Road
Belgrade, MT 59714

☐ **Please send me your free catalog on hunting and flyfishing books.**

Ship to:
Name _____

Address _____

City _____ State_____ Zip_____

Home Phone_____ Work Phone_____

Payment: ☐ Check   ☐ Visa   ☐ Mastercard   ☐ Discover   ☐ American Express

Card Number _____ Expiration Date_____

Qty	Title of Book and Author	Price	Total
	Wingshooter's Guide to Arizona	$26.95	
	Wingshooter's Guide to Iowa	$26.95	
	Wingshooter's Guide to South Dakota	$26.95	
	Wingshooter's Guide to Kansas	$26.95	
	Wingshooter's Guide to North Dakota	$26.95	
	Wingshooter's Guide to Montana	$26.00	
	Wingshooter's Guide to Idaho	$26.95	
	Wingshooter's Guide to Oregon	$26.95	
	Wingshooter's Guide to Minnesota	$26.95	
	Total Order + shipping & handling		

**Shipping and handling: $4.00 for first book,
$2.50 per additional book, up to $11.50 maximum**